Moving Culturally-Based Sororities and Fraternities Forward

This book is part of the Peter Lang Education list.
Every volume is peer reviewed and meets
the highest quality standards for content and production.

PETER LANG
New York • Bern • Berlin
Brussels • Vienna • Oxford • Warsaw

Moving Culturally-Based Sororities and Fraternities Forward

Innovations in Practice

Edited by
Crystal E. Garcia and Antonio Duran

PETER LANG
New York • Bern • Berlin
Brussels • Vienna • Oxford • Warsaw

Library of Congress Cataloging-in-Publication Control Number: 2021010291

Bibliographic information published by **Die Deutsche Nationalbibliothek**.
Die Deutsche Nationalbibliothek lists this publication in the "Deutsche
Nationalbibliografie"; detailed bibliographic data are available
on the Internet at http://dnb.d-nb.de/.

ISBN 978-1-4331-8824-4 (hardcover)
ISBN 978-1-4331-8763-6 (paperback)
ISBN 978-1-4331-8764-3 (ebook pdf)
ISBN 978-1-4331-8765-0 (epub)
DOI 10.3726/b18296

© 2021 Peter Lang Publishing, Inc., New York
80 Broad Street, 5th floor, New York, NY 10004
www.peterlang.com

All rights reserved.
Reprint or reproduction, even partially, in all forms such as microfilm,
xerography, microfiche, microcard, and offset strictly prohibited.

Table of Contents

List of Figures ix
List of Tables xi
Foreword xiii
Acknowledgments xxi

Section 1: Setting the Stage: Overview of Culturally-Based Sororities and Fraternities

Chapter One: Introduction: Historicizing and Contextualizing Culturally-Based Sororities and Fraternities 3
Crystal E. Garcia and Antonio Duran

Chapter Two: Developments in Research on Culturally-Based Sororities and Fraternities 21
Antonio Duran, Crystal E. Garcia, and Hannah L. Reyes

Section 2: Innovations in Practice: Opportunities and Challenges Facing Organizations

Member Vignette: Black Sororities and Fraternities 41
Nadrea Njoku

Chapter Three: A Practitioner's Perspective: Advising and Supporting Black Sororities and Fraternities — 45
Cameron C. Beatty, Ebony Wofford, and Chris Graham

Member Vignette: Asian-Interest Sororities and Fraternities — 61
Trang Bui

Chapter Four: A Practitioner's Perspective: Asian-Interest Sororities and Fraternities — 65
Bryan Dosono, Vigor W. H. Lam, and Bilal Badruddin

Member Vignette: Latinx/a/o-Based Sororities and Fraternities — 83
Janel Ramos

Chapter Five: *La Perspectiva de un Practicante* (A Practitioner's Perspective): Latinx/a/o-based Sororities and Fraternities — 87
Juan R. Guardia

Member Vignette: LGBTQ-Interest Sororities and Fraternities — 103
Avery Willis

Chapter Six: Queering Greek Life: LGBTQ-Interest Sororities and Fraternities — 105
Douglas N. Case

Member Vignette: Multicultural Sororities and Fraternities — 123
Javier Mena and Jessica Snell

Chapter Seven: Building Solidarity: A Guide for Supporting Multicultural Sororities and Fraternities — 125
Jessica Peñaranda and Jessica Snell

Member Vignette: Historically Native American Fraternities and Sororities — 135
Heather McMillan Nakai

Chapter Eight: Confronting Colonization: Moving Forward to Remove Barriers for Historically Native American Fraternities and Sororities — 139
Symphony Oxendine and Derek Oxendine

Section 3: Innovations in Practice: Issues in the Broader Landscape of Culturally-Based Sororities and Fraternities

Chapter Nine: Attending to Intersecting Identities in Culturally-Based Sororities and Fraternities — 159
Keith D. Garcia

Chapter Ten: Addressing Hazing Practices within Culturally-Based Sororities and Fraternities 175
Jenny Nirh and Marcos Guzman

Chapter Eleven: Bridging the Gap between Culturally-Based Sororities and Fraternities within Larger SFL Communities 193
Trace Camacho

Chapter Twelve: Interweaving Culturally-Based Sororities and Fraternities into the Campus Imagination 207
Crystal E. Garcia and Antonio Duran

Chapter Thirteen: Moving Forward: Concluding Thoughts on the Future of Culturally-Based Sororities and Fraternities 221
Antonio Duran and Crystal E. Garcia

About the Authors 235
Index 245

Figures

Figure 1.1. Sorority and Fraternity Organizational Structure   9
Figure 1.2. Example of a Campus Sorority and Fraternity Life
Organizational Structure   11
Figure 4.1. Geographic Spread of NAPA Chapter Locations in North America
as of 2020   70

Tables

Table 4.1. AAGLO Council Directory 67
Table 4.2. Directory of NAPA Organizations in 2020 69
Table 6.1. LGBTQ-Interest Sororities and Fraternities in the United States and Canada 107

Foreword

On February 6, 2020, Drs. Crystal Garcia and Antonio Duran congregated and facilitated the first meeting with all the contributors of this book. For some of the scholar-practitioners who agreed to contribute to the text, this was the first time meeting each other, while for others this convocation was an opportunity to reconnect. On this date, the group celebrated their individual and collective accomplishments and also commemorated Crystal and Antonio for bringing into fruition this book proposal, which brought together a number of experts in sorority and fraternity life (SFL) research and practice in the same room. *Moving Culturally-Based Sororities and Fraternities Forward: Innovations in Practice* provides a deep overview of the history and current landscape of culturally-based sororities and fraternities, as well as opportunities and challenges for growth and change within postsecondary education. This work facilitates a rich overview of the missing histories and experiences of culturally-based sororities and fraternities, as they have often been forgotten and buried in mainstream SFL and higher education. This book is long overdue.

Crystal and Antonio define culturally-based sororities and fraternities as:

> ... social organizations that were founded to serve marginalized student populations, such as Students of Color and individuals who identify as part of the LGBTQ community. More specifically, culturally-based sororities and fraternities include, but are not limited to, historically Black sororities and fraternities situated within

the National Pan-Hellenic Council as well as sororities and fraternities typically grouped within Multicultural Greek Councils (e.g., those created for Asian American, Latinx/a/o, LGBTQ, Multicultural, and Native American communities) (see Chapter One for more).

With this definition in mind, I advance that culturally-based sororities and fraternities are cultural productions that provide collegiate Black, Indigenous, and Students of Color spaces to (re)create and (re)imagine sorority and fraternity identities. In other words, culturally-based sororities and fraternities provide space for Students of Color and those with other minoritized identities (e.g., those within the Lesbian, Gay, Bisexual, Transgender, and Queer [LGBTQ] community) to feel visible and validated.

I am grateful for the intellectual labor of Crystal and Antonio, and all contributors of this book. Through theoretical and practice-based scholarship, the reader will be challenged to think about and lead critically on their campuses and Greek life organizations. In particular, readers who work with or have an interest in sororities and fraternities within the National Association of Latino Fraternal Organizations, Inc. (NALFO), National APIDA Panhellenic Association (NAPA), National Multicultural Greek Council (NMGC), National Pan-Hellenic Council (NPHC), as well as Native American, LGBTQ, and other culturally-based sororities and fraternities that are not part of national umbrella organizations, will find this text instrumental to research and practice. One example of how readers will be challenged and question their own behaviors is the critical use of language. When referring to Greek life organizations, Crystal and Antonio first refer to sororities and then fraternities (i.e., "sororities and fraternities," not "fraternities and sororities"). This intentional decision on the order of language generates a conversation about gender and privilege, and moves us towards challenging and dismantling the rigid gendered culture of sororities and fraternities. This book motivates readers to create and foster a culture of inclusivity in postsecondary education institutions, for culturally-based sororities and fraternities, and its members.

As I engage in reading and unpacking the scholarship of Crystal and Antonio, I recognize they are making a difference in our field, and the world. They offer a careful critique to how SFL has segregated and oppressed Black, Indigenous, and Students of Color. They complicate the SFL experiences of students by placing a race and ethnicity analysis at the center of this conversation, alongside sex assigned at birth, gender, and sexuality. All which start creating a social movement for justice and transformational change for and with Black, Indigenous, and Students of Color in culturally-based sororities and fraternities. This book situates, humanizes, and empowers many Black, Indigenous, and People of Color, and other minoritized communities (e.g., LGBTQ people) who are or have been part of culturally-based sororities and fraternities in research, practice, and leadership.

Before engaging in the practical context provided by all practitioner-scholars in each chapter, and with the help of bell hooks, Daniel Solórzano, Miguel Ceja, Tara Yosso, Iris Marion Young, Beverly Daniel Tatum, Kathleen E. Gillon, Cameron C. Beatty, Michelle Espino, James Barber, Daniel Bureau, Jeff Duncan-Andrade, Monica Miranda, Manuel Del Real, Stephen John Quaye, and Shaun R. Harper, in this *foreword* I contextualize and theorize racism and culture in context to culturally-based sororities and fraternities. The importance of theorizing racism and culture rests in "presuppose[ing] specific structural and institutional background conditions … how they affect distribution—what there is to distribute, how it gets distributed, who distributed, and what the distributive out is" (Young, 1990, p. 22).

Black, Indigenous, and Students of Color have not received an equitable distribution of resources in higher education due to racism. Racism is manifested in all aspects of society, from which, overt and covert racist policies have given greater access to white students in higher education. Solórzano et al. (2000) defined racism as "one group believes itself to be superior, 2) the group that believes to be superior has the power to carry out the racist behavior, and 3) racism, affects multiple racial and ethnic groups" (p. 61). Racist policies and practices have also recreated and reproduced oppression through sororities and fraternities. For example, since the establishment of Greek-letter organizations in the United States, these societies were organized by settler-colonial European notions of a gender construct as binary, and "White as a racial category was often linked to Christianity as a way to refuse membership to Jewish students" (Gillon, Beatty, & Salinas, 2019, p. 11). Furthermore, Gillon et al. (2019) explained that while white sororities and fraternities were expanding in higher education, "the participation of Students of Color in higher education continued to be regulated by racist laws that excluded them from attending college or segregated them into specific colleges and universities" (pp. 9–10). This form of racism and segregation creates a dystopic canon wherein "cultural images and messages that affirm the assumed superiority of Whites and the assumed inferiority of people of color [*sic*]" (Tatum, 2013, p. 65).

Cultural racism has played a significant impact on sororities and fraternities' history. Black, Indigenous and Students of Color were not allowed to join white sororities or fraternities. Therefore, Black, Indigenous, and Students of Color created their own Greek-letter organizations as a form of racial uplifting. Racial uplifting is manifested through the "aspirations to find activities in higher education to empower, uplift, and support [Black, Indigenous, and Students of Color] while receiving an education motivated them to create organizations for themselves" (Gillon et al., 2019, p. 11). Similar to Gillon et al., in the introduction to this text, Crystal and Antonio expand that culturally-based sororities and fraternities continue their racial uplifting by giving "attention to serving and lifting up Communities of Color and other marginalized populations" through their service, leadership, academics, and philanthropy.

Culturally-based sororities and fraternities have created their own cultural perspectives to develop their own sense of belonging and validation. These cultural perspectives are rooted in how Black, Indigenous, and Students of Color often experience cultural stereotypes, isolation, alienation, oppression, and marginalization from whiteness on- and off-campuses. Reflecting on the new cultural perspectives that these organizations bring to higher education can help one understand and define culture as a new form of *critical hope* (Duncan-Andrade, 2009). Culture as critical hope embraces inclusion of Black, Indigenous, and People of Color histories, epistemologies, beliefs, values, symbols, traditions, practices, meanings, leadership, habitual components, and stories of individuals and groups in an institution that express their experiences, and communicate with one other. With this definition of culture in mind, Young (1990) suggested that "Culture is ubiquitous, but nevertheless deserves distinct consideration in discussion of social justice" (p. 23). Therefore, the following questions should be asked to challenge the cultural perspectives of white sororities and fraternities: Who holds the status quo? Who is being oppressed, and what are the root causes? What factors shape the values and beliefs of organizations and institutions? How is prejudice and bias created? And what are people's individual biases, values, and beliefs towards culturally-based sororities and fraternities?

Higher education institutions have capitalized from Black, Indigenous and Students of Color, and now, they are trying to capitalize on culturally-based sororities and fraternities. For example, higher education institutions have benefitted from the contributions of service, philanthropy, and academic engagement from Black, Indigenous, and Students of Color and LGBTQ students, bolstering institutional success, but have failed to critique this political and cultural labor. Moreover, students push higher education institutions to actualize their set goals as a form of performativity to gain funding and prestige. Institutions set goals all the time, and students hold them accountable so that goals are not performative but become a reality (Quaye & Harper, 2015). Furthermore, institutions must practice effective methods of cultivating belonging and validation in order to maintain and affirm that culturally-based sororities and fraternities are spaces where various nationalities, races, ethnicities, sexual and gendered boundaries offer a space for students' development and experiences. One must acknowledge that not everyone within a culturally-based sorority and fraternity is a Student of Color or shares the same experience. Instead, culturally-based sororities and fraternities symbolize the breaking away from homogenized notions of sororities and fraternities as white spaces. To identify a part of a culturally-based sorority and fraternity is to identify with, and advocate with other students who have been rejected in mainstream higher education spaces. Culturally-based sororities and fraternities play a significant role for students' sense of belonging, retention and graduation.

This book transgresses the traditional knowledge on SFL. Though culturally-based sororities and fraternities have been ignored in most aspects of higher education, they have resisted and shaped higher education and have contributed to the culture, policies and economies of colleges, universities and communities (Barder, Espino, & Bureau, 2015; Miranda, Salinas, & Del Real, 2020). Therefore, we, higher education scholars and practitioners, must raise critical questions that disrupt the mainstream understandings of culturally-based sororities and fraternities in higher education. And not allow others to lessen the impact of culturally-based sororities and fraternities in higher education spaces for students, and in particular Black, Indigenous, and Students of Color as well as LGBTQ students. This book allows us to imagine the new possibilities that SFL has lacked to imagine—the act of becoming part of the culturally-based sisterhood, brotherhood, and siblinghood. Yet, we have to question, what does sisterhood, brotherhood, and siblinghood mean in culturally-based sororities and fraternities and in higher education? And how are these spaces also oppressive of people who do not identify with the gender binary? Further, we must ask how have culturally-based sororities and fraternities dismissed the conversations of access to trans* students, students of low social economic status, undocumented students (with and without Deferred Action for Childhood Arrival (DACA) status), homeless students, and students with disabilities?

Black, Indigenous, and Students of Color continue to resist erasure. In hooks' (2010) words, in order

> ... to resist this erasure, we must do all we can to document, to highlight, to study, to celebrate, and most importantly to crate work that is cutting-edge, that breaks through silences and the different walls that have been erected to block our vision, of ourselves and our futures. (p. 174)

As I read each book chapter, I recognized that this text is not merely about culturally-based sororities and fraternities, rather it is about how resistance is a way of knowing that connects us with others, the struggles and successes of students in culturally-based sororities and fraternities. The goal of this book is ultimately to help us center, remember, and revert the erasure and dehumanization Black, Indigenous, and Students of Color, and LGBTQ students have endured. Culturally-based sororities and fraternities have histories and need spaces in text and on campus to be valued, recognized, and celebrated.

I encourage all readers to reflect on (y)our own emotional and physical experiences in SFL, including, but not limited to racism, oppression, sexual harassment, hazing, and bullying. As stated earlier, question and challenge the status quo to stop racism and create uplifting culturally-based sororities and fraternities. *Moving Culturally-Based Sororities and Fraternities Forward: Innovations in Practice* is a symbol of how Black, Indigenous, and Students of Color, and LGBTQ SFL members are emerging as a force to reckoned with in white spaces, and serve as the rhetorical bridge by which they create community, challenging leadership and practice. Though justice looks different within each context of colleges and universities, I hope that the following chapters allow you to contextualize and envision justice for Black, Indigenous, and Students of Color, LGBTQ students, and culturally-based sororities and fraternities on your campus.

Cristobal Salinas Jr.
Associate Professor
Florida Atlantic University

References

Barber, J. P., Espino, M. M., & Bureau, D. (2015). Fraternities and sororities: Developing a compelling case for relevance in higher education. In P. A. Sasso & J. L. DeVitis (Eds.), *Today's college students: A reader* (pp. 241–255). Bern, Switzerland: Peter Lang.

Duncan-Andrade, J. M. R. (2009). Note to educators: Hope required when growing roses in concrete. *Harvard Educational Review, 79*(2), 181–194.

Gillon, K. E., Beatty, C. C., & Salinas, C., Jr. (2019). Race and racism in fraternity and sorority life: A historical overview. In K. E. Gillon, C. C. Beatty, & C. Salinas Jr. (Eds.), *Critical considerations of race, ethnicity, and culture in fraternity & sorority life* (New Directions for Student Services, no. 165, pp. 9–15). Hoboken, NJ: Jossey-Bass.

hooks, b. (2010). *Teaching critical thinking*. Oxfordshire, UK: Routledge.

Miranda, M., Salinas, C., & Del Real, M. (2020). The five phases of Latino/a fraternities and sororities: Historia y familia. In P. Sasso, P. Biddix, & M. Miranda (Eds.), *Fraternities and sororities in the contemporary era* (pp. 177–187). Gorham, ME: Myers Education Press.

Quaye, S. J., & Harper, S. R. (2015). *Student engagement in higher education: Theoretical perspectives and practical approaches for diverse populations* (2nd ed.). Oxfordshire, UK: Routledge.

Solórzano, D., Ceja, M., & Yosso, T. (2000). Critical race theory, racial microaggressions, and campus racial climate: The experiences of African American college students. *The Journal of Negro Education, 69(1),* 60–73.

Tatum, B. D. (2013). Defining racism: Can we talk? In M. Adams, W. J. Blumenfeld, R. Castañeda, H. W. Hackman, M. L. Peters, & X. Zúñiga (Eds.), *Readings for diversity and social justice* (3rd ed., pp. 65–68). Oxfordshire, UK: Routledge.

Young, I. M. (1990). *Justice and the politics of difference.* Princeton, NJ: Princeton University Press.

Acknowledgments

This book would not have been possible without the support of great friends, colleagues, and students who assisted us along the way. To begin, we want to thank and acknowledge the work of our contributors. These individuals were a pleasure to work with and produced chapters that are going to be integral to pushing culturally-based sororities and fraternities forward. Their thinking and recommendations are bound to have meaningful impacts on the ways that sorority and fraternity life (SFL) offices and student affairs practitioners work with culturally-based SFL organizations. Next, we see it imperative to thank the students that we have worked with throughout the years who have pushed us to center the stories of those in culturally-based sororities and fraternities. Finally, we wish to express gratitude to one another. This book is a culmination of years of critical conversations, collaborations on research projects, and friendship. We are deeply grateful to one another for the discussions that we had when imagining this text together all the way to putting the finishing touches on it. We look forward to continuing to think alongside one another to dream of equitable futures in and outside of postsecondary education.

Crystal is beyond grateful to all the family, friends, colleagues, and students that have supported and challenged her over the years to think more critically about the world and ways we can move toward equity. The relationships she developed within the University of Nebraska-Lincoln and Auburn University as well as the 2017 Faculty of Color Cohort and Chingona Scholar group along with the many other meaningful connections she has made at institutions across the nation have been crucial in her development as a scholar and ability to take on this project. She was also particularly inspired by her nieces and nephews; they demonstrate an understanding of social justice and human rights that give her hope for a better future. Over the last 2 years Crystal has been privileged to serve as the faculty advisor for the Beta Phi Chapter of Kappa Delta Chi Sorority, Inc. working with some phenomenal young women including Alena, Giovanna, Janet, Mia, Samantha, and Roshell. This role provided her direct insight to the incredible commitment these students harnessed to form a sisterhood and their work to keep it alive on campus. Often these efforts are working against the systemic ways SFL within historically white institutions was not built to center culturally-based groups. Based on our research, we know these patterns are not specific to any one institution, but they were a primary motivation for us to see the immense need for this text.

Finally, Crystal is grateful to have a partner, her husband Jacob Garcia, that supports her in everything she does including her work on this project. When Crystal had to work late or for long consecutive hours, Jacob supported her by offering to pick up coffee and alleviating her stress by taking care of household needs. Most importantly, he engaged in conversations with her about her scholarship and the state of the world, which served to further strengthen her writing. She considers herself fortunate to have his love and support.

Antonio values the assistance he received from colleagues at Auburn University and beyond during the book writing process. His network of friends located across the country contribute to the drive that Antonio has to imagine worlds more just for minoritized communities. Next, it is impossible not to thank the individuals affiliated with the Auburn colony of Omega Delta Phi. Witnessing their constant dedication to ODPhi has made Antonio a better advisor and advocate for culturally-based sororities and fraternities. Likewise, he appreciates his family and chosen family for giving him the motivation necessary to complete this project. And finally, Antonio wants to specifically thank his husband, Adam Zook Duran-Leftin, who has always offered crucial support to his academic pursuits. Adam was there for every step in this writing process, providing constant encouragement along the way. This book will forever be meaningful given that its submission date fell on Antonio and Adam's wedding day (October 30, 2020). Being surrounded by Adam's love and the snuggly personality of their dog, Michael P.W. Duran-Leftin, has made Antonio a better scholar, advocate, and person.

SECTION 1

SETTING THE STAGE: OVERVIEW OF CULTURALLY-BASED SORORITIES AND FRATERNITIES

CHAPTER ONE

Introduction: Historicizing and Contextualizing Culturally-Based Sororities and Fraternities

CRYSTAL E. GARCIA AND ANTONIO DURAN

Sorority and fraternity life (SFL) communities have a longstanding and complex relationship with higher education institutions and college students, a relationship that has been explored over time through the literature (Biddix, 2016; Biddix, Matney, Norman, & Martin, 2014; Perkins, Zimmerman, & Janosik Perkins, 2011). In particular, while SFL creates spaces for students to develop meaningful relationships, these organizations have been under fire from those in and outside of universities concerned about the problematic behaviors and practices furthered in SFL communities (Biddix et al., 2014; Rossman, 2017; Wade, 2017). Those who advocate for the utility of SFL organizations point to findings from studies that associate a number of positive outcomes with membership in SFL organizations. In fact, SFL involvement has been connected to leadership development and perspective taking (Atkinson, Dean, & Espino, 2010; Johnson, Johnson, & Dugan, 2015; Martin, Hevel, & Pascarella, 2012), social involvement and sense of belonging (Asel, Seifert, & Pascarella, 2009; Atkinson et al., 2010; Garcia, 2019a; Pike, 2003), academic performance and persistence (Delgado-Guerrero & Gloria, 2013; Long, 2012; Patton, Bridges, & Flowers, 2011; Walker, Martin, & Hussey, 2015), as well as involvement in community service (Asel et al., 2009) for college students. Although SFL can positively enrich the lives and aspirations of college students, it is important to recognize *who* these organizations benefit. Specifically, SFL has a history of exclusionary practices that shape who is permitted access to membership and, as a result, the effects of these practices still impact how organizations operate today.

Sororities and fraternities are often known for their selective membership practices and image of elitism. This aspect of SFL is often romanticized in the media as a way of recruiting the "popular" or "cool" students on campus to join, as seen in movies such as *Legally Blonde*, *Sydney White*, *Animal House*, and *House Bunny*. What is less commonly discussed are ways the selective nature of SFL organizations opened the door to discriminatory forms of gatekeeping and identity-based exclusion within SFL (Harris Combs, Stewart, & Sonnett, 2017; Hughey, 2009; Park, 2012; Ray, 2013; Ray & Rosow, 2012). For instance, it is not uncommon for particular sororities and fraternities to be deemed as "the white sororities and fraternities" (Hughey, 2009) or to be known as hostile to members of the Lesbian, Gay, Bisexual, Transgender, and Queer (LGBTQ) community (Case et al., 2005; Hesp & Brooks, 2009). This exclusion of potential members based on race, ethnicity, sexuality, and gender within SFL gave rise to culturally-based sororities and fraternities (CBSFs)—organizations that were founded to serve marginalized student populations, including Students of Color and individuals who identify as part of the LGBTQ community.

Although CBSFs have existed for over a hundred years (Torbenson & Parks, 2009), few people may be familiar with the historical development, purpose, current status, and potential future of these organizations. Our interest in writing this book comes from our own experiences working in student affairs and higher education, seeing the need for a text that explores CBSFs in depth. Crystal's pursuit of exploring CBSFs stemmed from her involvement in SFL as a member of a Panhellenic sorority. During her undergraduate experience she served as an officer in her sorority, a member of the Panhellenic Council, and was even awarded "Greek Woman of the Year" during her senior year by her campus SFL Office. Following graduation, she served as an advisor for her chapter for 5 years. Even though NPHC and MGC chapters were present on her campus, she had few interactions with members of these organizations. Moreover, she did not have any understanding of their history or purpose as an undergraduate student or during the first 4 years of her time as a chapter advisor. It was not until she took a position working as a graduate assistant in campus activities (which was within the same department as the SFL Office) at her alma mater that she started to understand what CBSFs were. This caused her to begin questioning the extent to which CBSFs were recognized within other college campuses. Antonio, on the other hand, came to an interest in SFL not being affiliated with an SFL organization. His undergraduate institution had a small SFL community and for this reason, Antonio never considered joining an organization. It was during his master's degree experience working at an institution which had a much larger SFL culture (where approximately one-third of the student population were affiliated) that Antonio gained a noticeable interest in SFL groups. Specifically, because much of his research examines how campuses (re)produce inequality for marginalized populations, Antonio is motivated to unearth how these organizations can serve as places for minoritized individuals to find a sense of belonging while also understanding why certain organizations/councils have excluded these very students. Both of us currently serve as chapter advisors for CBSFs based at Auburn University, which has further informed our research around these groups.

Through our practice and research, we have noticed that CBSFs are groups that most student affairs professionals are not well equipped to support. This text is dedicated to not only developing readers' understanding of CBSFs, but also to push the conversation forward regarding dynamics within these sororities and fraternities, as well as the interconnections among larger SFL and campus communities. In this introduction, we first provide some historical context to understand the emergence of CBSFs, followed by an explanation of how these organizations are situated within SFL communities locally within colleges and universities and their role (inter)nationally. We end with an overview of some ways research has problematized these organizations and how this book will examine these topics in more depth. Ultimately, it is our hope that this text will serve a number of different groups—those not affiliated with these organizations as well as current members—by moving the scholarly conversation forward about CBSFs.

The Emergence and Evolution of Culturally-Based Sororities and Fraternities

Throughout their history, sororities and fraternities have adopted implicit and explicit exclusionary practices based on factors including cost of membership, race, ethnicity, gender, sexuality, and religion (Garcia & Shirley, 2019; Harris Combs et al., 2017; Park, 2008; Ray, 2013; Soria, 2013; Torbenson, 2012). In fact, the first SFL organizations were catered to those originally permitted to enroll in and attend higher education institutions, namely white Christian men (James, 2000; Torbenson, 2012). Though the doors of SFL opened slightly with the establishment of sororities open to white women, exclusionary clauses written within organizational documents still prevented Students of Color from membership (Gillon et al., 2019; James, 2000; Torbenson, 2012).

Barone (2014) charted the history of sorority and fraternity exclusionary clauses, the first of which was published in 1879 by Delta Sigma Phi and read: "Membership is confined to men of the Caucasian race, whose 'ideals and beliefs are those of modern Christian civilization'" (p. 144). Over time, these exclusionary clauses faced challenges, much of which stemmed from World War II veterans (James, 2000). James (2000) traced this early SFL history detailing that one University of California, Los Angeles (UCLA) fraternity member wrote a letter to the campus paper arguing that racial discrimination "violates a major reason for which the last war was so bloodily fought. If Jews, Negros and gentiles could fight together, and die together, sometimes in each other's arms, why shouldn't they enter the houses along Hilgard and Gayley together?" (p. 306). Years of challenges to these exclusionary clauses did not ease their dismissal; removal of clauses were met with resistance from organizational members and national leaders (James, 2000). In fact, the national chairman of the North American Interfraternity Conference (NIC) in 1947 argued for the continuation of exclusionary clauses asserting "Individuals choose friends most like themselves socially and culturally" (James, 2000, p. 310). In response to the overt discriminatory practices in SFL membership, as well as within society broadly for those established in minority-serving institutions such as HBCUs, Students of Color and those from other minoritized populations established their own organizations, the origin of CBSFs that continue to grow today.

Early fraternities excluded Jewish students from membership, which gave rise to nonsectarian fraternities (Brown, Parks, & Phillips, 2012) and the first Jewish fraternity, Zeta Beta Tau, which began in 1898 (Zeta Beta Tau, 2019). Just a few years later, the first of the historically Black sororities and fraternities that were later known as the "Divine Nine" (Brown et al., 2012) was established. Specifically, in 1906, Alpha Phi Alpha was the first of the Divine Nine and was founded in response to racial discrimination. It originally served "as a study and support group" (Alpha Phi Alpha, n.d., para. 2) and over time the aims of the organization shifted to "[recognize] the need to help correct the educational, economic, political, and social injustices faced by African Americans" (para. 3). Shortly after Alpha Phi Alpha's establishment, in 1908, Alpha Kappa Alpha Sorority, Incorporated was established to serve the needs of Black women (NPHC, n.d.).

The early 1900s was a time for the development of other culturally-based fraternities and sororities as well. The first of the Asian Pacific Islander Desi American (APIDA) organizations began with Rho Psi Fraternity, a Chinese serving organization established in 1916 at Cornell University (NAPA, n.d.a). In 1929, the first APIDA sorority, Chi Alpha Delta, was established at UCLA to serve Japanese American women (NAPA, n.d.a). The first Latino fraternities were established in the early 1900s with the intent to serve the needs of "wealthy international students" (Fajardo, 2015, p. 69) from Latin American countries that were enrolled in colleges and universities in the U.S. These early fraternities died out over time and gave rise to a new generation of organizations intended to serve Latino students from the U.S. (Fajardo, 2015). Though its roots date back to organizations that began in the late 1800s, Phi Iota Alpha was founded in 1931 and claims to be the oldest still-existing Latino-based fraternity (Phi Iota Alpha, 2018). Many years later, the first Latina interest sorority, Lambda Theta Alpha, was established in 1975.

Distinct from sororities and fraternities that were founded to serve a single identity group (Wells & Dolan, 2009), organizations that branded themselves as multicultural and multiethnic broadly have early histories branching to the establishment of Beta Sigma Tau fraternity in the 1940s (see Wells & Dolan, 2009). However, present-day multicultural sororities and fraternities began with the founding of Mu Sigma Upsilon Sorority, Inc., known as the first multicultural sorority, in 1981 at Rutgers University (Mu Sigma Upsilon Sorority, Inc., n.d.; Wells & Dolan, 2009). Historically Native American sororities and fraternities emerged in the 1990s. Unlike other culturally-based predecessors where fraternities were founded first, the first Historically Native American Greek-letter organization, Alpha Pi Omega, was a sorority and was founded in 1994 (Alpha Pi Omega, 2016). Phi Sigma Mu was the first Historically Native American fraternity, founded in 1996 at the University of North Carolina at Pembroke (Phi Sigma Mu, n.d.; Still & Faris, 2019). Of note, there are currently eight fraternities and sororities labeled as Historically Native American sororities and fraternities within the U.S. (Still & Faris, 2019).

In addition to racial and ethnic discrimination in SFL, sororities and fraternities have a history of excluding and regulating membership based on gender and sexuality (Hesp & Brooks, 2009; Means & Jaeger, 2013; Rhoads, 1995; Welter, 2012). In fact, organizations have been found to reify issues of heterosexism and trans oppression through alcohol abuse (Iwamoto et al., 2011; Sasso, 2015), together with sexually aggressive and hypermasculine attitudes (Corprew & Mitchell, 2014). Hegemonic masculinity has also come to define how hazing and pledging rituals are carried out within culturally-based fraternities (Jenkins, 2012). While conversations at the national level have increasingly brought questions around inclusion for individuals that are transgender, gender fluid, gender queer, or gender non-binary (Campus Pride, 2013; Raymond, 2018; Van Syckle, 2016), many organizations still maintain stances that exclude these individuals from membership (see Washington State University Center for Fraternity and Sorority Life, 2018). Although scholarship shows that climates for LGBTQ students within SFL chapters have become less hostile over the last 30 years (Rankin et al., 2013), other studies have argued these behaviors still persist (Garcia &

Duran, 2020; Hall & La France, 2007; Hesp & Brooks, 2009; Worthen, 2014). In addition to excluding individuals from membership, these studies show that hegemonic expectations around gender and sexuality can create hostile environments for individuals that do not align with these expectations. LGBTQ sororities and fraternities were founded in response to these patterns of behavior. Delta Lambda Phi was an early LGBTQ fraternity that was "Founded by Gay men for all men" in 1987 (Delta Lambda Phi Social Fraternity, 2016). Founded in 2003, Gamma Rho Lambda National Sorority was the first national multicultural LGBTQ sorority (Gamma Rho Lambda National Sorority, n.d.).

We shared these highlights of the historical development of CBSFs to provide context for their existence, but we also note this brief history does not encapsulate every type of CBSF. Much of this history of exclusion within SFL is rarely discussed or even known to individuals within SFL communities, much less to those outside of SFL. However, these conversations are imperative for culturally-based organizations to be recognized and respected for their resistance to these oppressive practices within SFL. Furthermore, education around SFL's discriminatory history is key for historically white sororities and fraternities to continue to engage in meaningful systemic change.

An Organizational Overview of Culturally-Based Sororities and Fraternities

To understand how CBSFs are situated within SFL communities, it is important to first discuss sorority and fraternity governance structures. To begin, a chapter is a locally-based branch of a national/international sorority or fraternity (Virginia Tech, 2019). While most chapters are affiliated with (inter)national organizations, there are also some that are not; these chapters are often referred to as "locals" (Montclair State University, n.d.). The campus SFL office is made up of the professional staff members that oversee all sorority and fraternity chapters on a respective campus. These professionals communicate with the local chapter and (inter)nationals to ensure chapters abide by local and (inter)national policies.

Notably in SFL communities, (inter)national organizations are often referred to as "national" despite the fact that many of these organizations have established chapters internationally (Montclair State University, n.d.). The (inter)national organizations that oversee SFL chapters are often, but not always, affiliated with larger (inter)national umbrella associations. National umbrella associations are largely formed to connect (inter)national SFL organizations with one another for strength and opportunities to collaborate and share resources, which may be particularly useful for CBSFs since they often have smaller alumni bases compared to historically white organizations. The choice to affiliate with an umbrella association is made by the (inter)national organization and there are also requirements for membership such as minimum chapter numbers, liability insurance coverage, and anti-hazing and risk management policies among others (see NALFO, 2018; NAPA, n.d.b; NIC, 2019; NMGC, 2010); for those and other reasons, some organizations are not governed by umbrella associations. Furthermore, there is currently no formal umbrella association for historically Native American sororities and fraternities. Figure 1.1 illustrates SFL organizational structure. The dotted lines around the (inter)national organization and umbrella association indicates that chapters may or may not be part of these.

The aim of umbrella associations to forge communities of support is evident through their purpose statements. For instance, the National Asian Pacific Islander Desi American (APIDA) Panhellenic Association (NAPA) formed in 2005 (NAPA, n.d.c) and described part of its mission as, "to advocate the needs of its member organizations and provides a forum to share ideas and resources within its members" (NAPA, n.d.d, para. 1). Other umbrella associations for CBSFs include:

- The National Association of Latino Fraternal Organizations, Inc. (NALFO), established in 1998 and currently oversees 16 fraternities and sororities with the aim to "promote and foster positive interfraternal relations, communication, and development of all Latino fraternal organizations" (NALFO, 2019, About NALFO section, para. 1).

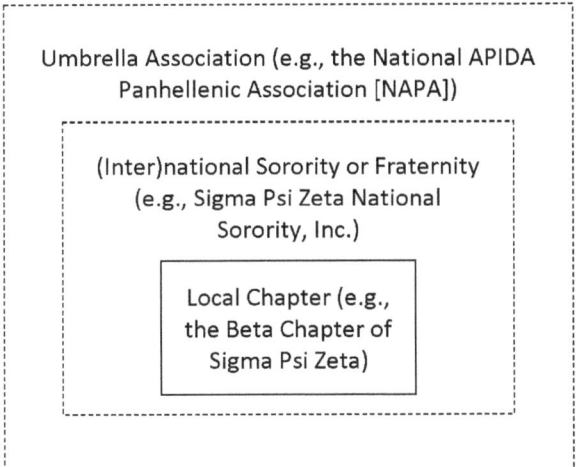

Figure 1.1. Sorority and Fraternity Organizational Structure

- The National Multicultural Greek Council (NMGC) was established in 1998 (NMGC, n.d.a) and is home to 10 multicultural sororities and fraternities (NMGC n.d.b).
- The National Pan-Hellenic Council, Incorporated (NPHC) was established in 1930 and oversees nine sororities and fraternities (NPHC, n.d.).

Though some inter(national) sororities and fraternities may not be associated with an umbrella association, some culturally-based fraternities are part of two. The umbrella association for historically white fraternities, the North American Interfraternity Conference (NIC), opened membership to culturally-based fraternities, permitting organizations to possess dual membership in their culturally-based umbrellas as well as within NIC. For example, Phi Iota Alpha Fraternity, Inc. is affiliated with NALFO and NIC. Alpha Phi Alpha is another example of an organization with dual affiliations with NPHC and NIC. NIC further established its commitment to culturally-based organizations by hiring a Director of Emerging & Culturally-Based Fraternal Initiatives in 2016 (NIC, 2016). NIC's expansion is distinct from the umbrella organization for historically white sororities, the National Panhellenic Conference. The NPC reports to be "the world's largest umbrella organization specifically charged with advancing the sorority experience" (NPC, n.d.a, para. 1). Two Jewish based sororities are members of the NPC including Alpha Epsilon Phi and its youngest member, Sigma Delta Tau, founded in 1917 (NPC, n.d.b). However unlike the NIC, other culturally-based sororities are not members of the NPC.

Now that we have discussed how sororities and fraternities are organized up to (inter)national umbrella associations, we would like to return to a discussion on how culturally-based chapters are situated within local campuses (see Figure 1.2). In a similar aim of national umbrella associations, chapters come together within campus communities to form SFL councils. Campus-based councils unify similarly-structured sororities and fraternities to provide opportunities to collaborate/communicate with one another. Each SFL office determines how councils are organized and these decisions also depend on the chapters present on the campus. However, there are commonly up to four councils loosely guided by national umbrella organization affiliation. When there are two or more NIC fraternities on a campus, an Interfraternity Council (IFC) is formed (NIC, 2017). Similarly, when two or more NPC sororities are present, a College Panhellenic Association is formed (NPC, n.d.c) though it may take on different monikers within a respective campus such as a Panhellenic Council (PC), National Panhellenic Council (NPC) or Collegiate Panhellenic Council (CPC or CPH). Within this text, we will refer to these councils as Panhellenic Councils (PC) for

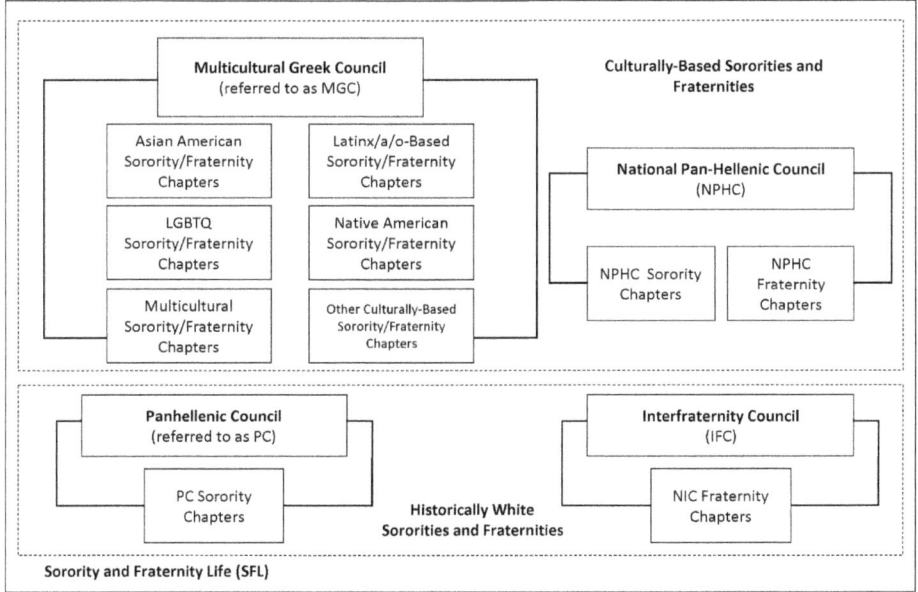

Figure 1.2. Example of a Campus Sorority and Fraternity Life Organizational Structure

consistency. Sororities and fraternities within the NPHC organizations are often grouped together under a council by the same name—NPHC (Ross, 2000). Asian American, Latinx/a/o, LGBTQ, Multicultural, and Native American organizations sometimes have councils dedicated to particular organization types such as a Latinx Greek Council, however in most cases these organizations are categorized within what are typically called Multicultural Greek Councils or United Greek Councils (MGC, UGC; Muñoz & Guardia, 2009). For the purposes of this text, we will refer to these councils as Multicultural Greek Councils (MGC).

Existing Research on Culturally-Based Sororities and Fraternities

Chapter Two will further elaborate on the existing research on CBSFs, but here we will first briefly overview some of the thematic areas of research within the literature. In the first area of research, studies have explored the characteristics of CBSFs and ways they are distinct from historically white SFL organizations. Second, researchers have examined ways CBSFs serve to affirm the identities of members from marginalized populations. In the final strand of scholarship, researchers have problematized issues that arise within CBSFs.

Although CBSFs are distinct from historically white organizations in many ways, they all share common ties that distinguish them as SFL organizations (further explained in Chapter Two of the text). These ties include a focus on leadership development and engagement in philanthropy; familial labels such as brotherhood, sisterhood, and siblinghood; the adoption of colors, Greek letters, and mascots to represent the organizations; secret rituals; and oversight by national organizational governance and often national umbrella associations (Muñoz & Guardia, 2009; Torbenson, 2012). Although CBSFs share similarities with historically white organizations, they also differ in a number of ways including their membership intake processes and costs of membership among other organizational traditions (Garcia, 2019b; Torbenson, 2012; Torbenson & Parks, 2009). Further, a crucial element that distinguishes these organizations from historically white sororities and fraternities is their attention to serving and lifting up Communities of Color and other marginalized populations (Arellano, 2020; Orta, Murguia, & Cruz, 2019).

Culturally-based sororities and fraternities have been shown to play a positive role in the experiences of minoritized student populations on college campuses (Dancy & Hotchkins, 2015; Garcia, 2019a; Guardia & Evans, 2008; Harper, 2007; McGuire, McTier, Ikegwuonu, Sweet, & Bryant-Scott, 2020; McCoy, 2011; Orta et al., 2019). Notably, scholars have underscored that these organizations can affirm collegians' gender and sexuality (Chan, 2017; McClure, 2006; Yeung & Stombler, 2000) as well as their racial/ethnic identities, especially for those at predominantly white institutions (e.g., Garcia, 2019a; Guardia & Evans, 2008; McCoy, 2011; Mitchell, 2014; Orta et al., 2019) and serve as spaces in which students can form community with other Students of Color (e.g., McGuire et al., 2020).

Researchers have also examined issues around CBSFs, highlighting challenges that are unique to their members. Members of these organizations often feel ostracized from and erased by the greater SFL community because of a lack of understanding of these organizations (Garcia, 2019b; Ray, 2013); observe a shortage of support from SFL professionals (Garcia, 2019b); and receive negative differential treatment when compared to members of historically white sororities and fraternities (Bourke, 2010; Ray & Rosow, 2012). Members of CBSFs experience hostile climates within the greater SFL community (Garcia, 2019b; Guardia & Evans, 2008). In addition to the unique ways these organizations interact with the greater SFL and campus community, researchers have also explored ways these organizations may impact members differently based on their multiple identities. Namely, although CBSFs were founded to center racial and ethnic identities, they often neglect to recognize problematic behaviors around identities such as gender and sexuality (Duran & Garcia, 2021; Garcia & Duran, 2020). For example, findings from various studies have pointed to ways culturally-based fraternities can cultivate hegemonic forms of masculinities that negatively impact sexual minorities (DeSantis & Coleman, 2008; Williams, 2017). This book will further unpack these issues, providing readers a deeper understanding of dynamics surrounding CBSFs and recommendations to support them on college campuses.

Setting the Stage for This Text

Members of CBSFs have historically been rendered invisible on college campuses and in the national media. Because historically white sororities and fraternities typically encompass the majority of SFL membership on local campuses and are often in the national attention due to issues concerning hazing, alcohol use, and racist incidents, professionals in SFL offices frequently focus their time and effort on these organizations specifically. Furthermore, SFL professionals at predominantly white institutions are often members of historically white sororities and fraternities themselves and may have little knowledge of ways culturally-based organizations differ. As campuses are becoming increasingly diverse as it relates to demographics of race, gender, and sexuality, organizations developed for these populations will continue to grow as will membership within CBSFs. This book will further unpack CBSFs in an effort to center their histories and the experiences of members within them.

We were intentional in positioning this text to highlight the voices and expertise of practitioners working directly with CBSFs as well as members of these organizations. Therefore, while the first two chapters present information around the history and context of culturally-based SFL as well as a discussion of scholarship around CBSFs, the remainder of the text presents two sections on innovations in practice from practitioners and members. In the first section, *Innovations in Practice: Opportunities and Challenges Facing Organizations*, each chapter is dedicated to exploring issues that emerge uniquely by organizational type. These chapters are presented in alphabetical order as follows: African American/Black Sororities and Fraternities, Asian American Sororities and Fraternities, Latinx/a/o-Based Sororities and Fraternities, LGBTQ-Interest Sororities and Fraternities, Multicultural Sororities and Fraternities, and Historically Native American Fraternities and Sororities.[1] Each of these chapters is introduced with

---

[1] Although we intentionally placed sororities before fraternities throughout this text, here we honor the term the chapter authors have used to name these organizations.

a member vignette from the respective organizational type followed by content from practitioners' perspectives. The second section, *Innovations in Practice: Issues in the Broader Landscape of Culturally-Based Sororities and Fraternities*, focuses on issues that span across all CBSFs. These chapters examine intersecting identities, hazing practices, the relationship among CBSFs and the larger SFL community, and other considerations for building inclusive SFL communities. The book will conclude with a chapter on concepts addressed within the text and a discussion of the path forward for CBSFs.

References

Alpha Phi Alpha. (n.d.) *The founding of Alpha Phi Alpha*. https://apa1906.net/our-history/

Alpha Pi Omega. (2016). *Home*. http://www.alphapiomega.org

Arellano, L. (2020). Why Latin@ s become Greek: Exploring why Latin@ s join Latino Greek-letter organizations. *Journal of Hispanic Higher Education, 19*(3), 280–302.

Asel, A. M., Seifert, T. A., & Pascarella, E. T. (2009). The effects of fraternity/sorority membership on college experiences and outcomes: A portrait of complexity. *Oracle: The Research Journal of the Association of Fraternity/Sorority Advisors, 4*(2), 1–15.

Atkinson, E., Dean, L. A., & Espino, M. M. (2010). Leadership outcomes based on membership in multicultural Greek council (MGC) organizations. *Oracle: The Research Journal of the Association of Fraternity/Sorority Advisors, 5*(2), 34–48.

Barone, R. (2014). White clauses in two historically white fraternities: Documenting the past and exploring future implications. *Oracle: The Research Journal of the Association of Fraternity/Sorority Advisors, 9*(1), 54–73.

Biddix, P. (2016). Moving beyond alcohol: A review of other issues associated with fraternity membership with implications for practice and research. *Journal of College Student Development, 57*(7), 793–809.

Biddix, J. P., Matney, M. M., Norman, E. M., & Martin, G. L. (Eds.). (2014). The influence of fraternity and sorority involvement: A critical analysis of research (1996–2013). *ASHE Higher Education Report, 39*(6), 1–156.

Bourke, B. (2010). Experiences of Black students in multiple cultural spaces at a predominantly white institution. *Journal of Diversity in Higher Education, 3*(2), 126–135.

Brown, T. L., Parks, G. S., & Phillips, C. M. (Eds.) (2012). *African American fraternities and sororities: The legacy and the vision* (2nd ed.). Lexington, KY: University Press of Kentucky.

Campus Pride. (2013). *Transgender membership in fraternities and sororities and Title IX*. https://www.campuspride.org/resources/transgender-membership-in-fraternities-sororities-and-title-ix/

Case, D. N., Hesp, G. A., & Eberly, C. G. (2005). An exploratory study of the experiences of gay, lesbian, and bisexual fraternity and sorority members revisited. *Oracle: The Research Journal of the Association of Fraternity/Sorority Advisors, 1*(1), 15–31.

Chan, J. (2017). "Am I masculine enough?": Queer Filipino college men and masculinity. *Journal of Student Affairs Research and Practice, 54*(1), 82–94.

Corprew, C. S., III, & Mitchell, A. D. (2014). Keeping it frat: Exploring the interaction among fraternity membership, disinhibition, and hypermasculinity on sexually aggressive attitudes in college-aged males. *Journal of College Student Development, 55*(6), 548–562.

Dancy, T. E., & Hotchkins, B. K. (2015). Schools for the better making of men? Undergraduate Black males, fraternity membership, and manhood. *Culture, Society and Masculinities, 7*(1), 7–21.

Delgado-Guerrero, M., & Gloria, A. M. (2013). La importancia de la hermandad Latina: Examining the psychosociocultural influences of Latina-based sororities on academic persistence decisions. *Journal of College Student Development, 54*(4), 361–378.

Delta Lambda Phi Social Fraternity. (2016). *Our mission.* https://dlp.org/about/purposes/

DeSantis, A. D., & Coleman, M. (2008). Not on my line: Attitudes about homosexuality in Black fraternities. In G. S. Parks (Ed.), *Black Greek-letter organizations in the twenty-first century: Our fight has just begun* (pp. 291–312). Lexington, KY: The University Press of Kentucky.

Duran, A., & Garcia, C. E. (2021). Quaring sorority life: Identity negotiation of Queer Women of Color in culturally-based sororities. *Journal of College Student Development, 62*(2), 186-202.

Fajardo, O. (2015). A brief history of international Latin American student fraternities: A movement that lasted 86 years (1889–1975). *Journal of Hispanic Higher Education, 14*(1), 69–81.

Gamma Rho Lambda National Sorority. (n.d.). *Home.* http://gammarholambda.org

Garcia, C. E. (2019a). Belonging in a predominantly White institution: The role of membership in multicultural fraternities and sororities. *Journal of Diversity in Higher Education.* Advance online publication. https://doi.org/10.1037/dhe0000126

Garcia, C. E. (2019b). "They don't even know that we exist": Exploring sense of belonging within sorority and fraternity communities for Latina/o members. *Journal of College Student Development, 60*(3), 319–336.

Garcia, C. E., & Duran, A. (2020). "In my letters, but I was still by myself": Highlighting the experiences of Queer Men of Color in culturally based fraternities. *Journal of Diversity in Higher Education.* Advance online publication. https://doi.org/10.1037/dhe0000167

Garcia, C. E., & Shirley, Z. E. (2019). Race and privilege in fraternity and sorority life: Considerations for practice and research. In P. Sasso, P. Biddix, & M. Miranda (Eds.), *Fraternities and sororities in the contemporary era* (pp. 155–163). Sterling, VA: Stylus.

Gillon, K. E., Beatty, C. C., & Salinas, C., Jr. (2019). Race and racism in fraternity and sorority life: A historical overview. In K. E. Gillon, C. C. Beatty, & C. Salinas Jr. (Eds.), *Critical considerations of race, ethnicity, and culture in fraternity and sorority life* (New Directions for Student Services, no. 165, pp. 9–16). Hoboken, NJ: Jossey-Bass.

Guardia, J. R., & Evans, N. J. (2008). Factors influencing the ethnic identity development of Latino fraternity members at a Hispanic serving institution. *Journal of College Student Development, 49*(3), 163–181.

Hall, J. A., & La France, B. H. (2007). Attitudes and communication of homophobia in fraternities: Separating the impact of social adjustment function from hetero-identity concern. *Communication Quarterly, 55*(1), 39-60. https://doi.org/10.1080/01463370600998673

Harper, S. R. (2007). The effects of sorority and fraternity membership on class participation and African American student engagement in predominantly white classroom environments. *College Student Affairs Journal, 27*(1), 94–115.

Harris Combs, B., Stewart, T. L., & Sonnett, J. (2017). People like us: Dominance-oriented racial affiliation preferences and the white Greek system on a southern US campus. *Sociological Spectrum, 37*(1), 27–47.

Hesp, G. A., & Brooks, J. S. (2009). Heterosexism and homophobia on fraternity row: A case study of a college fraternity community. *Journal of LGBT Youth, 6*(4), 395–415.

Hughey, M. W. (2009). Rushing the wall, crossing the sands: Cross-racial membership in US college fraternities and sororities. In C. L. Torbenson & G. S. Parks (Eds.), *Brothers and sisters: Diversity in college fraternities and sororities* (pp. 237–277). Cranbury, NJ: Rosemont Publishing & Printing Corp.

Iwamoto, D. K., Cheng, A., Lee, C. S., Takamatsu, S., & Gordon, D. (2011). "Man-ing" up and getting drunk: The role of masculine norms, alcohol intoxication and alcohol-related problems among college men. *Addictive Behaviors, 36*(9), 906–911.

James, A. W. (2000). The college social fraternity antidiscrimination debate, 1945–1949. *The Historian, 62*(2), 303–324.

Jenkins, R. D. (2012). Black fraternal organizations: Understanding the development of hegemonic masculinity and sexuality. *Journal of African American Studies, 16*(2), 226–235.

Johnson, M. R., Johnson, E. L., & Dugan, J. P. (2015). Developing socially responsible leadership and social perspective-taking in fraternities and sororities: Findings from a national study. *Oracle: The Research Journal of the Association of Fraternity/Sorority Advisors, 10*(1), 1–13.

Long, L. D. (2012). A multivariate analysis of the relationship between undergraduate fraternity/sorority involvement and academic performance. *Oracle: The Research Journal of the Association of Fraternity/Sorority Advisors, 7*(2), 37–48.

Martin, G. L., Hevel, M. S., & Pascarella, E. T. (2012). Do fraternities and sororities enhance socially responsible leadership? *Journal of Student Affairs Research and Practice, 49*(3), 267–284.

McClure, S. M. (2006). Improvising masculinity: African American fraternity membership in the construction of a Black masculinity. *Journal of African American Studies, 10*(1), 57–73.

McCoy, D. L. (2011). Black men, fraternities, and Historically Black Colleges and Universities. In R. T. Palmer & J. L. Wood (Eds.), *Black men in college* (pp. 138–147). Oxfordshire, UK: Routledge.

McGuire, K. M., McTier Jr, T. S., Ikegwuonu, E., Sweet, J. D., & Bryant-Scott, K. (2020). "Men doing life together" Black Christian fraternity men's embodiments of brotherhood. *Men and Masculinities, 23*(3–4), 579–599.

Means, D. R., & Jaeger, A. J. (2013). Black in the rainbow: "Quaring" the Black gay male student experience at Historically Black Universities. *Journal of African American Males in Education, 4*(2), 124–140.

Mitchell, D., Jr. (2014). Does gender matter in Black Greek-lettered organizations? *Oracle: The Research Journal of the Association of Fraternity/Sorority Advisors, 9*(1), 20–32.

Montclair State University. (n.d.). *Greek life glossary*. https://www.montclair.edu/greek-life/greek-life-glossary/

Muñoz, S. M., & Guardia, J. R. (2009). Nuestra historia y futuro (our history and future): Latino/a fraternities and sororities. In C. L. Torbenson & G. S. Parks (Eds.), *Brothers and sisters: Diversity in college fraternities and sororities* (pp. 104–132). Cranbury, NJ: Rosemont Publishing & Printing Corp.

Mu Sigma Upsilon Sorority, Inc. (n.d.). *Our history*. http://www.msu1981.org/history/

NALFO. (2018). *National Association of Latino Fraternal Organizations constitution and bylaws*. http://nalfo.org/wp-content/uploads/NALFO-Constitution-and-Bylaws-Final-2018.pdf

NALFO. (2019). *About us*. http://nalfo.org

NAPA. (n.d.a). *APIDA Greek history*. http://www.napahq.org/about/#apia-greek-history

NAPA. (n.d.b). *Membership*. http://www.napahq.org/membership/

NAPA. (n.d.c). *NAPA history*. http://www.napahq.org/about/#napa-history

NAPA. (n.d.d). *Overview*. http://www.napahq.org/about/#overview

NIC. (2016). *Veronica Moore to join NIC team as Director of Emerging & Culturally-Based Fraternal Initiatives*. https://nicfraternity.org/moore-joins-nic-team/

NIC. (2017). *About Interfraternity Conference (IFC)*. https://nicfraternity.org/about-interfraternity-council-ifc/

NIC. (2019). *Guiding fraternity*. https://nicfraternity.org/nic-standards/

NMGC. (n.d.a). *About*. https://nationalmgc.org/about/

NMGC. (n.d.b). *Member organizations*. https://nationalmgc.org/about/member-organizations/

NMGC. (2010). *The amended and restated bylaws of the National Multicultural Greek Council, Incorporated*. http://nationalmgc.org/wp-content/uploads/2017/12/Amended-and-Restated-NMGC-Bylaws-2016.pdf

NPC. (n.d.a). *About the National Panhellenic Conference*. https://www.npcwomen.org/about/

NPC. (n.d.b). *National Panhellenic Conference member organizations*. https://www.npcwomen.org/about/our-member-organizations/

NPC. (n.d.c). *Our member organizations and affiliates*. https://www.npcwomen.org/about/our-members/

NPHC. (n.d.). *Our history*. https://www.nphchq.org/quantum/our-history/

Orta, D., Murguia, E., & Cruz, C. (2019). From struggle to success via Latina sororities: Culture shock, marginalization, embracing ethnicity, and educational persistence through academic capital. *Journal of Hispanic Higher Education, 18*(1), 41–58.

Park, J. (2008). Race and the Greek system in the 21st century: Centering the voices of Asian American women. *NASPA Journal, 45*(1), 103–132.

Park, J. J. (2012). Asian American women's perspectives on historically white sorority life: A critical race theory and cultural capital analysis. *Oracle: The Research Journal of the Association of Fraternity/Sorority Advisors, 7*(2), 1–18.

Patton, L. D., Bridges, B. K., & Flowers, L. A. (2011). Effects of Greek affiliation on African American students' engagement: Differences by college racial composition. *College Student Affairs Journal, 29*(2), 113–123.

Perkins, A. B., Zimmerman, D., & Janosik, S. M. (2011). Changing trends in the undergraduate fraternity/sorority experience: An evaluative and analytical literature review. *Oracle: The Research Journal of the Association of Fraternity/Sorority Advisors, 6*(1), 57–73.

Phi Iota Alpha. (2018). *Fact sheet*. https://www.phiota.org/fact-sheet

Phi Sigma Mu. (n.d.). *Home*. https://phisigmanu.com

Pike, G. R. (2003). Membership in a fraternity or sorority, student engagement, and educational outcomes at AAU public research universities. *Journal of College Student Development, 44*(3), 369–382.

Rankin, S. R., Hesp, G. A., & Weber, G. N. (2013). Experiences and perceptions of gay and bisexual fraternity members from 1960 to 2007: A cohort analysis. *Journal of College Student Development, 54*(6), 570–590.

Ray, R. (2013). Fraternity life at predominantly white universities in the US: The saliency of race. *Ethnic and Racial Studies, 36*(2), 320–336.

Ray, R., & Rosow, J. A. (2012). The two different worlds of Black and white fraternity men: Visibility and accountability as mechanisms of privilege. *Journal of Contemporary Ethnography, 41*(1), 66–94.

Raymond, N. (2018, December 5). Fraternities, sororities sue Harvard over single-sex club crackdown. *Reuters*. https://af.reuters.com/article/worldNews/idAFKBN1O41XG

Rhoads, R. A. (1995). Whales tales, dog piles, and beer goggles: An ethnographic case study of fraternity life. *Anthropology & Education Quarterly, 26*(3), 306–323.

Ross, L. C. (2001). *The divine nine: The history of African American fraternities and sororities*. New York, NY: Kensington Publishing Corp.

Rossman, S. (2017, November 22). Greek life suspensions keep coming on college campuses. Here's all of them from 2017. *USA Today*. https://www.usatoday.com/story/news/nation-now/2017/11/22/greek-life-suspensions-keep-coming-college-campuses-heres-all-them-2017/875699001/

Sasso, P. (2015). White boy wasted: Compensatory masculinities in fraternity alcohol use. *Oracle: The Research Journal of the Association of Fraternity/Sorority Advisors, 10*(1), 14–30.

Soria, K. M. (2013). Social class reconsidered: Examining the role of class and privilege in fraternities and sororities. *AFA Essentials*, 1–4.

Still, C. M., & Faris, B. R. (2019). Understanding and supporting historically Native American fraternities and sororities. In K. E. Gillon, C. C. Beatty, & C. Salinas Jr. (Eds.), *Critical considerations of race, ethnicity, and culture in fraternity and sorority life* (New Directions for Student Services, no. 165, pp. 51–59). Hoboken, NJ: Jossey-Bass.

Torbenson, C. L. (2012). The origin and evolution of college fraternities and sororities. In T. L. Brown, G. S. Parks, & C. M. Phillips (Eds.), *African American fraternities and sororities: The legacy and the vision* (2nd ed., pp. 33–62). Lexington, KY: University Press of Kentucky.

Torbenson, C. L. & Parks, G. S. (Eds.). (2009). *Brothers and sisters: Diversity in college fraternities and sororities*. Cranbury, NJ: Rosemont Publishing & Printing Corp.

Van Syckle, K. (2016, September 25). Pledging change: The transgender college students integrating Greek life. *The Guardian*. https://www.theguardian.com/society/2016/sep/25/transgender-students-fraternities-and-sororities

Virginia Tech. (2019). *Greek definitions*. https://fsl.vt.edu/resources/definitions.html

Wade, L. (2017, May 19). Why colleges should get rid of fraternities for good. *Time*. https://time.com/4784875/fraternities-timothy-piazza/

Walker, J. K., Martin, N. D., & Hussey, A. (2015). Greek organization membership and collegiate outcomes at an elite, private university. *Research in Higher Education*, *56*(3), 203–227.

Washington State University Center for Fraternity and Sorority Life. (2018). *Trans* inclusivity policies*. https://gogreek.wsu.edu/how-to-join/trans-inclusivity-policies/

Wells, A. E., & Dolan, M. K. (2009). Multicultural fraternities and sororities: A hodgepodge of transient multiethnic groups. In C. L. Torbenson & G. S. Parks (Eds.), *Brothers and sisters: Diversity in college fraternities and sororities* (157–183). Cranbury, NJ: Rosemont Publishing & Printing Corp.

Welter, E. (2012). College Greek life: Perceptions and lived experiences of lesbian, gay, bisexual, transgender, questioning, and queer (LGBTQ) students. *Journal of the Indiana Academy of the Social Sciences*, *15*(1), 111–139.

Williams, J. M. (2017). *Ostracized insiders: Exploring the experiences of Black gay men in historically Black Greek letter fraternities* (Doctoral dissertation). https://oaktrust.library.tamu.edu/

Worthen, M. G. (2014). Blaming the jocks and the Greeks?: Exploring collegiate athletes' and fraternity/sorority members' attitudes toward LGBT individuals. *Journal of College Student Development*, *55*(2), 168–195.

Yeung, K. T., & Stombler, M. (2000). Gay and Greek: The identity paradox of gay fraternities. *Social Problems*, *47*(1), 134–152.

Zeta Beta Tau. (2019). *About Zeta Beta Tau*. https://zbt.org/about-zbt/

CHAPTER TWO

Developments in Research on Culturally-Based Sororities and Fraternities

Antonio Duran, Crystal E. Garcia, and Hannah L. Reyes

The preceding chapter of this book provided insight into the emergence and structure of culturally-based sororities and fraternities at higher education institutions, highlighting the role that they play for students as well as larger sorority and fraternity life (SFL) communities. Understanding the histories of these organizations is important and has been the subject of formative texts like Torbenson and Parks' (2009) *Brothers and Sisters: Diversity in College Fraternities and Sororities*. Additionally, scholars have detailed these histories through other books and chapters including but not limited to works specific to African American (e.g., Brown, Parks, & Phillips, 2012; Parks & Hughey, 2020), Asian American (Dosono, Badruddin, & Lam, 2020), Latinx/a/o (Miranda, Garcia, & Guardi, 2020), and Historically Native American (Oxendine, Oxendine, & Minthorn, 2013) sororities and fraternities. Although comprehending the stories of how these organizations came to be is necessary to contextualize the values of these groups, especially considering their place within oppressive environments, this presents a narrow view of their overall functioning and contributions to individuals.

Although limited, the research on culturally-based sororities and fraternities has risen in the past couple of decades. This body of literature is significant because it provides contemporary perspectives on how members experience their organizations. Moreover, this scholarship showcases how professionals work to support these groups. Aligning with the goals of this present text, we argue that in order to move culturally-based sororities and fraternities forward, educators in postsecondary settings must explore up-to-date research that shines a light on these organizations. When professionals pair knowledge of the historical genealogies of these sororities and fraternities with a grasp on novel scholarship conducted on these organizations, they are better equipped to attend to the unique needs of these groups.

Therefore, the purpose of this chapter is to survey the emerging literature depicting culturally-based sororities and fraternities on college campuses specifically. Much of this research focuses in on students' experiences within these organizations with a smaller body of literature examining how higher education professionals support these SFL groups. In exploring the scholarship on culturally-based sororities and fraternities, several themes emerge. First, we examine how students make the decisions to join these organizations, the ways these groups influence students' identities, and how researchers discuss the outcomes associated with affiliation. Next, we describe contemporary issues facing culturally-based sororities and fraternities, including issues of hazing and attending to intersecting identities. Finally, we conclude with literature articulating the roles of practitioners in supporting these organizations. Reflecting on these areas of inquiry currently present in scholarship subsequently allows us to identify gaps in order to move research forward.

Joining Culturally-Based Sororities and Fraternities

Although culturally-based sororities and fraternities afford their members valuable opportunities to connect and build bonds with people of similar backgrounds and/or interests, some students on college campuses may not know about these organizations or be able to articulate why they may join such a group. Driven by this dilemma, researchers have started to answer the question of why individuals seek out and affiliate with culturally-based sororities and fraternities (e.g., Arellano, 2020; Delgado-Guerrero, Cherniack, & Gloria, 2014; Garcia & Duran, 2020, Greyerbiehl & Mitchell, 2014; Hughey, 2007; Tran & Chang, 2013). What is evident from this body of scholarship is that people who join culturally-based sororities and fraternities frequently do so for the lifelong connections that they anticipate, desiring to establish familial bonds and social networks.

Notably, scholars detailed that some individuals choose to join culturally-based sororities and fraternities as they see them as a way to construct relationships, especially as they encounter social isolation from other places on campus (e.g., Arellano, 2020; Tran & Chang, 2013). For example, in describing the many challenges that Latin@ college students experienced when transitioning to the collegiate environment (e.g., being away from campus, having to develop cross-racial friendships), Arellano (2020) stated the following: "The social isolation suffered forced these students to seek external support that materialized in the form of LGLOs [Latino Greek-Letter Organizations]" (p. 287). The same type of phenomena of lacking ties to the broader campus community also applied to Asian American men in Tran and Chang's (2013) study.

On a similar, yet related note, another reason why individuals choose to join culturally-based sororities and fraternities involves wanting to build relationships with those from similar cultural backgrounds and who hold similar values (Delgado-Guerrero et al., 2014; Greyerbiehl & Mitchell, 2014). Delgado-Guerrero's (2014) project on undergraduate Women of Color who affiliate with a cultural-specific sorority emphasized that these individuals joined because their organizations spoke to their specific needs to be empowered as Women of Color in addition to providing them the support necessary to persist in their college environment. Summarily, Delgado-Guerrero (2014) pointed to an internal desire to create a home-like group that would both assist and challenge them. In a likewise fashion, Greyerbiehl and Mitchell's (2014) study on African American women who join historically Black sororities emphasized that participants sought to join because they knew they would be held to high standards while also having access to a strong community. Of particular importance, individuals had the knowledge that this would be the case due to having mentors, families, and role models who were affiliated with these organizations. The reason why this is of significance is that it highlights how people can learn the value of the familial relationships formed within these groups through their own family or other role models.

One final noteworthy study that also stands out is Hughey's (2007) earlier project in which the author investigated why non-Black individuals join Black sororities and fraternities. In this project, Hughey (2007) discovered that those who do so affiliate with these organizations in order to tap into the social networks present in these groups but also join in order to benefit from Black Greek-Letter Organizations' histories of building bonds that last beyond the college years. As participants noticed major alumni activity, they too wanted to create these connections. Thus, even in instances in which people are affiliating with organizations whose histories of serving racial communities that are not their own, they still desire authentic and strong friendships.

Organizations' Influence on Social Identities

Central to the founding of culturally-based sororities and fraternities was the need for individuals to experience the bonds of siblinghood in a group more attentive to the lived realities of minoritized individuals (Gillon, Beatty, & Salinas, 2019; Torbenson & Park, 2009). Such communities came together to uplift individuals connected by particular social identities. Therefore, it is unsurprising that researchers have examined how these organizations influence how individuals see themselves and their specific identities (e.g., race/ethnicity, gender, and sexuality).

Race/Ethnicity

First, researchers have examined how culturally-based sororities and fraternities serve as settings that can inform how people view their racial/ethnic identity (e.g., Delgado-Guerrero et al., 2014; Garcia, 2020a; Greyerbiehl & Mitchell, 2014; Guardia & Evans, 2008; Orta et al., 2019). What is clear from these investigations is that culturally-based SFL organizations can provide individuals the opportunity to view their racial/ethnic identity in a more empowering way, especially for those who have experienced oppressive interactions on the basis of their race/ethnicity. For example, studies conducted on Latinx/a/o-based organizations underline how members are able to see their Latinx/a/o identity in a more positive light as they connect with individuals who come from similar backgrounds as one's self; this also extends to their ethnic identity specifically (e.g., Guardia & Evans, 2008; Orta et al., 2019). Similarly, the contributions of Greyerbiehl and Mitchell (2014) described how historically Black sororities created opportunities for individuals "to explore who they were as Black women [which] were powerful for the participants because it was not happening in other spaces on campus" (p. 291). Therefore, these organizations can be pivotal settings where Black women reflect on their Black identity and how it intersects with their gender.

Nevertheless, scholars have showcased how these organizations may present narrow views related to race and ethnicity. For example, the work of Chambers (2017) represents one critique of the ways that culturally-based sororities and fraternities may privilege certain types of members. Namely, in her discussion of Black Greek-Letter Organizations (BGLOs), Chambers (2017) contended that in striving to obtain acceptance into U.S. society, these sororities and fraternities have privileged the socially elite. Relevant to this discussion on race and ethnicity, she named that BGLOs showed a preference toward lighter-skinned individuals, thus marginalizing those with darker skin. Although this does not represent all

BGLOs, it is an important consideration to keep in mind when thinking about these organizations' influence on matters of race and ethnicity.

Gender

As inherently gendered organizations, culturally-based sororities and fraternities are also sites that shape people's conceptualization of masculinities (e.g., Anderson, Buckley, & Tindall, 2011; Duran & Garcia, 2020a; Jenkins, 2012; Jones, 2015; Khoury, 2013; McClure, 2006a; McGuire, McTier, Ikegwuonu, Sweet, & Bryant-Scott, 2018; Tran & Chang, 2013, 2019; Yeung, Stombler, & Wharton, 2006) and femininities (Hernandez, 2012; Literte & Hodge, 2012). For instance, the scholarship within the context of culturally-based fraternities showcases how these organizations can reify hegemonic beliefs on what it means to perform masculinities. These pieces of research communicate how Men of Color may perpetuate visions of masculinities in which they must be strong, engage in hypersexual behaviors, and suppress pain—especially in the initiation process (Jenkins, 2012). However, researchers have cautioned against painting these organizations and Men of Color in a one-dimensional point-of-view concerning masculinities. Namely, other scholars have argued that Men of Color in culturally-based organizations in fact can gain more productive and healthy perspectives on masculinities given the strong focus on brotherhood fostered by these organizations (Duran & Garcia, 2020a; McGuire et al., 2018). Although the literature on Asian American-interest fraternities is smaller compared to other kinds of organizations, Tran and Chang (2019) argued that the same positive influence can occur for Asian men affiliated with these groups. Of note, by participating in these organizations, these organizations encourage individuals to challenge racialized and gendered stereotypes, viewing their gender in a more empowering way. Across these studies, researchers emphasize the racialized nature of masculinities present in these culturally-based fraternities.

Comparatively, research on femininities within culturally-based sororities is lesser, but reveals similar patterns of individuals adhering to gendered norms. For example, in Hernandez' (2012) look at on appearance enforcement within historically Black sororities, she found that members are held to high gendered standards as it relates to their dressing, as well as behavior. These expectations emerged in order to challenge the unfair and oppressive ways Black women are seen in U.S. society. However, Hernandez (2012) argued that these norms can have deleterious effects on how members express their femininities, leading to negative attitudes rooted in classism. Put simply, sorority members can start to regulate who is considered womanly and who is not depending on how they perform their gender. This phenomenon also appeared in Literte and Hodge's (2012) examination of historically Black sororities in which some queer members felt that they had to perform in more feminine ways given the fear of being treated differently because of their sexuality. Related to this point, select pieces of scholarship have named how culturally-based sororities and fraternities influence people's view of their sexuality.

Sexuality

Finally, a smaller body of research has taken a look at how culturally-based sororities and fraternities inform how individuals think of their sexuality (Duran & Garcia, in press; Garcia & Duran, 2020; Yeung & Stombler, 2000). Of note, very few articles exist specific to Lesbian, Gay, Bisexual, Transgender, and Queer (LGBTQ) organizations (Yeung & Stombler, 2000; Yeung et al., 2006), a reality emphasized in Chapter Six by Douglas N. Case. What is present showcases how LGBTQ fraternities present a paradoxical nature concerning how members understand their gay identity. Specifically, though LGBTQ fraternities provide safe spaces for people to explore their gay identity, members also have to reconcile navigating heterosexism within the broader SFL community. Therefore, the influence that these organizations have on sexuality for members is complex and multi-faceted. Beyond attending to LGBTQ sororities and fraternities, researchers have also communicated how other culturally-based SFL organizations can provide affirming environments for Queer Men of Color (Garcia & Duran, 2020) and Queer Women of Color (Duran & Garcia, 2021) to express and relate to their sexuality.

Outcomes of Joining: Connections to Belonging, Engagement, Success, and Leadership

In addition to detailing the reasons why individuals join culturally-based sororities and fraternities, as well as their influence on members' social identities, scholars have described how affiliation with these organizations leads to significant student outcomes. Specifically, research has centered on topics of belongingness, student engagement and success, as well as on leadership.

Students' Sense of Belonging

One of the central outcomes that higher education institutional leaders hope to develop is a sense of belonging for students, a construct defined by experiencing a mutual sense of mattering between a group and an individual (Strayhorn, 2019). Hence, it is unsurprising that researchers interested in culturally-based sororities and fraternities have explored how these organizations influence belongingness (e.g., Atkinson et al., 2010; Delgado-Guerrero et al., 2014; Garcia, 2020a, 2020b; Greyerbiehl & Mitchell, 2014; Hunter & Hughey, 2013; Shalka & Jones, 2015). Connected to points made above concerning the influence on social identities, scholars have showcased how the validation that people receive concerning their racial and ethnic identity is meaningful for how they experience belongingness on campus (Delgado-Guerrero et al., 2014). But still, the research on students' success of belonging for those in these culturally-based SFL organizations is complex.

For example, the work of Garcia (2020a) on Latina/o sororities and fraternities highlighted how membership in these organizations can lead to different experiences of belongingness. In particular, participants in her study differed in how they reported their sense of belonging on an institutional level versus that in their Latina/o sorority and fraternity, as well as other campus subgroups. For some, their belongingness was connected to their campus subcultures including their SFL organization, as well as their institution as whole, while for others, it was one or the other. Consequently, this finding portrays culturally-based sororities and fraternities as meaningful for students but not able to fully solve the issues that exist on an institutional level. Other studies like Hunter and Hughey's (2013) provide even more nuanced perspectives on belongingness for members of culturally-based SFL organizations. In their research on Multicultural Greek Organizations, they found that some members felt that rather than embrace their individual differences, their group portrayed multiculturalism as one-dimensional. In turn, this affected how students reported a sense of belonging within their organization.

Student Engagement and Success

Beyond attending to belongingness, researchers have also examined how culturally-based sororities and fraternities shape other important metrics including student engagement (Harper, 2007; Patton, Flowers, & Bridges 2011; Yearwood, 2012) and success (e.g., Delgado-Guerrero & Gloria, 2013; McClure, 2006b; Moreno & Banuelos, 2013). In the scholarship specific to student engagement, results oftentimes point to positive effects created by affiliation with culturally-based SFL organizations. Patton et al.'s (2011) research on African American students emphasized that involvement with BGLOs seemed to "stimulate increased levels of engagement among African American students" (p. 119).

Specifically, Patton et al. (2011) described how affiliation with these organizations led to noticeable influences on faculty-student interactions, as well as collaborative learning.

Related to this interest in engagement, other studies centered on metrics of student success related to culturally-based sororities and fraternities. Research on Latinx/a/o-based SFL organizations articulates how involvement with these organizations frequently leads to important sources of motivation (Moreno & Banuelos, 2013), which in turn can also benefit students when it comes to measures of academic persistence (Delgado-Guerrero & Gloria, 2013). Connected to these findings, an earlier study conducted by McClure (2006b) argued that affiliation with historically Black fraternities may be a formative influence for members that prevents their attrition from predominantly white institutions. The reason being is that these organizations can provide the social support and mentorship necessary to navigate oppressive contexts within these types of institutions.

Leadership Outcomes

Lastly, another area of research has examined how culturally-based sororities and fraternities contribute to the leadership experiences of their members (e.g., Armstrong & Jackson, 2017; Atkinson et al., 2010; Mitchell, Gipson, Marie, & Steele Mitchell, 2017). Present in these studies is the acknowledgment that culturally-based SFL organizations provide leadership opportunities for minoritized individuals that may not otherwise have access to on campus. Atkinson et al. (2010) emphasized this point in their study on those affiliated with Multicultural Greek Council (MGC) organizations, as they noted how members of these sororities and fraternities are more likely to hold leadership roles (e.g., chapter president or vice president) because of the smaller size of these chapters. However, other scholars have showed how members exercise their leadership potential beyond the confines of their individual organizations.

An example of this can be seen in the contributions of Mitchell et al. (2017) who examined the experiences of African American women in historically Black sororities versus non-historically Black organizations. Notable findings from this study included that those affiliated with historically Black sororities were more likely to be involved with culturally-based student groups and with their SFL organizations compared to their counterparts in non-historically Black organizations. What these results showcase are the ways that these sororities encourage and empower Black women to achieve their leadership potential. Other studies offer additional perspectives on how members of culturally-based sororities and fraternities grow in their leadership development as a result of their affiliation. Armstrong and Jackson (2017), for instance, conveyed how Black men in Black Greek-letter fraternities had more access to mentors who in turn supported them in their leadership abilities. Evident in all of these examples is the beneficial role that culturally-based sororities and fraternities play for individuals' leadership capacities, both within and outside of their individual organizations.

Contemporary Issues Facing Culturally-Based Sororities and Fraternities

Although culturally-based sororities and fraternities afford students the opportunity to explore their social identities and also contribute to significant college outcomes, these organizations still wrestle with certain issues in contemporary times. These areas for improvement mirror many of the problems expressed as it relates to historically white sororities and fraternities, including oppressive behaviors, hazing, and illicit drug or alcohol use (Biddix, 2016; Rossman, 2017; Wade, 2017). However, scholars writing in this area of research showcase how these difficulties manifest differently in the context of culturally-based sororities and fraternities. For the purposes of this chapter, we focus on two contemporary issues: hazing and attending to intersecting forms of oppression within culturally-based sororities and fraternities.

Hazing in Culturally-Based Sororities and Fraternities

In the broader landscape of SFL, one subject matter that regularly appears is that of hazing, an issue that is present across various types of student organizations (Allan, Kerschner, & Payne, 2019). Scholars have examined hazing specifically within the culturally-based sorority and fraternity context (e.g., Foster, 2008; Jones, 2000; Kimbrough, 2009; Parks, Jones, Ray, Hughey, & Cox, 2015; Parks, Ray, Jones, & Hughey, 2014; Rogers, Rogers, & Anderson, 2012). Namely, those who have taken a more historical approach to understanding this phenomenon have argued that the ways hazing manifests in spaces like BGLOs is different than it was in the past. For instance, Kimbrough (2009) named how BGLOs once relied on more of a problematic pledging process while they now embrace a membership intake process that does not incorporate hazing to the same extent. Nevertheless, this too has resulted in older members perceiving the process and new members as softer. What is important to note is that even though most of the hazing research on culturally-based sororities and fraternities attends to historically

Black fraternities, this is certainly not to say that the same issues are not present in other kinds of organizations.

More contemporary research has showed several noteworthy findings as it relates to hazing. An example of this includes the work of Parks et al. (2015) who provided both a historical and contemporary analysis of historically Black sororities and fraternities. In this comprehensive manuscript, Parks et al. (2015) described the differences between the types of hazing that manifest in sororities and fraternities with the former being more emotionally driven while the latter is traditionally physical in nature. Interestingly, in their study of members affiliated with BGLOs, they discovered that those who had attended predominantly white institutions were more likely to be hazed when compared to those who were from Historically Black Colleges and Universities. For this reason, it is imperative to underscore as always that these practices within BGLOs are always tied back to histories of white supremacy and colonialism. Parks et al. (2015) put it succinctly when they stated: "Colonialism and racial hegemony have had a direct negative effect on the rights of passage traditions established in BGLOs, which are heavily rooted in the warped concept of masculinity" (p. 154). This kind of contextualization is important to attend to the realities of hazing within these organizations and other kinds of culturally-based sororities and fraternities, an argument taking up in Chapter Ten written by Jenny Nirh and Marcos Guzman.

Attending to Intersecting Forms of Oppression

Another topical subject matter that has appeared in the research on culturally-based sororities and fraternities includes critically analyzing how these organizations address intersecting forms of oppression. What is evident about these groups from their histories is that their leaders established them given the experiences of marginalization that minoritized individuals (e.g., People of Color, LGBTQ community members) encountered on- and off-campus (Torbenson & Parks, 2009). This type of commitment to supporting those who face marginalization stands strong today. Nevertheless, some scholars have argued that it is important to analyze how organizations address oppressive behaviors and beliefs in areas that are outside of their explicit area of focus. For instance, how do LGBTQ-interest sororities and fraternities not only attend to heterosexism and trans oppression, but also racism and ableism? How do Latinx/a/o-based sororities and fraternities create welcoming spaces on the basis of race and ethnicity, but also sexuality? Albeit limited, researchers have begun answering these questions.

In particular, the research that does exist on this topic frequently examined how culturally-based sororities and fraternities founded to uplift racially minoritized populations perpetuate or mitigate oppressive realities for those within the LGBTQ community (DeSantis & Coleman, 2008; Duran & Garcia, 2020a, 2020b, 2021; Garcia & Duran, 2020; Jenkins, 2012; Literte & Hodge, 2012; Williams, 2017). For instance, research has primarily examined the attitudes toward queerness in historically Black sororities and fraternities, pointing to how these organizations at times display homophobic beliefs that marginalize prospective and current members (DeSantis & Coleman, 2008; Jenkins, 2012; Literte & Hodge, 2012; Mahoney, 2019; Williams, 2017). Yet, this should by no means paint a monolithic picture of these organizations. Literte and Hodge (2012), for example, argued that these types of beliefs were predominantly held by older members of historically Black sororities. Moreover, Mahoney (2019) contended that the presence of homophobia within Black fraternities emerged as a result of white supremacy and whiteness. Namely, by mobilizing Queer of Color Critique, Mahoney (2019) named that it was historically Black fraternities' striving to succeed in a society dominated by whiteness that caused them to acquiesce to respectability politics that position queer people as deviant.

In our own work examining the experiences of Queer Cisgender Women and Men of Color (see Duran & Garcia, 2020a, 2020b, 2021; Garcia & Duran, 2020), we have attempted to make a similar argument. Namely, Queer Men of Color encountered marginalization in these organizations (in the case of our work, Black and Latinx/a/o-based fraternities) and at times, reified these behaviors by deciding to vote against queer individuals in addition to feeling as though they needed to prove their strength and worth more so than heterosexual members (Garcia & Duran, 2020). However, at the same time, some participants reported feeling accepted by their fraternity members (Garcia & Duran, 2020) or their sorority sisters (Duran & Garcia, 2021) when they actively showed their acceptance toward queer individuals. What these findings showcase is that culturally-based sororities and fraternities are more than capable to create inclusive spaces for LGBTQ individuals when they actively work in search of this aim.

Practitioner Roles in Supporting Culturally-Based Sororities and Fraternities

In the broader landscape of research on culturally-based sororities and fraternities, the central focus in studies involves the experiences of members. However, there are some scholars who have started to address the realities of practitioners who advise and advocate for these organizations (e.g., Parks & Spencer, 2013; Patton & Bonner, 2001; Strayhorn & McCall, 2012). Of note, these pieces of scholarship have almost exclusively centered on professionals working with BGLOs, suggesting a gap in the literature relevant to other culturally-based sororities and fraternities. What these studies highlighted was a need for practitioners to do their due diligence in understanding the unique nature of BGLOs.

Specifically, scholars argued that advisors should seek to comprehend how issues present in broader SFL communities (e.g., alcohol use, public perceptions, hazing) manifest in the BGLO context (Patton & Bonner, 2001). Expanding upon this point of view, Parks and Spencer's (2013) manuscript on civil liability and advising BGLOs suggested that student affairs practitioners can cause harm if they are not well-informed on how to work with BGLOs, especially as it relates to hazing. In particular, they contended that BGLO advisors may lack crucial knowledge on BGLO culture, recommending that these practitioners seek out current literature on these SFL organizations. Part of the work involved in advising these groups includes having a high degree of cultural competence, a finding asserted by Strayhorn and McCall (2012). Therefore, practitioners interested in serving in an advisor capacity for BGLOs, and culturally-based sororities and fraternities more generally, must be prepared in seeking out resources that will broaden their content knowledge and cultural competency.

Conclusion

Culturally-based sororities and fraternities are complex organizations that require further attention from practitioners and scholars alike. Though their histories are present in texts available to the general public (e.g., Brown et al., 2012; Dosono et al., 2020; Miranda et al., 2020; Oxendine et al., 2013; Parks & Hughey, 2020; Torbenson & Parks, 2009), the amount of scholarship detailing contemporary experiences is not as bountiful. That being said, several researchers have begun to illustrate how these organizations continue to support minoritized communities, in addition to detailing areas of improvement for these groups. As readers move through the rest of this book and hear from the voices of practitioners who support culturally-based sororities and fraternities, we encourage them to keep this broader area of research in mind. This knowledge, paired with the recommendations from the chapter authors, will be crucial to move culturally-based sororities and fraternities forward.

Questions for Reflection

- What areas of research concerning culturally-based sororities and fraternities are you most unfamiliar with? How can you create a plan to learn more about these topic areas?
- What gaps do you notice in the existing scholarship on culturally-based sororities and fraternities?
- How do you see yourself translating scholarly perspectives on culturally-based sororities and fraternities to your practice?

References

Allan, E. J., Kerschner, D., & Payne, J. M. (2019). College student hazing experiences, attitudes, and perceptions: Implications for prevention. *Journal of Student Affairs Research and Practice*, 56(1), 32–48.

Anderson, R., Buckley, P. M., & Tindall, N. T. J. (2011). Black Greek-letter fraternities and masculinities. In M. W. Hughes & G. S. Parks (Eds.), *Black Greek-letter organizations 2.0: New directions in the study of African American fraternities and sororities* (pp. 114–132). Jackson, MS: University Press of Mississippi.

Arellano, L. (2020). Why Latin@s become Greek: Exploring why Latin@s join Latino Greek-letter organizations. *Journal of Hispanic Higher Education*, 19(3), 280–302.

Armstrong, J., & Jackson, B. A. (2017). "They expect you to be better": Mentoring as a tool of resistance among Black fraternity men. *Oppression and Resistance: Structure, Agency, Transformation*, 48, 175–190.

Atkinson, E., Dean, L. A., & Espino, M. M. (2010). Leadership outcomes based on membership in Multicultural Greek Council (MGC) organizations. *Oracle: The Research Journal of the Association of Fraternity/Sorority Advisors*, 5(2), 34–48.

Biddix, P. (2016). Moving beyond alcohol: A review of other issues associated with fraternity membership with implications for practice and research. *Journal of College Student Development*, 57(7), 793–809.

Brown, T. L., Parks, G. S., & Phillips, C. M. (Eds.) (2012). *African American fraternities and sororities: The legacy and the vision* (2nd ed.). Lexington, KY: University Press of Kentucky.

Chambers, A. D. (2017). The failure of the Black Greek Letter Organization. *Journal of Black Studies*, 48(7), 627–638.

Delgado-Guerrero, M., Cherniack, M. A., & Gloria, A. M. (2014). Family away from home: Factors influencing undergraduate Women of Color's decisions to join a cultural-specific sorority. *Journal of Diversity in Higher Education*, 7(1), 45–57.

Delgado-Guerrero, M., & Gloria, A. M. (2013). La importancia de la hermandad Latina: Examining the psychosociocultural influences of Latina-based sororities on academic persistence decisions. *Journal of College Student Development, 54*(4), 361–378.

DeSantis, A. D., & Coleman, M. (2008). Not on my line: Attitudes about homosexuality in Black fraternities. In G. Parks (Ed.), *Black Greek-letter organizations in the twenty-first century* (pp. 291–312). Lexington, KY: The University Press of Kentucky.

Dosono, B., Badruddin, B., & Lam, V. W. H. (2020). History of Asian American Greek-letter organizations. In P. A. Sasso, J. P. Biddix, & M. L. Miranda (Eds.), *Foundations, research, and assessment of fraternities and sororities: Retrospective and future considerations* (pp. 25–37). Gorham, ME: Myers Education Press.

Duran, A., & Garcia, C. E. (2020a). Narratives of Queer Men of Color in culturally-based fraternities making meaning of masculinities. *International Journal of Qualitative Studies in Education.* Advance online publication. doi: 10.1080/09518398.2020.1828652

Duran, A., & Garcia, C. E. (2020b). Post-undergraduate narratives of Queer Men of Color's resistance in culturally-based fraternities. *Journal of Student Affairs Research and Practice.* Advance online publication. doi: 10.1080/19496591.2020.1772083

Duran, A., & Garcia, C. E. (2021). Quaring sorority life: Identity negotiation of Queer Women of Color in culturally-based sororities. *Journal of College Student Development, 62*(2), 186–202.

Foster, K. M. (2008). Black Greeks and underground pledging: Public debates and communal concerns. *Transforming Anthropology, 16*(1), 3–19.

Garcia, C. E. (2020a). Belonging in a predominantly white institution: The role of membership in Latina/o sororities and fraternities. *Journal of Diversity in Higher Education, 13*(2), 181–193.

Garcia, C. E. (2020b). "They don't even know we exist": Exploring sense of belonging within sorority and fraternity communities for Latina/o members. *Journal of College Student Development, 60*(3), 319–336.

Garcia, C. E., & Duran, A. (2020). "In my letters, but I was still by myself": Highlighting the experiences of Queer Men of Color in culturally based fraternities. *Journal of Diversity in Higher Education.* Advance online publication. http://dx.doi.org/10.1037/dhe0000167

Gillon, K. E., Beatty, C. C., & Salinas, C., Jr. (2019). Race and racism in fraternity and sorority life: A historical overview. In K. E. Gillon, C. C. Beatty, & C. Salinas Jr. (Eds.), *Critical considerations of race, ethnicity, and culture in fraternity & sorority life* (New Directions for Student Services, no. 165, pp. 9–16). Hoboken, NJ: Wiley.

Greyerbiehl, L., & Mitchell, D., Jr. (2014). An intersectional social capital analysis of the influence of historically Black sororities on African American women's college experiences at a predominantly white institution. *Journal of Diversity in Higher Education, 7*(4), 282–294.

Guardia, J. R., & Evans, N. J. (2008). Factors influencing the ethnic identity development of latino fraternity members at a Hispanic serving institution. *Journal of College Student Development, 49*(3), 163–181.

Harper, S. R. (2007). The effects of sorority and fraternity membership on class participation and African American student engagement in predominantly white classroom environments. *College Student Affairs Journal, 27*(1), 94–115.

Hernandez, M. D. (2011). Challenging controlling images: Appearance enforcement within Black sororities. In M. W. Hughey & G. S. Parks (Eds.), *Black Greek-letter organizations 2.0: New directions in the study of African American fraternities and sororities* (pp. 212–229). Jackson, MS: University Press of Mississippi.

Hughey, M. W. (2007). Crossing the sands, crossing the color line: Non-Black members of Black Greek Letter Organizations. *Journal of African American Studies, 11*(1), 55–75.

Hunter, J. S., & Hughey, M. W., (2013). "It's not written on their skin like it is ours": Greek letter organizations in the age of the multicultural imperative. *Ethnicities, 13*(5), 519.

Jenkins, R. D. (2012). Black fraternal organizations: Understanding the development of hegemonic masculinity and sexuality. *Journal of African American Studies, 16*(2), 226–235.

Jones, R. L. (2015). *Black haze: Violence, sacrifice, and manhood in Black Greek-letter fraternities* (2nd ed.). Albany, NY: State University of New York Press.

Khoury, I. (2013). "It's a manhood thing": Pledging, masculinity, and identity development in Black Greek fraternities. In M. C. Brown II, T. E. Dancy II, & J. E. Davis (Eds.), *Educating African American males: Contexts for consideration, possibilities for practice* (pp. 139–156). Bern, Switzerland: Peter Lang.

Kimbrough, W. M. (2009). The membership intake movement of historically Black Greek-Letter Organizations. *Journal of Student Affairs Research and Practice, 46*(4), 603–613.

Literte, P. E., & Hodge, C. (2012). Sisterhood and sexuality: Attitudes about homosexuality among members of historically Black sororities. *Journal of African American Studies, 16,* 674–699.

Mahoney, A. D. (2019). *Queering Black Greek-lettered fraternities, masculinity and manhood: A Queer of Color critique of institutionality in higher education* (Paper 3286) (Doctoral dissertation, University of Louisville, Louisville, KY). University of Louisville Electronic Theses and Dissertation.

McClure, S. M. (2006a). Improvising masculinity: African American fraternity membership in the construction of a Black masculinity. *Journal of African American Studies, 10*(1), 57–73.

McClure, S. M. (2006b). Voluntary association membership: Black Greek men on a predominantly white campus. *Journal of Higher Education, 77*(6), 1036–1057.

McGuire, K. M., McTier, T. S., Jr., Ikegwuonu, E., Sweet, J. D., & Bryant-Scott, K. (2018). "Men doing life together": Black Christian fraternity men's embodiments of brotherhood. *Men and Masculinities.* Advance online publication. doi: 10.1177/1097184X18782735

Miranda, M. L., Garcia, K. D., & Guardia, J. D. (2020). NALFO: A retrospective y hacia adelante. In P. A. Sasso, J. P. Biddix, & M. L. Miranda (Eds.), *Foundations, research, and assessment of fraternities and sororities: Retrospective and future considerations* (pp. 39–46). Gorham, ME: Myers Education Press.

Mitchell, D., Jr., Gipson, J., Marie, J., & Steele, T. (2017). Intersectional value? A pilot study exploring educational outcomes for African American women in historically Black sororities versus non-historically Black sororities. *Oracle: The Research Journal of the Association of Fraternity/Sorority Advisors, 12*(2), 44–58.

Moreno, D. R., & Banuelos, S. M. S. (2013). The influence of Latina/o Greek sorority and fraternity involvement on Latina/o college student transition and success. *Journal of Latino-Latin American Studies (JOLLAS), 5*(2), 113–125.

Orta, D., Murguia, E., & Cruz, C. (2019). From struggle to success via Latina sororities: Culture shock, marginalization, embracing ethnicity, and educational persistence through academic capital. *Journal of Hispanic Higher Education, 18*(1), 41–58.

Oxendine, D., Oxendine, S., & Minthorn, R. (2013). The historically Native American fraternity and sorority movement. In H. J. Shotton, S. C. Lowe, & S. J. Waterman (Eds.), *Beyond the asterisk: Understanding Native students in education* (pp. 67–80). Sterling, VA: Stylus.

Parks, G. S., & Hughey, M. W. (2020). *A pledge with purpose: Black sororities and fraternities and the fight for equality*. New York, NY: NYU Press.

Parks, G. S., Jones, S. E., Ray, R., Hughey, M. W., & Cox, J. M. (2015). White boys drink, Black girls yell …: A racialized and gendered analysis of violent hazing and the law. *Journal of Gender, Race & Justice, 18*(1), 93–158.

Parks, G. S., Ray, R., Jones, S. E., & Hughey, M. W. (2014). Complicit in their own demise? *Law & Social Inquiry, 39*(4), 938–972.

Parks, G. S., & Spencer, D. (2013). Student affairs professionals, Black "Greek" hazing, and university civil liability. *College Student Affairs Journal, 31*(2), 125–138.

Patton, L. A., & Bonner, F. A., II. (2001). Advising the Historically Black Greek Letter Organization (HBGLO): A reason for angst or euphoria? *National Association of Student Affairs Professionals Journal, 4*(1), 17–30.

Patton, L. D., Flowers, L. A., & Bridges, B. K. (2011). Effects of Greek affiliation on African American students' engagement differences by college racial composition. *College Student Affairs Journal, 29*(2), 113–123.

Rogers, S., Rogers, C., & Anderson, T. (2012). Examining the link between pledging, hazing, and organizational commitment among members of a Black Greek fraternity. *Oracle: The Research Journal of the Association of Fraternity/Sorority Advisors, 7*(1), 43–53.

Rossman, S. (2017, November 22). Greek life suspensions keep coming on college campuses. Here's all of them from 2017. *USA Today*. https://www.usatoday.com/story/news/nation-now/2017/11/22/greek-life-suspensions-keep-coming-college-campuses-heres-all-them-2017/875699001/

Shalka, T. R., & Jones, S. R. (2015). Differences in self-awareness related measures among culturally based fraternity, social fraternity, and non-affiliated college men. *Oracle: The Research Journal of the Association of Fraternity/Sorority Advisors, 5*(1), 1–11.

Strayhorn, T. L. (2019). *College students' sense of belonging: A key to educational success for all students* (2nd ed.). Oxfordshire, UK: Routledge.

Strayhorn, T. L., & McCall, F. C. (2012). Cultural competency of Black Greek-Letter Organization advisors. *Journal of African American Studies, 16*(4), 700–715.

Torbenson, C. L., & Parks, G. S. (Eds.). (2009). *Brothers and sisters: Diversity in college fraternities and sororities.* Cranbury, NJ: Rosemont Publishing & Printing Corp.

Tran, M. C., & Chang, M. J. (2013). To be mice or men: Gender identity and the development of masculinity through participation in Asian American interest fraternities. In S. D. Museus, D. C. Maramba, & R. T. Teranishi (Eds.), *The misrepresented minority: New insights on Asian Americans and Pacific islanders, and the implications for higher education* (pp. 67–85). Sterling, VA: Stylus.

Tran, M., & Chang, M. (2019). Asian American interest fraternities: Fulfilling unmet needs of the loneliest Americans. In K. E. Gillon, C. C. Beatty, & C. Salinas Jr. (Eds.), *Critical considerations of race, ethnicity, and culture in fraternity & sorority life* (New Directions for Student Services, no. 165, pp. 99–108). Hoboken, NJ: Wiley.

Wade, L. (2017, May 19). Why colleges should get rid of fraternities for good. *Time.* https://time.com/4784875/fraternities-timothy-piazza/

Williams, J. M. (2017). *Ostracized insiders: Exploring the experiences of Black gay men in historically Black Greek letter fraternities* (Doctoral dissertation, Texas A&M University, College Station, TX). Texas A&M University Libraries. https://oaktrust.library.tamu.edu/

Yearwood, T. L., & Jones, E. A. (2012). Understanding what influences successful Black commuter students' engagement in college. *JGE: The Journal of General Education, 61*(2), 97–125.

Yeung, K.-T., & Stombler, M. (2000). Gay and Greek: The identity paradox of gay fraternities. *Social Problems, 47(1)*, 134–52.

Yeung, K.-T., Stombler, M., & Wharton, R. (2006). Making men in gay fraternities: Resisting and reproducing multiple dimensions of hegemonic masculinity. *Gender and Society, 20*(1), 5–31.

SECTION 2

INNOVATIONS IN PRACTICE: OPPORTUNITIES AND CHALLENGES FACING ORGANIZATIONS

Member Vignette: Black Sororities and Fraternities

NADREA NJOKU

I knew rather early that I wanted to join Alpha Kappa Alpha Sorority, Inc. (AKA). When I was in second grade my mother enrolled in her first college course at a local Historically Black College and University (HBCU) specializing in full-time working adults. Accompanying her to class, doing my homework in the Dean's office, and attending student events meant I met other adult Black women—but those AKA ladies stood out. From students to administrators, they were poised, campus queens, and leaders. So, when I arrived at Xavier University of Louisiana, I knew for sure I wanted to pledge.

I pledged in the fall of 2003 after two women lost their lives pledging a suspended chapter in California, which resulted in a year-long moratorium. I had classmates who were supposed to be initiated the year prior but were unable to because of this tragedy. Some of those women made my line; others watched from the audience of our neophyte show.

Since the sorority had a heightened sense of alarm around hazing post-2002, sorority membership intake occurred under a microscope. Our movements as young members were intensely scrutinized (from my entrance at rush until I graduated in 2006). We consistently faced relentless and dogged panels of graduate sorors (sorority sisters) who were questioning our motives, our conversations with non-members interested in joining, and the language we used—that may or may not promote an environment of hazing. On one hand, they were instructing us to follow the rules and regulations of the organization, and on the other penalizing us for not having been "made in their day." If it were not for the joys of attending an HBCU as a Black sorority girl—a connection to history personified, step shows, sisterhood, and comradery between other Black sororities and fraternities—my experiences with the graduate members would have tainted my view of AKA. The dichotomy of experiencing these women from afar as a child and my interactions with them as a college-age member was traumatic.

I took my experiences—both good and challenging—into constant consideration as I embarked on membership and advising as a graduate student at Indiana University. By day, I advised Indiana University's National Pan-Hellenic Council (NPHC) and mentored younger women on campus at night. They seemed to be facing some of the same highs and lows I faced as a student. As members of the NPHC faced allegations of hazing, I centered my experiences as I counseled them to abide by the student conduct code of the university by aiming to listen first. I was 5 years removed from undergrad, so I did not have the space to act oblivious to the pressures of campus life and tradition. Yet, I used my growing knowledge of student affairs practice to help safeguard them from themselves. The ideas I began to formulate as a graduate student balancing my coursework, graduate membership, and advising NPHC students were bringing me to a higher plane of preparation. Though I did not have the exact phrasing and critical language at that time, I was equipped in ways my advisors were not.

As a scholar of Black feminisms and Black women's college experiences, I am reflective of what we learn, and, in turn, teach young women about their behaviors and bodies through sorority membership. To demonstrate my ideas around this, I will turn to my own writing at 21 years of age. To articulate for my undergraduate chapter the type of woman we should initiate, I wrote a manual to guide us. Our neos (new members) were struggling to "get it." We were seeing proposals to take interest in a variety of women, but few seemed worthy of the chapter's standard. In this guide, I wrote extensively on the characteristics of a good soror. Pulled from the campus norms, my point of view, and an Ivy Primer published by our sorority in 1970 that we found in the chapter's storage facility, a portion of "A Good Soror" stated the following:

> A good soror is fair in making decisions and does what is best to benefit the sorority, not herself. A soror is a selfless person who gives her time to improve her sorority. She is one who takes pride in her chapter and always remembers who she is representing when she is in the public eye. She understands that being in a sorority is not all about strutting at parties and having the prettiest line jacket; she knows that being in a sorority is about being a part of a sisterhood, being a service to mankind, and striving for scholastic achievement.

I go on about more characteristics and behaviors becoming of an Alpha Kappa Alpha woman and I end with "most importantly, a good soror is RESPEKFUL at all times!"

This writing and my notions of the role sorority played in the lives of my sorors highlight several themes. My time as an undergraduate member of AKA equipped me with fight and drive, and it shaped my Black feminist politics—sisterhood has saved *me at every juncture of my adulthood. Yet, this training also stifled my dream making beyond respectable and conventional ideas of Black womanhood. At critical junctures of my life post-initiation, I was far too concerned with my behavior and people's perceptions than maintaining my joy, dreams, and self-integrity. These worries caused me to make personal and professional choices that were not authentic, yet today, I have successfully obtained three degrees, maintain a robust professional portfolio, and am growing a beautiful family. All of these things should equal happiness, but as a Black woman, I am riddled with "what-ifs." Sorority membership has helped and harmed me. However, I know that if improved and re-envisioned, the model could rise to the expectations of both the founders and current membership—truly freeing us all. Historically Black sororities have to be nimble and evolving organizations that embed the best principles we learn from history and instill tactics to combat racism and patriarchy.*

CHAPTER THREE

A Practitioner's Perspective: Advising and Supporting Black Sororities and Fraternities

CAMERON C. BEATTY, EBONY WOFFORD, AND CHRIS GRAHAM

During the 19th century, Greek-letter social organizations, which were organized and separated by normative notions of the gender binary and legal race segregation, began to emerge and expand on college campuses (Kimbrough, 2003). The creation and expansion of historically white sororities and fraternities were regulated by both formal and informal racist practices and policies that allowed for broader access to higher education for white students, and limited access for Black students (Hughey, 2009). While historically white sororities and fraternities were growing and expanding, the participation of Black students in higher education continued to be regulated by racist laws that excluded them from attending college or segregated them into specific colleges and universities (Kimbrough 2003, 2009). Some Black students found educational homes at private historically Black colleges and universities (HBCUs) and then public HBCUs, often referred to as the 1890s schools (Hughey, 2009). Additionally, some Students of Color—Black, Latinx/a/o, Native American, Asian—although small in number, were attending historically white institutions (HWIs; Hughey, 2009; Kimbrough, 2003).

For those students, access did not translate to full opportunities to participate in university life at HWIs. Rather, access was often intertwined with exclusion, including for Black students (Gillon, Beatty, & Salinas, 2019). By the turn of the 20th century, this exclusion had manifested in specific ways on college campuses, including denied access to residential housing and recreational spaces and at institutions where Greek-letter organizations were present, exclusion from sorority and fraternity life (SFL; Rogers, 2012). These restrictive policies at HWIs created conditions in which Students of Color were "socially homeless, invisible to the majority, with no virtual or physical dwelling" (Rogers, 2012, p. 20). Racist policies such as these took a toll on Black students and provided an impetus for creating new social organizations specifically for Black people.

Historically, African Americans' aspirations to find activities in higher education to empower, uplift, and support them while receiving an education motivated them to create organizations for themselves (Gillon et al., 2019; Kimbrough, 2003). Black Greek-letter organizations (BGLOs) were formed in America at a time when racial segregation and white supremacy were a way of life. The 1896 U.S. Supreme Court ruling of Plessy v. Ferguson constitutionally upheld racial segregation in public places (specifically railroads) and legalized the doctrine of "separate but equal" (Fireside, 2004). It is important to note that while Black men were organizing for racial uplift at HWIs, Black women were also organizing in response to racism and sexism at HBCUs (Gillon et al., 2019). This separate but equal doctrine meant that society must be racially segregated, but allegedly ensure equal opportunities to all races (Fireside, 2004). The themes of exclusion, racial uplift, and cultural relevance/validation are woven throughout the histories of Black Greek-letter organizations and are important to consider when understanding their present-day missions and values and how practitioners can support them in upholding these themes. For Black students who found educational homes at HBCUs, National Pan-Hellenic Council (NPHC) organizations became venues for service and beacons of Black history and culture to be celebrated (Kimbrough, 2003). This chapter offers innovative approaches for working with NPHC chapters as advisors, alumni, national organizations, and campus professionals. The chapter centers on the role of NPHC on college campuses and the history of the member organizations. Finally, the chapter offers opportunities to support NPHC through recruitment, collaboration, and addressing toxic behavior.

Innovations in Practice

Having a solid understanding of the history, foundations, and purposes of Black Greek-lettered organizations is essential. Though essential, it is just the beginning of developing effective advising practices. Although Black sororities and fraternities are similar in many ways to historically white sororities and fraternities, there are many unique aspects to the BGLO community that add to the dynamic nature of advising them. BGLOs are organizations born from a desire to help Black collegiate students develop and succeed holistically. Before discussing best practices for success when advising NPHC, we would be remiss if we did not introduce ourselves and our experiences.

Cameron Beatty joined Alpha Phi Alpha Fraternity, Inc. as an undergraduate student at Indiana University. Cameron held multiple chapter executive leadership roles and went on to be the campus NPHC president. Professionally, for 3 years Cameron worked as an advisor to both the NPHC and Multicultural Greek Councils (MGC) at Iowa State University. Cameron also has experience as a house director for IFC chapter Theta Xi Fraternity at Iowa State University. Cameron's involvement and advising of NPHC organizations led to his interests in leadership education and research that centers the experiences of Students of Color developing their leadership identity, capacity, and efficacy.

Ebony Wofford has had a passion for sororities and fraternities since joining Zeta Phi Beta Sorority, Inc. in 2012 at North Carolina A&T State University. Throughout her time as an undergraduate member, this passion was fostered through the opportunities she was afforded in leadership at the organizational level. Navigating the complexities of higher education as a student while working closely with organizational volunteers inspired her down a path of exploration into the fraternal experience and ultimately to pursue a master's degree in higher education. Working as a graduate assistant for sororities and fraternities, and specifically with a very small NPHC, and then having the opportunity to work at an institution like Florida State broadened her understanding of the experiences of BGLOs and helped formulate the advising strategy included in this chapter.

Chris Graham joined Alpha Phi Alpha while attending Winston-Salem State University. He earned his Master of Science in Counseling, with an emphasis on student development in higher education from the University of North Carolina at Greensboro and went on to work professionally within the fraternal industry. Chris has served as Director of Fraternity and Sorority Life at Florida State University for five years. In his role, he has led one of the largest fraternal communities in the country. He also has extensive experience serving as a consultant and volunteer for a number of universities and fraternity and sorority headquarters in a variety of capacities, including educational programs, curriculum development, organizational structure, and more. He currently serves on the Board of Directors and is the 2020 president-elect for the Association of Fraternity and Sorority Advisors (AFA).

Understanding Institutional Context

As council culture varies from institution to institution, understanding institutional context and how it impacts the NPHC on your campus is critical to the success of the council and will provide insights for your advising strategy.

From personal experience and as Nadrea highlighted through her vignette, we know that NPHC involvement contributes to the holistic success of students that choose to join including higher retention, graduation rates, and grade point averages (GPAs). How successful NPHC can be in contributing to this success is based on several factors. One of these factors is the geographic location of your institution. Where the institution is located will give those individuals that work with the chapter such as full-time staff, state/regional volunteers, and chapter advisors insight into what type of members join NPHC organizations. For example, Black student enrollment at a regional state institution differs from that of an elite private institution or HBCUs; assessing the type of student that is enrolled is important to understanding the complexity of Black Greek-letter organizations. One instance that knowledge of student type has been helpful relates to Pell Grant rates. Students at a state regional institution where most Students of Color receive Pell Grants could impact the number of students that are financially able to join a chapter within NPHC in contrast to an elite private school where some Students of Color are paying full tuition out of pocket. Another example of this is seen with first-generation college students. This population of students may not have had exposure to SFL. Even if they know they may want to join a chapter, this lack of knowledge can make it difficult to navigate the process of joining an organization and therefore put prospective members at a disadvantage compared to students who have family members that are members of NPHC organizations. First-generation college students might not be aware of the process of expressing interests in a local NPHC chapter by attending interest meetings, building relationships, and understanding the history of the national organization.

An additional factor to assess before jumping into advising and supporting NPHC campus organizations is considering the campus involvement history of the students being served. This is a great time to elicit assistance from university historians, like past/current chapter advisors, enrollment management, case managers, and Black student union advisors and multicultural center directors. As the African proverb states, "It takes a village," and this is especially beneficial when working with NPHC. Use your village of advisors, headquarter staff, regional/state volunteers, and alumni to help reinforce expectations and guide chapters. Additionally, the campus partners previously listed will provide a more holistic view of the students being served from an institutional standpoint. Gaining insight on the culture of the Black students at the institution, perceptions of the NPHC chapters, the current GPAs of students, lists of admitted self-identified Students of Color, institutional resources, and much more can be invaluable. For example, identifying the Students of Color who are graduating from local high schools and who will be enrolling at an institution can assist in outreach efforts and recruitment. Regardless of the direction or the expectations of NPHC, it is highly recommended that supporters of NPHC identify these partnerships that are a part of their "village" and cultivate them in the same way institutions keep good partnerships with the headquarter (HQ) staff of organizations. These partnerships will assist in determining barriers to success for NPHC chapters on campus and enforce the expectations that have been set.

Chapter advisors are on the frontlines and can be the biggest advocates for NPHC chapters, so take the time to invest in the relationship; this means not only reaching out when there is a problem. Having standing advisor meetings, sending emails recognizing when a chapter wins an award, and forwarding institutional resources before a crisis arises are all ways to foster this relationship. Understanding the advising structure for chapters will benefit the individual working with the chapter. Understanding the advisor's role in the chapter will help filter out legitimate issues that may need follow up versus personality conflicts and complaints about the way the advisor fulfills their role. Additionally, the proximity of the local NPHC organization graduate/alumni chapter can enhance or hinder the experience for undergraduate members. Considering many organizations require chapter advisors to be present at chapter programming, intake planning, new member education sessions, and other chapter operations, if the graduate chapter is further than an hour away, there may be some issues keeping a chapter healthy and operating. Therefore, building a relationship with the graduate chapter president can also prove beneficial as a check and balance of the graduate advisor and as an additional contact within the organization.

The Role of the Advisor

Once chapter advisors and the organizations have started coalition building for the NPHC council and chapters, it is time to discuss the campus advisor's role in the chapter/council's success. Campus-based advisors take up the mantle of many things for a sorority and fraternity community such as mentor, role model, judge, and jury; but if they hope to be a successful advising NPHC, and specifically Black and Brown students, they should expect to have dual responsibilities as a campus partner for other entities in the community. These dual responsibilities may include liaison for their local NPHC council, a community organizer if the council is involved political activism, liaisons to other on-campus entities such as Dance Marathon or Relay for Life, and assisting in events such as an elementary school "Greek Day," accommodating grandparents at NPHC new member presentations, and in general being an advocate for the NPHC experience in areas that campus advisors have influence. Having a pulse on what is affecting Students of Color on campus will help campus-based NPHC advisors build credibility with the organizations and the main stakeholders. This pulse will sometimes come from the meeting after the meeting, where NPHC members are hanging out talking about other things that are happening on campus; things like the latest student government decision or the new Black-owned establishment in town.

Many Black students are looking for familial bonds on their campuses, which is why they may join an NPHC organization, and campus-based advisors become an extension of their support system. From being a mentor, role model, caseworker, community liaison, and advocate, campus-based advisors are called upon for almost any type of situation. One model that has helped those who work with NPHC navigate their roles is intrusive advising (Glennen & Baxley, 1985; Maxwell, 2003). The premise of this model is that students who have an ongoing relationship with one or more individuals at an institution are more likely to persist and graduate (Glennen & Baxley, 1985). The goal of intrusive advising is that students have agency over their experience and recognize that someone supports and cares for them (Glennen & Baxely, 1985). Students should know that their organization is just as important to their campus-based NPHC advisors as any other chapter or council in the community. Furthermore, considering that Black students are often tokenized and subjected to racial microaggressions and racism (Linder et al., 2019; Smith, 2009; Solórzano, Ceja, & Yosso, 2000), having someone who cares about them is the key to success. Sometimes, NPHC students may feel overlooked in comparison to IFC and Panhellenic chapters. Considering IFC and Panhellenic have large national joining processes like formal recruitment that campus advisors help manage and typically have larger chapter sizes, it can be difficult to invest as much time as they would like into NPHC chapters. However, when campus-based advisors show they genuinely care about a student's well-being, they will build trust that will transcend many mistakes/missteps they may make in advising.

Knowing this, it will take some time to build that trust, but meeting the students in their own space and showing up for the students first is a great way to start. Going to programs, encouraging students to hang out in the SFL office, offering resources, building relationships with multiple chapter members, and sharing personal experiences make campus-based advisors seem human to a student and they are more apt to engage with that advisor in meaningful ways. When campus-based advisors have conversations with students, it is encouraged that they ask the hard questions, and not just about their chapter. Asking personal questions about their families, their interests, what they want to do upon graduation, and genuinely seeking to build a relationship with NPHC chapter members allows council members to see their campus-based advisor as an ally to their experience. Students may not tell their campus-based advisors everything but they will come to these individuals when it counts if they know they can rely on them. Admittedly, this can be difficult to balance with the campus advisors' role and responsibility as an administrator, but it can be done by being transparent with students and garnering support from supervisors. The mission of institutions of higher education is to educate students first so our values and vision when advising should align with this aim. Knowing how taxing the role of advisor can be, taking care of your mental health as an advisor is imperative because it is easy to take on the burdens students are bearing when you genuinely care. It may be true that students do not care how much an advisor knows until they know how much they care (Maxwell, 2003), but taking care of one's self must be a priority as well.

To reiterate the previously stated points, campus-based advisors should be active, present, supportive, and engaged with NPHC chapters. Chapters might not actively seek out an advisor and may need clarity on their role and the benefit they provide to NPHC organizations. Though there may only be one campus-based advisor, advisors should be aware that others around campus might frequently provide advice to the NPHC council and chapters on a range of issues, so they could be able to rely on them as well for support. The knowledge, skills, and awareness needed to successfully advise these organizations are multi-layered and the approach should be centered on organizational context, institutional history, environmental factors, support, and engagement.

Organizational Context

Each of the nine NPHC organizations has very similar purposes, backgrounds, and missions. Understanding the distinct differences in the founding history when supporting and advocating for the BGLO experience is important context. Though much progress has been made in the 114-year history of the organizations, the connection to the culture of the campuses on which they were founded continues to permeate through to its members today. As an advisor, advocate, or supporter of these organizations, one must start with that understanding, regardless of institutional type or history. A great place to start is by reading some of the fundamental texts for NPHC such as *Black Greek 101* by Dr. Walter Kimbrough (2003) and *The Divine Nine: The History of African American Fraternities and Sororities* by Lawrence Ross (2001).

As shared previously, the history of each organization is foundational as it relates to successfully advising the members of the BGLO community; however, it is additionally important to understand the institutional history of a respective chapter in context of the campus where the chapter resides. For example, advising at an institution with a single-letter chapter(s), chapters that have one Greek letter as a chapter designation instead of two or three, is a critical context because often these chapters are the oldest in the NPHC organization. Older chapters have a long legacy and understanding chapter history will offer important context as it relates to the alumni base, historical practices of the chapter, points of pride, and level of commitment and service a chapter has provided to the campus and the local community. Conversely, advising at an institution with a novice BGLO community could highlight the different resources needed by each local NPHC organization. For example, if the BGLO chapters on campus are less than a decade old, there might not be an alumni base to provide a full-time local advisor, or the alumni base might be overly active in the business and function of the chapter due to their experience and the chapter both being so new in the respective organization. Additionally, while the history of BLGOs is rich in tradition, chapters in the community may struggle to find their identities as campuses today are more diverse than they were when these organizations began to expand at HWIs. NPHC chapters were built for Black students but as organizations grew, some non-Black members have joined these organizations.

Institution Type, History, and Purpose

The unique purpose and mission of an institution add critical dynamics to the BGLO community and advisors' roles. Knowing if the campus is a commuter campus, regional or flagship, or minority-serving institution is foundational knowledge that should be provided in the onboarding process for advisors. Each institution type has its own culture as it relates to the type of students it serves, faculty it recruits, and staff it hires to support the student experience. This contextual information will impact the daily operations of a chapter. A prime example of this is chapter sizes at HBCUs compared to HWIs. Chapter sizes for organizations at HWIs tend to be smaller but are proportional to the number of Black students and can still be a typical size for the organization considering there are more HWIs in the country than HBCUs. The resources provided to these chapters such as risk management workshops, intake seminars, and executive board meetings do not require as many hours to execute. Chapter sizes at HBCUs tend to be significantly larger so the resources must match. The same is true of how students engage with the advisor, the office or department, and the institution. Take for example policy changes a SFL office may create. A chapter with a large population and political connections within the institution may push back on these changes and/or require that the office include them in the decision making process. This push back might be supported from alumni members when holding the institution accountable to the needs of Black students. Both the culture of the institution and NPHC must inform policy creation and revisions to ensure a universal design that will enhance the experience for chapters. Having an understanding of institutional history and NPHC history will serve as a foundation of how to serve, support, and be resourceful for the community on campus.

Support and Student Engagement

Understanding the support and engagement dynamics for BGLOs is imperative in helping them maximize their potential and continue to create relevant examples of positive contributions to the campus and the local community. It often takes several support systems to resource and serve BGLOs. The range of impact will vary greatly depending on your relationship with the support unit and its influence and connection to the BGLO community. Here are a few examples of individuals, groups, organizations, and associations that can support you in your role of advocating for BGLOs: campus partners, community partners, alumni or campus advisors, faculty and staff, Alumni Associations (both chapter and university), graduate students, local NPHC chapters, the National Pan-Hellenic Council President, National Pan-Hellenic Council of Presidents, regional leadership of each respective organization, and other campus-based professionals or inter/national organization's headquarters staff. Ways an advisor can partner with these entities include mentorship networks with Black Alumni Associations, scholarships from local NPHC chapters, and campus-based workshops provided by regional leadership to the entire NPHC community or SFL staff. Providing potential advisor training to those individuals that are interested in serving as campus student organization advisors for chapters can encourage those who may be interested in an organization to join a graduate chapter which proves beneficial to the national organization.

Defining the Role of the Council in Relation to the Chapter

Conversations about the role of NPHC as an umbrella organization and its role on a college campus have been ongoing (Ross, 2000). It is important to note, there are only 9 members of the NPHC, and the last time the council "expanded" or took on new members was in 1997 with the addition of Iota Phi Theta Fraternity, Incorporated. Understanding that there will only be nine member organizations of this council at any given time will help to manage the expectations of other organizations that may be looking for a home on your campus under the NPHC umbrella. As a point of reference, whenever a campus has two or more NPHC chapters, they are technically considered a council (NPHC, 2020). How chapters interact with the NPHC as a council varies greatly from institution to institution, but the pride that members have in being NPHC members is universal. In this context, dual citizenship refers to an individual's membership in both their respective organization and the NPHC. Understanding the concept of what we call dual citizenship will help support NPHC members and NPHC as a collective council; however, it is important to note that unlike Panhellenic and NIC, NPHC is not a governing council. Thus, at a national level, organizations do not interfere with the business of other national organizations. On a campus level, whichever of the nine organizations make up the NPHC on a respective campus would have the authority to hold one another accountable through the utilization of a council executive board that is elected by the chapters to serve the community and the local council's constitution and bylaws.

Understanding how to utilize the umbrella NPHC council and their executive board as a way to advise the chapters within is critical. For example, hosting a retreat at the council level will give students insight as to how a quality retreat is planned and they will take that information back to their chapter and this information to enhance their own chapter retreat.

As we mentioned earlier, the relationships you build with executive officers of the campus chapter and at the graduate/alumni chapter level is a great way to understand what is important to their chapter and get ahead of potential issues. The umbrella council is also an extension of the chapters that will give you insight into chapter culture and can be used as an additional leadership pipeline for students to strengthen their respective chapters. This strategy provides necessary training to chapter leaders as many individuals serving on the council executive board (depending on council/chapter size) will also have a leadership role in their chapter. Walking students through sharing a vision, goal setting, an election process, program planning, and all the other ways we advise a student, will support chapters in the long run by providing them a positive example to follow.

Considering NPHC organizations have a shared history and have many similarities between them, it can be easy to create uniform policies and procedures. When it comes to the examples mentioned, it would be more beneficial to the advisor to gain insight into the culture for each specific chapter that is being advised so the advising strategies can be more precise. We encourage advisors to have more of an individualistic approach when it comes to the member organizations and to leave space for chapters to get their individual chapter needs addressed. Every chapter operates independently from each other and it is important to seek out information to understand those differences. One example of this strategy is when considering intake deadlines. Typically an institution or national organization may make a window for intake and within that window, chapters have to complete their new member education, initiation, and new member presentation. Providing chapters with opportunities to adjust these timelines if this is an institutional policy or having a larger window that chapters can create their own intake calendar while adhering to their national policies will give chapters the opportunity to create a calendar that is best for their chapter.

When looking to make advising more chapter-specific, asking the students is not always the best and only approach to do this research. Reading fundamental texts included earlier in the chapter, researching using reputable sources, and contacting chapter advisors and/or regional staff will be more productive as sometimes students are learning the business side of their organization alongside you.

Honoring Black History

If you have been around NPHC chapters for a while, you have undoubtedly seen their paraphernalia that reads "I am Black History." In our current world filled with systemic racism and police brutality, it is important to acknowledge that under the letters, these are Black students. Honoring their Blackness and their history will be imperative for those that hope to support effectively. There are a few ideas to accomplish this:

- Help chapters honor their founding and chartering dates, even if that is simply showing up to their programs. These dates are important not just because it is the start of their organization, but because they are Black businesses built in a time where Black people were supposed to be invisible; these dates are Black history.
- Encourage chapters to connect with local predominately Black businesses and organizations, such as Title I schools, Black-owned restaurants, and hair stores. These spaces provide jobs and resources for the community and are also great locations to organize service projects to give back directly to the Black community.
- Civic engagement is a cornerstone of all NPHC organizations. There are many avenues a council can take to address the issues that continue to plague the Black community so teaching them how to use their platform to be civically engaged and advocate for others is quintessential.

- Participating and engaging in dialogue with the university during, not only Black History month, but all year long. Students must have the opportunity to be in spaces to advocate for themselves and others. If there are meetings, committees, or programs that students should be a part of, encourage them to attend and create space for them to have a voice.

Recruitment, Collaboration, and Addressing Toxic Behavior

For NPHC organizations, recruitment, new member education, and membership retention have to be thought of as relationships with one another. These pieces work in tandem to create a healthy environment for interested students to join BGLOs. New members are the lifeblood of our organizations and so conducting membership intake is an act of loving-kindness; it is a gift of brother/sisterhood/siblinghood for a lifetime. These processes have changed over time from pledging which was as long as a year process (Ross, 2000), to a present-day 2–4 week process where students can opt-out of their new member presentations if they choose. No matter how NPHC chapters bring new members into their organizations, we recommend having intake on a yearly basis. It is not healthy for a chapter to only have intake sporadically. A few reasons for chapters engaging in intake sporadically are that it is a chapter tradition to only have intake a certain interval like every other year. Disciplinary issues such as hazing allegations that prevent the chapter from being approved for intake is another common issue.

Chapters that have multiple intake classes of new members in the chapter consistently have the opportunity to be more productive with service to the community and campus programming. Having three intake classes in the chapter at a time helps the chapter to disperse work evenly and allows members to engage in other campus organizations besides just the work of the chapter. Seniors can become brand ambassadors by being in leadership in other areas of the institution, while the new members are enthusiastic about executing the work of the chapter. The class between made up of new members and graduating seniors can focus on being the planners and organizers as they have experienced some time in the chapter and have hopefully learned strategies to be a successful chapter.

Recruitment

What recruitment looks like to NPHC is providing space at the council level for interested individuals to be introduced to chapters without being pressured to pick one right away. Events such as "NPHC 101" or "Meet the Greeks" where organizations have an opportunity to showcase themselves is imperative. Our experience is that some chapters still have an antiquated mindset that if students attend their chapter's program, then they are interested in that chapter. Some aspiring members feel that they could be blackballed from the NPHC community if they attend another chapter's events. NPHC 101 or its likeness is a great way to educate potential members on NPHC and give them the opportunity to see what is available on that respective campus, especially because some of the individuals joining these chapters are first-generation college students with no background knowledge of NPHC. This blackballing culture should also be addressed with the council prior to said events and remain a continued conversation.

Cross-Council Collaboration

Encourage collaborations across campus councils and city/regional local chapters. Giving students the opportunity to see the experience of members in other councils and at other institutions allows them to reflect on their own council or chapter's successes and areas for growth. Oftentimes SFL councils operate in silos, so encourage NPHC leaders to disrupt these silos instead of continuing to perpetuate them and, as an advisor, facilitate dialogue with the students to bring attention to this opportunity for growth. There is a lot of information from the other councils that can be used to provide their members with a better experience if given the opportunity. Additionally, toxic behavior can be disrupted with all council chapter president meetings, cross-council collaboration awards, incentives for funding, and conference travel to programs like the Association for Fraternal Leadership and Values (AFLV), home of the National Black Greek Leadership Conference (NBGLC).

Disrupting Toxic Behavior

There is a delicate line between calling students out for their behavior and helping them process a mistake or misstep. Depending on the egregious nature of the behavior, other agencies on your campus may have to get involved but this reference is for toxic behavior that chapters could begin to address themselves. Helping students to understand where their education gaps are, what practices are outdated, and how they can use their voice to advocate for the invisible in their chapters is a great step in the right direction. Council retreats are a great way to start this process. Exercises like a SWOT (Strengths, Weaknesses, Opportunities, and Threats) analysis (Gunn & Williams, 2007), hosting open dialogue sessions where facilitated dialogue occurs, or using tools like Strengths Quest (Clifton & Anderson, 2016), to formulate an action-based plan can prove beneficial. If we consistently call students out on their behavior but do not help them process why these behaviors occur, we will never get to the root cause to make sustainable change.

Another layer to disrupting toxic behavior is to address alumni that may be contributing to a chapter's dynamic. Considering that alumni are no longer under the purview of the campus, a solid partnership with the chapter advisor and sponsoring graduate chapter is imperative to be able to address concerns. Many national organizations have strict guidelines about the ways in which alumni can be involved in chapter processes; however, current members will always seek validation from alumni and the voice of a campus-based advisor may be muted if it comes down to choosing a side. The key is to not let the students have to choose, but to help students make up their own mind about what is best for their chapter and instill in them the autonomy to decide which type of interactions will be healthier when dealing with alumni in general. Giving students the tools necessary to address toxic behavior in conjunction with their chapter advisor is a must. Sometimes the tools necessary boil down to helping students be able to identify toxic behavior and how to address it while maintaining a relationship with the alumni members. For example, many students may not know that alumni can be held accountable for their actions regardless if they are currently involved in a graduate chapter or how to report them for toxic behavior. If students knew how to approach difficult conversations with these alumni or what to do if a conversation is not helpful, it will help to protect the chapter in the long run. Giving students these tools to advocate for themselves and for the best interest of the chapter is important.

On the other side, the best way to prevent toxic behavior as an alumni advisor is to have conversations with current students before they graduate. Strong alumni start as current students, so campus professionals should have conversations with graduate advisors about resources that they are providing to graduating seniors. This member development can help curb toxic behavior before it begins. Additionally, offering a program at the council level such as a senior sendoff can give the campus-based professional an opportunity to offer resources to these soon-to-be alumni regarding healthy ways to interact with their undergraduate chapter.

All of these suggestions take time and assistance from an ever-vigilant and forward-thinking coalition of international headquarter staff, campus staff, and advisor support to actualize. Changes in chapter culture only occur once issues are actually seen as an issue by the current members of the undergraduate chapter and proposed changes are supported by the aforementioned coalition. To quote the great Maya Angelou from her posthumous 2018 tweet, "Do the best you can until you know better. Then when you know better, do better."

Conclusion

The factors discussed in this chapter offer considerations for advisors, campus-based professionals, and IHQ staff supporting NPHC chapters, councils, and students. This chapter offers key recommendations for innovative practices to address recruitment and create healthy environments for interested students to join BGLOs and sustain the legacies of these organizations. The chapter also highlights the importance of cross-council collaboration for the purpose of sharing experiences and reflecting on one's own council or chapter's successes and areas for growth. Finally, toxic behaviors are addressed by offering recommendations for practice that disrupt the toxicity that can be perpetuated by alumni members and current members. These innovative practices create momentum for chapters that leads to continued contributions and success as it relates to the original founding purposes of BGLOs, which is to support Black collegiate students develop and succeed holistically beyond the collegiate experience.

Questions for Reflection

- How can you enhance your level of understanding as it relates to the Black sorority and fraternity chapters and council on your campus?
- How can your SFL office build an intrusive advising model to adequately support and service its chapters and council?
- How do you create and call BGLOs into learning moments versus just calling them out for not following policy, procedures, and protocols on your campus?
- How can you leverage partnerships to enhance the experience of BGLO students on your campus?

References

Angelou, M. [@DrMayaAngelou]. (2018, August 12). *Do the best you can until you know better. Then when you know better, do better—#MayaAngelou* [Tweet]. Twitter. https://twitter.com/drmayaangelou/status/1028663286512930817?lang=en

Clifton, D. O., & Anderson, E. C. (2016) *StrengthsQuest*. London, UK: Gallup Press.

Eschner, K. (2017, March 2). The horrors of the 'Great Slave Auction'. *Smithsonian Magazine*. https://www.smithsonianmag.com/smart-news/horrors-great-slave-auction-180962287/

Fireside, H. (2004). *Separate and unequal: Homer Plessy and the Supreme Court decision that legalized racism*. New York City, NY: Carroll & Graf.

Gillon, K. E., Beatty, C. C., & Salinas, C., Jr. (2019). Race and racism in fraternity and sorority life: A historical overview. In K. E. Gillon, C. C. Beatty, & C. Salinas Jr. (Eds.), *Critical considerations of race, ethnicity, and culture in fraternity/sorority life* (New Directions for Student Services, no. 165, pp. 9–16). Hoboken, NJ: Jossey-Bass.

Glennen, R. E., & Baxley, D. M. (1985). Reduction of attrition through intrusive advising. *NASPA Journal, 2*(3), 10–14.

Gunn, R., & Williams, W. (2007). Strategic tools: an empirical investigation into strategy in practice in the UK. *Strategic Change, 16(5),* 201–216.

Hughey, M. W. (2009). Rushing the wall, crossing the sands: Cross-racial membership in U.S. college fraternities and sororities. In C. L. Torbenson & G. Parks (Eds.), *Brothers and sisters: Diversity in college fraternities and sororities* (pp. 237–276). Plainsboro, NJ: Associated University Presses.

Kimbrough, W. (2003). *Black Greek 101: The culture, customs, and challenges of black fraternities and sororities*. Plainsboro, NJ: Associated University Presses.

Kimbrough, W. F. (2009). The membership intake movement of historically Black Greek-letter organizations. *NASPA Journal, 46*(4), 603–613.

Linder, C., Quaye, S. J., Lange, A. C., Roberts, R. E., Lacy, M. C., & Okello, W. K. (2019). "A student should have the privilege of just being a student": Student activism as labor. *The Review of Higher Education, 42*(5), 37–62.

Maxwell, J. (2003). *Relationships 101*. Nashville, TN: Thomas Nelson.

National Pan-Hellenic Council. (2020, September). *National Pan-Hellenic Council Website*. https://nphchq.com/millennium1/

Rogers, I. H. (2012). *The Black campus movement: Black students and the racial reconstitution of higher education 1965–1972*. London, UK: Palgrave Macmillan.

Ross, L. (2000). *The divine nine: The history of African-American fraternities and sororities*. Fountain Valley, CA: Kingston.

Smith, W. A. (2009). Campus wide climate: Implications for African American students. In L. Tillman (Ed.), *A Handbook of African American Education* (pp. 297–309). Thousand Oaks, CA: Sage.

Solórzano, D., Ceja, M., & Yosso, T. (2000). Critical race theory, racial microaggressions, and campus racial climate: The experiences of African American college students. *The Journal of Negro Education, 69*(1/2), 60–73.

Member Vignette: Asian-Interest Sororities and Fraternities

Trang Bui

Getting into college was the easy part, but no one could have prepared me for the transition into life after high school. In that first semester, I found myself feeling out of place, working multiple jobs, and studying alone as most of my close friends had left town to other institutions. I did not know where to begin getting involved on campus or whom I could connect with. I realized an unfortunate truth: my voice was missing in the student body and in the administration itself. As a first-generation student and a Person of Color at a predominately white institution (PWI), I was lost in understanding my identity. I was just a single individual. Simply put, it seemed as though I did not belong anywhere. Juggling my studies and work, along with uncovering my identity, felt like a balancing act that would come crashing down at any moment. These challenges were especially challenging when there was not a mentor I could connect with that could provide direction.

However, all that changed for the better after my introduction to sorority and fraternity life (SFL). This became a turning point for me. I attended multiple fraternity mixers with a friend from class and met several sorority members. But still, I felt lost in the crowd and as a result, I was hiding a big part of myself. I knew the next 4 years would be crucial in defining who I would become, but I never realized how much I would take pride in my cultural roots until I found a community of womxn who shared my beliefs, values, and aspirations. After coming together, we knew we wanted to have a place to call home, to be recognized as strong Womxn of Color, and to pave the way for future members to join our mission for years to come. In the fall of 2013, we chartered Sigma Psi Zeta Sorority, Inc. at Wichita State University, which was the only Asian-interest sorority in the state of Kansas at that time. Through this organization, I found mentors that identified with my struggles and inspired me to be a proud Asian American womxn.

Following my initiation, I found confidence in my voice to be an activist for my community and to continue building a foundation for our local chapter. I became involved as an Ambassador for the Office of Diversity and Inclusion, where I helped build InspirA-SIAN month to celebrate our APIDA students. I also became a part of Kappa Delta Pi Educational Honors Society, Order of Omega, and Asian Student Conference. Through all of these different leadership opportunities, I became a better student and was able to leave behind a legacy that inspired resiliency, social advocacy, and an appreciation of cultural differences.

Even though our sorority and fraternity community was starting to build unity between the different councils, there was still more work that needed to be done and hard conversations to have in order to evoke prominent change. I remember having an active membership of 10 members, and while it was disheartening to be compared to other sororities with more than 100 members, we persisted. Despite all the skepticism, we never let our numbers define us and the work we would do. We had to lead by example and remember that quantity does not equate quality. Every doubt that others had of us to be considered a "real sorority" gave us the fire and drive to work even harder to get where we are today. The journey that I embarked on initially so I could find a place to fit in has come full circle. Now I have the opportunity to mentor and connect with undergraduates who were once in my shoes. I hope that this cycle continues forward, positively affecting generations to come. As an alumna, I am proud of who we used to be, who we are today, and where we will be in the future as progressive sorority members.

Undoubtedly, being part of an Asian-interest sorority helped push me to the career path I am on as it opened doors to opportunities I am passionate about in teaching, mentoring, and activism. I chose to pursue a career in education because of the lack of representation of those who look like me in this field—especially in Kansas. When I was a classroom teacher, I stayed involved with my local undergraduate chapter as an advisor and was recruited back to campus to be part of the first cohort of graduates in the higher education/student affairs program. With the experience, knowledge, and skills I have acquired since then, I recognize the need for continued research in student development. As new generations of students enter college, institutions should hire student-centered professionals and develop programs to help students build self-awareness, life skills, leadership, and the confidence to reach their goals. Student development theories serve as the foundation to help guide professionals to understand how students think and evolve through time. There needs to be research in not only how the new generation learns, but *the multiple identities they identify with in order to have a holistic understanding of their experiences.*

My presence on campus matters because every student deserves a chance at a great education. Not only that, but there are also cultural and social advantages. All too often, Asian American students are generalized and viewed under the myth of being hardworking, high-achieving, and non-confrontational members of the "model minority." These stereotypes are a harmful misconception as it leads to a disservice to provide the right academic, social, and emotional support for Asian American students. With my work as a practitioner in student affairs, I intend to use my experiences and advocate for missing voices at the table. I will work to ensure that we are no longer the silent minority. Our students deserve individual support, resources and services, and an opportunity to grow outside of the classroom through involvements such as SFL. Creating spaces for students to learn, express themselves freely, and find confidence in their identity is at the heart of all my work as a student affairs professional.

CHAPTER FOUR

A Practitioner's Perspective: Asian-Interest Sororities and Fraternities

BRYAN DOSONO, VIGOR W. H. LAM, AND
BILAL BADRUDDIN

In this chapter, the co-authors will provide a brief review on the history of Asian American Greek Letter Organizations (AAGLOs), discuss the relevance of culture and values within these organizations, and share recommendations for practitioners who work with AAGLOs. Dr. Bryan Dosono, Vigor Lam, and Bilal Badruddin have all served on the National Asian Pacific Islander Desi American Panhellenic Association (NAPA) Board and the (inter)national boards for their respective AAGLO. They possess foundational knowledge and extensive experience serving Asian American sororities and fraternities from the alumni, headquarters staff, and researcher perspective.

Review: Timeline and Trajectory

An institution over a century old, AAGLOs preserve a storied history that dates back to the early 1900s (Dosono, Badruddin, & Lam, 2019). Tied to institutions of higher education and inspired by the legacy of Black Greek-Letter Organizations (BGLOs), AAGLOs provided a platform for Asian American college students to collaborate alongside individuals with like-minded interests.

Early AAGLOs were founded with a specific ethnic identity. Flip Flap Fraternity and Rho Psi Fraternity, the two first fraternities for Chinese members, were both deeply rooted in Chinese culture and values (Dosono et al., 2019). In the 1930s, the formation of sororities and fraternities grounded in Japanese culture began. And while the higher education industry experienced low enrollment during and immediately after World War II—causing many fraternal organizations to cease operations—the growing Anti-Asian sentiment reached an all-time high, making it increasingly difficult for Asian American students and organizations to organize and sustain on PWI campuses.

From Organizational Growth to Council Development

The ethnic composition of Asian American sororities and fraternities evolved with the ever-changing social dynamics of a racialized nation, and previous scholarship has classified their growth into four distinct waves (Dosono et al., 2019). In the First Wave of AAGLO history (1910s), Chinese men formed tightly knit communities within American universities, knowing that they would eventually return to China. In the Second Wave (1930s), ethnic enclaves spurred fraternal organizations that sought to promote belonging at Predominantly White Institutions (PWIs). In the Third Wave (1980s), the burgeoning Asian American movement united a wide range of ethnicities from the Asian diaspora into a political umbrella, resulting in a new generation of sororities and fraternities with diverse lineages of founding mothers and fathers. Finally, in the Fourth Wave (2000s), South Asian Americans rose to prominence in making the Desi presence within Asian American Pacific Islander Desi American (APIDA) organizations more known.

Since the early 1990s, over 110 distinct AAGLOs spanning more than 800 chapters have formed across 160 and counting North American colleges and universities (Dosono, 2020b; Dosono et al., 2020). AAGLOs particularly thrive in states with noticeable Asian American student enrollment, such as California, New York, and Texas. In the latter two waves of growth, councils formed on campuses that were home to a sizable presence of AAGLOs and were recognized by their local sorority and fraternity life (SFL) offices (see Table 4.1).

The Asian Greek Council of Southern California comprised of 16 organizations chartered at eight different universities around Southern California: Cal State Long Beach; Cal State Los Angeles; Cal State Northridge; Cal State Pomona; University of California, Los Angeles; UC Irvine; UC Riverside; University of Southern California (Chen, 2008). According to online archives, their purpose was to "be a guiding force which strives to foster the high ideas of friendship and cooperation, and to develop the best qualities of character among the member councils" (Chen, 2008, para. 1). In providing a model for universities to adopt Asian Greek Councils at their own institutions, the Fourth Wave of AAGLOs established dedicated councils—albeit with their own naming variants—at campuses like the University of Illinois at Chicago (Greeks of the Pan-Asian American Council) and the University of Texas at Austin (Texas Asian Pan-Hellenic Council).

Though AAGLO unity may have originated in regional pockets of the United States, an even larger national coalition of sororities and fraternities would soon form into what is now known as the National APIDA Panhellenic Association (NAPA). Initially conceived as the APIA Greek Alliance in the summer of 2004 as a collective voice of 2,500 undergraduates to register young voters for the 2004 U.S. Presidential Election (Gee, Seoh, & Dosono, 2019), NAPA established more formally a year later in the summer of 2005 after realizing its potential to mobilize its members beyond the political sphere. In 2020, NAPA has grown to represent 20 (inter)national organizations (see Table 4.2) with over 6,000 current undergraduates and over 45,000 alumni. The association champions a commitment to fraternal unity and supports its organizations in advancing the fraternal experience (Gee et al., 2019), particularly in higher education.

Table 4.1. AAGLO Council Directory

Name of Council	Institution	Founding Year	Chapters
Asian Greek Council of Southern California	Regionally open to students at universities in Southern California Metropolitan Area	1982	16
Asian Greek Council	University of California, Los Angeles	*1990	4
National APIDA Panhellenic Association Council	State University of New York at Binghamton	1994	6
Asian Greek Council	University of Southern California	1997	5
Greeks of the Pan-Asian American Council	University of Illinois at Chicago	2011	8
Texas Asian Pan-Hellenic Council	University of Texas at Austin	2011	10
Asian Sorority and Fraternity Council	University of California, Davis	2013	8
National Asian Panhellenic Council	State University of New York at Albany	2013	7

* The earliest published recording of UCLA AGC is printed in the 1990–1991 volume of *BruinLife Yearbook*.

Modern Day AAGLOs

By providing its member organizations resources and expertise to continually improve their operations, NAPA sets the gold standard for APIDA sororities and fraternities. NAPA hosts an in-person Annual Meeting in conjunction with the Association of Fraternity/Sorority Advisors Annual Meeting to recognize the success of its members. In 2017, NAPA unveiled its inaugural Standards of Excellence Awards to recognize outstanding individuals, chapters, councils, and organizations for their merit, impact, and unity demonstrated in their community.

In 2020, NAPA issued progressive statements to vocalize the collective concerns of AAGLOs to the broader public on issues like xenophobia and racism. For instance, at the onset of the COVID-19 pandemic, NAPA denounced President Trump's racist remarks and affirmed its commitment "to working with its member organizations and institutional partners in ensuring the safety of its students and the fraternal community" (Badruddin, 2020a, para. 4). NAPA also expressed firm solidarity and spoke out against anti-Black racism upon the death of George Floyd, insisting that "APIDA-identifying individuals not remain complicit or be passive bystanders when seeing racist actions or policies" (Badruddin, 2020b, para. 4). Created to challenge the status quo and advocate for change, NAPA continues to provide resources for educating its communities on the importance of social justice.

AAGLOs continue to chart new paths for belonging within PWIs. NAPA organizations are physically expanding their geographic footprint (see Figure 4.1) and rely on NAPA's collegial spirit of open expansion to provide more opportunities for students to bring new AAGLOs to their campus. APIDA students also manifest belonging in online spaces through shared expressions of solidarity, and they utilize social media platforms to mobilize collectively for philanthropic fundraising and the promotion of social causes (Dosono, 2019; Dosono, 2020a). Trang Bui's aforementioned member vignette illustrates one of the numerous diverse journeys students embark on to start a new chapter at their university. Through involvement with SFL, students develop interpersonal and professional skills necessary to lead and serve their communities.

Defining AAGLOs

As NAPA continues to grow in resources, its Executive Board has identified research on AAGLOs as a core area of work to pursue. No scholarly work to date has explicitly defined the characteristics of AAGLOs. We offer the following five criteria—who, what, when, where, why—as operational parameters for outlining

Table 4.2. Directory of NAPA Organizations in 2020

Organization	Founding Institution	Year Established	Charters Granted
alpha Kappa Delta Phi International Sorority, Inc.	University of California, Berkeley	1990	60
Alpha Phi Gamma National Sorority, Inc.	Cal Polytechnic University, Pomona	1994	17
Alpha Sigma Rho National Sorority, Inc.	University of Georgia	1998	11
Beta Chi Theta National Fraternity, Inc.	University of California, Los Angeles	1999	29
Chi Sigma Tau National Fraternity, Inc.	University of Illinois at Chicago	1999	9
Delta Epsilon Psi National Fraternity, Inc.	University of Texas at Austin	1998	35
Delta Kappa Delta National Sorority, Inc.	Texas A&M University	1999	17
Delta Phi Lambda National Sorority, Inc.	University of Georgia	1998	23
Delta Phi Omega National Sorority, Inc.	University of Houston	1998	49
Delta Sigma Iota National Fraternity, Inc.	Pennsylvania State University	2000	8
Iota Nu Delta National Fraternity, Inc.	Binghamton University	1994	30
Kappa Phi Gamma National Sorority, Inc.	University of Texas at Austin	1998	19
Kappa Phi Lambda National Sorority, Inc.	Binghamton University	1995	37
Kappa Pi Beta National Fraternity, Inc.	Northern Illinois University	2000	5
Lambda Phi Epsilon International Fraternity, Inc.	University of California, Los Angeles	1981	70
Pi Alpha Phi National Fraternity, Inc.	University of California, Berkeley	1929	28
Pi Delta Psi National Fraternity, Inc.	Binghamton University	1994	31
Sigma Beta Rho National Fraternity, Inc.	University of Pennsylvania	1996	57
Sigma Psi Zeta National Sorority, Inc.	University at Albany	1994	39
Sigma Sigma Rho National Sorority, Inc.	St. John's University	1998	26

Figure 4.1. Geographic Spread of NAPA Chapter Locations in North America as of 2020

their breadth and impact. Affiliated sororities and fraternities must meet a majority of the following criteria to be considered an AAGLO:

- Founded historically by enrolled college students who are descendants of the Asian diaspora.
- Represented as a social fraternal organization traditionally by Greek letters.
- Established as early as the 20th century and offer lifetime membership for initiated members.
- Chartered across North American institutions of higher education and commonly affiliated with a Greek council.
- Concerned with the cultural advancement of an Asian-based ethnicity or group of ethnicities (e.g., APIDA).

Our definition does not consider AAGLOs as sororities and fraternities that are founded outside of North America (e.g., fraternal organizations in the Philippines) or religious fraternal groups with no affiliation to a university (e.g., Cross and Sword, David and Jonathan Christian Fraternity, Cheng Zhi Hui). By defining the AAGLO community, we also identify pockets of AAGLOs that have not been adequately served by either their university or through NAPA. Smaller Greek organizations, such as Armenian sisterhoods or Filipino brotherhoods, face the challenge of making their presence known and may fall through the cracks in the institutions that were meant to serve them.

Existing Literature and Implications on Advising AAGLOs

Current literature on AAGLOs theorizes the experiences of members based on historical narratives recorded from interviews and existing literature. This is particularly important to note because although there is a growing number of collegiate students joining Asian American sororities and fraternities or forming their own organizations, the individuals who are working with these organizations, including advisors, have not been able to expand their knowledge of the community (Gonzalez, 2012; Torbenson & Parks, 2009). For this reason, when conducting research on AAGLOs, it is important to also take the advisor's role and knowledge of AAGLOs into consideration. As a result, Dosono and colleagues (2019) called for more members of AAGLOs to pursue higher education administration as a career choice.

To guide a positive growth trajectory for AAGLOs, Tran and Chang (2019) recommended "more oversight and attention ideally through mentorship from Asian American staff and faculty who understand their challenges and can provide culturally sensitive reference points" (p. 83). The pursuit of a career in higher education will then provide the opportunity for students and advisors to have a shared experience through their belonging to an AAGLO.

In the sections that follow, we discuss how BGLOs paved a path forward in the trajectory of AAGLOs, articulate the extent to which collective APIDA values shape the AAGLO experience, share introspective insights for how AAGLOs can move forward as a community, and provoke reflection questions for practitioners to innovate the culturally-based sorority and fraternity landscape.

Relevance: Furthering Collective APIDA Values

Values, customs, and traditions have been foundational to culturally-based sororities and fraternities—which are inclusive of AAGLOs—since their inception. AAGLO members commonly lived with each other. Such "communal living" provided supportive values in those days when segregation and discrimination against racial minority groups and People of Color in the United States were explicit (Wong, 2015, p. 58). AAGLOs are among the youngest organizations compared to sororities and fraternities in broader umbrella groups, and much of their traditions and values have been appropriated and/or borrowed from BGLOs.

NAPA sororities and fraternities extend structures and practices established from organizations in National Association of Latino Fraternal Organizations, Inc. (NALFO), National Multicultural Greek Council (NMGC), National Pan-Hellenic Council (NPHC), National Panhellenic Council (NPC), and North

American Interfraternity Council (NIC). All members of NAPA organizations use hand signs, step, and place letters on clothing, jewelry, pins, and other paraphernalia. These customs convey a sense of pride and unity of membership across a variety of occasions. Themes of tradition that are valued in the AAGLO community include cultural aspects like family and language, and social customs such as paraphernalia, calls, and hand signs.

Family and Language

AAGLOs advance the tradition of mentoring relationships commonly structured in sororities and fraternities. A "big sister"/"big brother" refers to an active member of a sorority or fraternity who mentors a new member throughout their new membership education (or "intake") process leading up to initiation. These terms are oftentimes gendered and can further introduce the language of siblings. The active member assigned to oversee the education in the chapter's traditions, history, and ritual is commonly referred to as the "New Member Educator" and more colloquially referenced as the "pledge mom"/"pledge dad." A "line sister"/"line brother" (or "pledge brother"/"pledge sister") are terms used to reference a fellow member who was part of the same new member class and/or intake period.

Though these familial terms are shared vocabulary across a number of fraternal organizations (Javier, 2018), AAGLOs commonly apply cultural signifiers to pay deference to older members within their ranks. Examples include:

- "Dailo 大佬" and "Sailo 細佬" (Cantonese for "Older Brother" and "Younger Brother")
- "Ate" and "Kuya" (Tagalog for "Elder Sister" and "Elder Brother")
- "Bhai" and "Bahan" (Hindi/Urdu for "Brother" and "Sister")
- "Chettan," "Chechi," "Aniyathi," "Aniyan" (Malayali for "Elder Brother," "Elder Sister," "Younger Sister," "Younger Brother")

Members of AAGLOs were often raised from ethnic cultures that function in "high context," that is, cultures that uphold a system of values that prioritize the identity of the group over the identity of the individual (Hall, 1989). High context societies, such as those originating from Asia, are hierarchical in nature and emphasize honor and respect-based practices that maintain positive impressions both within interpersonal networks and outwardly in public (Semaan, Dosono, & Britton, 2017).

Language within AAGLOs evolved from a form of cultural identification (Bauman, 2016) to resistance from white hegemony. AAGLO-specific terminology surfaces in external-facing new member presentations (e.g., in greetings to organizations and esteemed audience members) and internal-facing online forums (e.g., the "Subtle Asian Greeks" Facebook group). Complementary research will further examine possibilities for creating new traditions as AAGLOs highlight their culture and spread awareness.

Paraphernalia

According to Kimbrough (2003), by the mid-1980s, jackets became more than paraphernalia, and in many instances, walking artwork. Students began to use the jackets as showcases to provide detailed information about their experience as a member of their sorority or fraternity. Not only did the jackets have Greek letters, one would typically see the name of the chapter where the member was initiated, the member's alma mater, the member's line number, and the line name of the person, solidifying the tradition of giving line names or nicknames since the late 1970s (Kimbrough, 2003).

AAGLOs have adopted similar practices in having custom designs, line names, numbers, and chapters showcased on the jacket. Entrepreneurial AAGLO alumni even started their own businesses (e.g., StitchZone, SleekAttire, OneGreekStore, DangPaddles) to create customized apparel, graduation stoles, and engraved gifts for members of the broader sorority and fraternity community. On a broader level, NAPA celebrates International Badge Day during National Women's History Month in March annually with the National Panhellenic Conference to honor female leaders who make an impact on their chapters, organizations, campuses, and communities (NAPA, 2016). Locally, councils including the National Asian Panhellenic Council at the University at Albany display unity through events like "Para Day" to show their unified pride in their sorority and fraternity experience.

Calls

Calls are audible sounds made by members as a means to signify or acknowledge membership in a particular organization, or to acknowledge or "call" a member who may be in range where they could hear the sound and respond. Instead of yelling the person's name, the sorority or fraternity sibling would use the call to get the person's attention. These actions are also steeped in African as well as African American traditions (Kimbrough, 2003). Alternately named whoops, hollers, cries, and artwhoolies, they were a form of yodeling employed in the Congo and Angola among tribes (whooping), or sung by slaves (cries and artwhoolies). The call was also the name of the practice of Black vendors who peddled and advertised their products (Kimbrough, 2003). Other forms of symbolic communicative practices include the adaptation of BLGO practices of engaging calls and hand signs that signify the respective identities of various organizations, as does stepping (Olivas, 2006).

Members within AAGLOs grew to adopt these practices and use calls to signal their presence on campus-wide cultural shows, dance performances, installation ceremonies, and commencement exercises. AAGLOs also use chants as a response to their organizations being called into a roll call when attending sorority and fraternity events, which may allude to the organization's mascot, motto, colors, founding year of establishment, and additional factors that set historical context in a catchy call-and-response format. Chants may be created at the regional and chapter level to locally differentiate members who were initiated from their respective universities and broader geographic areas.

Hand Signs

The compliment to the call is the hand sign, or hailing signal. The oral history of BGLO customs questions the exact origin of this custom; theories include an introduction of gang hand signs as more former gang members entered colleges and universities (Kimbrough, 2003). Although hand signs are considered a 1970s invention, within a decade, hand signs became ubiquitous and proliferated on college campuses. Since that time, the majority of Greek-affiliated undergraduates pose for pictures while using their respective hand signs (Kimbrough, 2003). AAGLO members project their own hand signs as visual signaling in chapter photos, recruitment videos, and group gatherings. Hand signs commonly replicate the shape or formation of an organization's primary Greek letter with one hand or set of letters with both hands.

Performances

Sharing a tradition across culturally-based sororities and fraternities, AAGLOs and Latinx/a/o organizations learned and adopted stepping practices from BGLOs. As Latina Greek-Letter Sororities (LGLS) have learned from BGLOs the performance of hand signs and calls, they have also adapted stepping. The art of stepping is believed to draw on African American folk traditions and communication patterns as well as materials from popular culture, such as advertising jingles, televisions theme songs, and Top 40 hits (Fine, 1991, as cited in Kimbrough, 2003). Each BGLO that engages in stepping develops "'trade steps' (also known as signature steps) that add to the organization's identity"

(Fine, 1991, as cited in Kimbrough, 2003, p. 46). Similarly, LGLS can draw from the same materials as BGLO, but they add elements specific to the influences of Latin dance and music (Olivas, 2006). Those engaging in step dancing have often competed alongside BGLO at step shows hosted by members of one organization or a group of organizations. These step shows promote cultural awareness and often serve as vehicles in unifying minority CBSFs participating in these events (Olivas, 2006).

AAGLOs deliver step and stroll performances at campus talent shows, dance competitions, culture nights, and new member presentations. These performances have evolved to embed artistic elements originating from Asian culture. For example, Pi Delta Psi fraternity members performed Chinese lion dancing during the Lunar New Year (Rosene, 2005) and Kappa Phi Gamma sorority members fused popular hip-hop routines with traditional South Asian dance (Kirchner, 2019). By incorporating movements and expressions from traditional dance styles—e.g., bharatanatyam, bhangra, fan dancing, and lion dancing—into their performance showcases, AAGLOs spotlight and share their cultural heritage to their broader campus and community.

While the precise chronology of co-opting of these traditions and customs within Asian American fraternal organizations is unknown, the frequent use of these practices continues to be discussed amongst organizational leadership to prevent the perpetuation of anti-Blackness. We speculate the use of these traditions, adopted from BGLOs, were acts of resistance against being viewed as a model minority, "honorary white" (Tuan, 1998), or white-adjacent. By extending these organizational traditions, we honor the anti-Asian racism our ancestors faced in America.

Research: Introspective Insights

The institutional memory of AAGLOs are preserved through embodied memory-keeping practices such as crafting scrapbooks (Wong, 2015) and attending annual conventions (Stillman, 2017) where stories outlining history are passed down to members as wisdom. Although there is such a vast history of AAGLOs, even within the larger context of SFL, there continues to be a dearth in literature centering their stories and the experiences of members of these organizations. Just as general sorority and fraternity research cannot be done effectively without taking other factors or perspectives into consideration, research on AAGLOs needs to also speak to the experience of the APIDA community (Badruddin, 2017).

Dispelling the Model Minority Stereotype

Despite the diversity in the APIDA community, the community is often lumped together as a model minority. Scholars including Museus and Kiang (2009) asserted "the exclusion of [Asian Americans and Pacific Islanders] AAPIs from scholarly inquiry in postsecondary education is in part due to the pervasive influence of the model minority myth" (pp. 5–6). The model minority myth pits Asian Americans against other racial minorities, promoting the concept of meritocracy and minimizing the impact of racial discrimination (Suzuki, 2002). The model minority myth also promotes the idea that the APIDA community is monolithic (Chan & Hune, 1995; Chou & Feagin, 2008), when in reality, APIDAs are composed of different ethnicities, socioeconomic backgrounds, and political ideologies.

AAGLOs work to dismantle the stereotypes associated with the model minority myth through the cultural, educational, and philanthropic programs they organize on a local and national level (NAPA, 2019). Below are several excerpts from the 2019 NAPA Standards of Excellence Awards that encapsulate the impact of local AAGLO programming:

- Kappa Phi Lambda at Rutgers University hosted an event called "Signs of Love" as a way to open up a dialogue about the LGBTQIA+ community as well as the deaf community. In collaborating with the Rutgers American Sign Language Club, alpha Kappa Delta Phi, Delta Lambda Phi, and Delta Kappa Delta, they taught audience members the American Sign Language for queer terminology. They held this event in order to discuss homophobia within the Greek community and how to combat homophobia while learning the beauty of American Sign Language.
- Delta Epsilon Psi at the University of Illinois-Chicago is heavily involved with the surrounding downtown Chicago community. S.H.I.N.E. (Spreading Harmony in Neighborhoods Everywhere) is an event created in hopes of inspiring confidence and harmony for those in need. This chapter distributed hygiene products, gave free haircuts, and provided clothing to help those in need to see a brighter future.
- Lambda Phi Epsilon at the University of Nebraska–Lincoln collaborated with registered student organizations to host their annual Asian Student Leadership Conference, which is a student-led, non-profit, one-day event founded by a charter brother that promotes the diversity within APIDA cultures to nearby high school communities. This chapter hosted workshops on sharpening interpersonal skills and educating students about

the bamboo ceiling, Asian masculinity and femininity, and the model minority myth.

The programs mentioned above highlight the diversity of the APIDA population and the opportunity for impact for the greater community. In the pursuit of creating a greater sense of belonging on their campuses, members of AAGLOs remake space socially and physically to reshape their institutional landscapes through prolonged collective action (Samura, 2016).

Through active collaboration, AAGLOs leverage their campus networks to uplift their community and shift public perception of stereotypes surrounding APIDAs. While these partnerships are mutually beneficial, "AAGLOs can mobilize their members more effectively than many other Asian American groups—they can be great allies and leaders in building a stronger Asian American community on campus" (Gonzales, 2012, p. 225).

Next Steps for AAGLOs and Recommendations for Practitioners

By parsing through data by subculture, a researcher would simultaneously highlight the diversity of the APIDA community and increase awareness of the different cultural practices. By creating awareness of the wide variety of cultural traditions within the APIDA community, an organization can more easily utilize these customs instead of co-opting traditions of the African American and Black community. Historically, BGLOs brought stepping and strolling into the sorority and fraternity realm; Latinx/a/o Greek-letter organizations introduced saluting. It is now time for APIDA folks and AAGLOs to make their contribution to the ever-evolving sorority and fraternity community.

Practitioners advising and working with AAGLOs should consider the following recommendations to build rapport and trust within the student and alumni community:

- Advocate for the hiring of a full-time staff member within the SFL Office to advise local councils serving AAGLOs.
- Promote the formation of NAPA councils among student leaders at PWIs to affirm and uplift the collective APIDA sorority and fraternity experience.
- Foster trust and strong relationships with headquarter staff and volunteers as well as the local chapters of AAGLOs being advised by attending AAGLO events on campus to show visibility and willingness to serve as a resource to students.

- Learn organizational history, culture, and values of AAGLOs by reviewing resources on the NAPA website (National APIDA Panhellenic Association, 2021).
- Encourage AAGLO chapters to partner and collaborate with their peer multicultural sororities and fraternities in co-hosting educational programs.
- Allocate departmental funding for students to attend conferences like the National Cultural Greek Leadership Conference at the Association of Fraternal Leadership and Values West and the Northeast Greek Leadership Association Conference.
- Listen and direct students to the Honestly, Asian Greeks podcast that launched in January 2021, which spotlights the untold stories, hxstories, and narratives of AAGLO alumni and current students (Lam, Wang, Phoumivong, & Chen, 2021). The podcast provides talking points for generating discussion, reflection, and action to help AAGLOs realize their original founding vision and mission.

Questions for Reflection

Customs adopted from BGLOs continue to drive traditions in AAGLOs. As traditions continue to change and evolve over time, we pose the following questions to open dialogue with SFL professionals:

- How should practitioners advise AAGLO chapters to honor their culture's traditions while learning the history of other cultures as it relates to culturally-based sororities and fraternities?
- How should AAGLOs honor the traditions of BGLOs and infuse their own culture into their respective organizations?
- How could AAGLOs be better partners in honoring the traditions of BGLOs they have appropriated and/or borrowed and also advocate in solidarity for the Black community?

References

Badruddin, B. (2017). Lions, tigers, and South Asian Greeks: Oh, my! The opportunity for more research! *Texas Education Review*, 5(2), 17–20.

Badruddin, B. (2020a). *NAPA condemns racist coronavirus remarks*. National APIDA Panhellenic Association. https://www.napahq.org/napa-condemns-racist-coronavirus-remarks/

Badruddin, B. (2020b). *Asian American solidarity against anti-Black racism*. National APIDA Panhellenic Association. https://www.napahq.org/asian-american-solidarity-against-anti-black-racism/

Bauman, C. (2016). *Speaking of sisterhood: A sociolinguistic study of an Asian American sorority* (Doctoral dissertation, New York University, New York, NY). https://proquest.com/docview/1769841034

Chan, K., & Hune, S. (1995). Racialization and panethnicity: From Asians in America to Asian Americans. In W. Hawley & A. Jackson (Eds.), *Toward a common destiny* (pp. 205–233). Hoboken, NJ: Jossey-Bass.

Chen, J. (2008). *Asian Greek Council of Southern California*. https://web.archive.org/web/20080310233935/http://www.asiangreekcouncil.com/members.htm

Chou, R., & Feagin, J. (2008). *The myth of the model minority: Asian Americans facing racism*. New York, NY: Paradigm.

Dosono, B. (2019). *Identity work of Asian Americans and Pacific Islanders on Reddit: Traversals of deliberation, moderation, and decolonization* (Doctoral dissertation, Syracuse University, New York, NY). https://proquest.com/docview/2241646214

Dosono, B. (2020a). Identity work in online fraternal spaces. *Association of Fraternity/Sorority Advisors Perspectives*, 29–31. https://issuu.com/afa1976/docs/afa-perspectives-2019-issue4-final-nobleed/28

Dosono, B. (2020b). Directory of NAPA organization chapter locations. *National APIDA Panhellenic Association*. http://bit.ly/napachapterlocations

Dosono, B., Badruddin, B., Lam, V. (2019). History of Asian American Greek-Letter Organizations. In P. Sasso, J. P. Biddix, & M. L. Miranda (2019), *Foundations, research, and assessment of fraternities and sororities: Retrospective and future consideration*s (pp. 25–37). Sterling, VA: Stylus.

Dosono, B., Badruddin, B., & Lam, V. (2020). *Directory of Asian American Greek letter organizations*. http://bit.ly/aaglo

Gee, B., Seoh, H., & Dosono, B. (2019). The National Asian Pacific Islander Desi American Panhellenic Association. In P. Sasso, J. P. Biddix, & M. L. Miranda (2019), *Supporting fraternities and sororities in the contemporary era: Advancements in practice* (pp. 225–231). Gorham, ME: Myers Education Press.

Gonzalez, A. (2012). Redefining racial paradigms: Asian American Greek-letter organizations in American higher education. In D. Ching & A. Agbayani (2012), *Asian Americans and Pacific Islanders in higher education* (pp. 213–229). Washington, DC: NASPA-Student Affairs Administrators in Higher Education.

Hall, E. T. (1989). *Beyond culture*. New York, NY: Anchor Books.

Javier, K. N. (2018). *Asian American women: The influence of sororities and little sister programs* (Doctoral dissertation, Alliant International University, San Diego, CA). https://proquest.com/docview/2047520557

Kimbrough, W. M. (2003). *Black Greek 101: The culture, customs, and challenges of Black fraternities and sororities*. Vancouver, British Columbia, Canada: Fairleigh Dickinson University Press.

Kirchner, K. (2019). Kulture Night: A night of appreciation and expression. *Fourth Estate*. https://gmufourthestate.com/2019/11/04/kulture-night-a-night-of-appreciation-and-expression/

Lam, V., Wang, C., Phoumivong, T., & Chen, N. (2021). Audio podcast. AAGLO Education Collective. https://anchor.fm/honestly-asian-greeks/episodes/Episode-1-History-of-AAGLOs-eok3em

Museus, S. D., & Kiang, P. N. (2009). Deconstructing the model minority myth and how it contributes to the invisible minority reality in higher education research. In S. D. Museus (Ed.), *Conducting research on Asian American in higher education* (New Directions for Institutional Research, no. 142, pp. 5–15). Hoboken, NJ: Wiley.

National APIDA Panhellenic Association. (2016). *International Badge Day 2016: A time to remember*. https://www.napahq.org/international-badge-day-2016/

National APIDA Panhellenic Association. (2019). *2019 NAPA standards of excellence award recipients*. https://www.napahq.org/2019-napa-standards-of-excellence-award-recipients/

National APIDA Panhellenic Association. (2021). *NAPA website*. https://www.napahq.org/

Olivas, M. R. (2006). *Straddling the organizational borderland: Negotiating identity in Latina Greek-letter organizations* (Doctoral dissertation, University of Colorado Boulder, Boulder, CO). https://proquest.com/docview/305353277

Rosene, H. (2005). Fraternity celebrates Chinese New Year. *Daily Collegian*. https://www.collegian.psu.edu/archives/article_e8c3080d-c09f-5cad-b720-b5ff865842ad.html

Samura, M. (2016). Remaking selves, repositioning selves, or remaking space: An examination of Asian American college students' processes of "belonging." *Journal of College Student Development*, *57*(2), 135–150.

Semaan, B., Dosono, B., & Britton, L. M. (2017). Impression management in high context societies: 'Saving face' with ICT. In *Proceedings of the 2017 ACM Conference on Computer Supported Cooperative Work and Social Computing* (pp. 712–725). Portland, OR: ACM.

Stillman, A. (2017). Living memory: What it portends when the founders still live. *Oracle: The Research Journal of the Association of Fraternity/Sorority Advisors*, *12*(1), 62–72.

Suzuki, B. (2002). Revisiting the model minority stereotype: Implications for student affairs practice and higher education. In M. McEwen, C. M. Kodama, A. N. Alvarez, S. L. Lee, & C. T. H. Liang (Eds.), *Working with Asian American college students* (New Directions for Student Services, 2002, no. 97, pp. 21–32). Hoboken, NJ: Wiley.

Torbenson, C. L., & Parks, G. (Eds.). (2009). *Brothers and sisters: Diversity in college fraternities and sororities*. Cranbury, NJ Associated University Press.

Tran, M., & Chang, M. (2019). Asian American interest fraternities: Fulfilling unmet needs of the loneliest Americans. In K. E. Gillon, C. C. Beatty, & C. Salinas Jr. (Eds.), *Critical *considerations of race, ethnicity, and culture in fraternity & sorority life* (New Directions for Student Services, no. 165, pp. 73–85). Hoboken, NJ: Wiley.

Tuan, M. (1998). *Forever foreigners or honorary whites?: The Asian ethnic experience today*. New Brunswick, NJ: Rutgers University Press.

Wong, V. L. (2015). *Asian Greek sisterhoods: Archives, affects, and belongings in Asian American sororities, 1929–2015* (Doctoral dissertation, UCLA, Los Angeles, CA). https://proquest.com/docview/1691346009

Member Vignette: Latinx/a/o-Based Sororities and Fraternities

JANEL RAMOS

The true value of sorority and fraternity life (SFL) is something I was introduced to at a young age. I had the privilege of watching, first hand, as beautiful relationships were fostered over many years and college friends turned into chosen family. My mother has always been surrounded by inspirational women who my siblings and I call our "Tías" or aunts. They were present for every important event and in every way, they are our family. I came to learn that in 1989, at the University of Albany, SUNY, my mother and her friends recognized a need for a space where Latinas could call home and created one. My mom is one of the 17 Radiant Founders of Omega Phi Beta, Sorority, Inc. (OPBSI) and the legacy she created was one I was blessed enough to recognize from an early age. After my mom's move from New York to Florida, she stayed active in the sorority but there wasn't a single active chapter in the state and the lack of sisterhood left her feeling lonely. She decided to start the journey of expanding OPBSI in Florida at Florida State University (FSU) and the University of South Florida (USF).

My mother, while raising 3 kids, decided to be the Membership Educator for the charter line at USF. As a middle schooler, this was my first real introduction to the sorority and I grew relationships with the women going through the process and looked up to them in every way. I finally understood the bond that surrounded my mother and at 12-year old. I knew I wanted to join this sisterhood. Seven years later, I did exactly that. In spring 2017, I became the first Founder-Legacy of Omega Phi Beta Sorority,

Inc. at the University of South Florida, the exact same school my mom fought so hard to charter years before.

I had an extremely difficult transition to college. My first semester, I went through a bad breakup, had a terrible roommate, and did not make many friends. I remember calling my mom and crying about how badly I wanted to leave the university and go back home. My roommate and I did not get along and because of that I grew extremely close to my suitemate. A few months into my first semester, I invited her to an OPBSI informational, a professional presentation of the organization and its history by sisters. She had never heard of Omega Phi Beta Sorority, Inc. and insisted she was not interested in joining a sorority, but she still attended the informational with me. After we met the sisters and heard their stories, we were hooked and became line sisters[1] the next spring. What started as a random suitemate assignment ended up turning into my best friendship and my sister for life.

When I joined the sorority, I did not realize the work does not truly begin until you enter the chapter and begin to plan events, community service, and socials while also trying to foster sisterhood. We have always been a smaller chapter so every event requires the full effort of each sister. We depend on each other for everything so my biggest struggle came when my line sisters graduated and we were left with a chapter of two members. I became chapter president and it was one of the hardest semesters of my life. My vice president and I had to hold every position in chapter and were in contact almost all day, every day, because there was so much to do, especially as it relates to recruitment. Thankfully, I was involved all over campus, so I was able to exemplify my organization and its values through my leadership, and our recruitment was the best it had ever been. Although we knew it would be extremely difficult, we decided to put on the biggest class since our chapter was chartered at USF. We were able to bring nine women into our chapter and it was one of the most rewarding experiences to date. We saw all of our hard work and non-stop dedication pay off in the way those women loved our sisterhood, together with the way they looked up to us on how to run the chapter in the future.

As a graduating senior, I look back on my experience with nothing but pride and gratitude. Legacy is a term that holds so much weight in my life. The legacy my mom left in 1989 allowed me to create my own. My sorority and my university gave me more than I could have ever imagined and I did my best to leave a legacy behind. At the end of this journey, I left with so many lessons, friends, and sisters for life. I had the honor of being awarded the NALFO Campus Leadership Excellence Award and Undergraduate Excellence Award, two of the highest undergraduate achievements from the National Association of Latino Fraternal Organizations, Inc.. Even though it did not seem like it at times, people were watching and recognizing the work and dedication I put into my

---

[1] A line sister(s) is defined as a fellow woman/women completing the new member educational process simultaneously in a Latinx/a-based sorority.

organization and my community. Many times, I had imposter syndrome and thought because I am Latina, I had to prove myself 10 times more than others. It was difficult to find my place, but my involvement helped me blossom and my organization turned me into the woman I am today. My sorority taught me confidence, professionalism, and leadership. It brought me my future bridesmaids, the God-moms of my future children, my sisters. SFL, like everything else in this world, is entirely what you make it. If you decide to put in hard work, sacrifice, love and passion, then you will receive all those things back 10 times over and I am so grateful to say that although my undergraduate career is over, my sisterhood is forever.

CHAPTER FIVE

La Perspectiva de un Practicante (A Practitioner's Perspective): Latinx/a/o-based Sororities and Fraternities

JUAN R. GUARDIA[1]

According to the U.S. Census Bureau, Hispanic/Latinx/a/os represent the nation's largest minoritized group. In 2019, Hispanic/Latinx/a/os constituted 60 million people—18.3% of the nation's population (U.S. Census Bureau, 2020). It is important to note that Latinx/a/os identify as an ethnic group and not a racial group. Accordingly, Bernal, Knight, Ocampo, Garza, and Cota (1993) defined how "ethnicity refers to an organization of people with their cultural, racial, and linguistic characteristics, whereas race refers to inherited physical qualities" (p. 34). Further expounding on ethnicity, Suro (2005) described Hispanic/Latino identity as:

> not a racial group, nor does it share a common language or culture. The single overarching trait that all Hispanics share in common is a connection to Latin America. The population, in fact, traces its origins to many countries with varied cultures, and while some Latinos have family histories in the United States that date back centuries, others are recent arrivals. Some speak only English, others only Spanish, and many are bilingual. (p. 3)

---

[1] The author would like to thank Dr. Mónica Lee Miranda for her valuable comments and feedback on the early draft of this book chapter. Dr. Miranda is a proud, Lifetime Member of Omega Phi Beta Sorority, Inc.

As such, Latinx/a/os may choose to identify in a variety of ways, inclusive of culture, languages, and with one or more racial groups. In addition, the inclusion of additional intersectional identities including socioeconomic status, sexual orientation/gender identity, and immigration status further adds to the rich, diverse identities of Latinx/a/os (Nuñez, 2014).

As the nation's largest minoritized group, it is not surprising that a significant amount of Latinx/a/o college students are enrolled in higher education. Since 2011, Latinx/a/o college students have been the largest minoritized group at 4-year college and university campuses (Fry & Lopez, 2012; Fry & Taylor, 2013). Latinx/a/o college students account for 19.5% of all students enrolled in degree-granting postsecondary institutions in the United States (National Center for Education Statistics, 2018). Latinx/a/o students may be involved in co-curricular activities on 4-year college and university campuses in a variety of ways, including admissions ambassador, orientation leader, peer advisor, and sorority and fraternity life (SFL), specifically Latinx/a/o-based sororities and fraternities. Latinx/a/o-based sororities and fraternities are an important subculture to highlight as an integral part of a campus' tapestry as they contribute to the knowledge, information sharing, and inclusivity that strengthens the campus community. Therefore, this chapter will cover a brief history of Latinx/a/o-based sororities and fraternities, the strengths of these organizations, including ethnic identity development and cultural empowerment, leadership development, and sexual orientation and gender inclusivity. Finally, I offer insights and recommendations for practitioners to better assist them when working with Latinx/a/o-based sororities and fraternities on their respective campuses.

Brief History of Latinx/a/o-Based Sororities and Fraternities

The foundation of Latinx/a/o-based sororities and fraternities dates back to the late 1800s as secret societies. These secret societies "later became fraternities founded to provide cultural and intellectual spaces for Latino/a students" (Miranda, Salinas, & Del Real, 2020, p. 180). Two early such organizations were Sigma Iota (formerly the Sociedad Hispano-Americana in 1904), founded at Louisiana State University in 1912, and Phi Lambda Alpha, founded at the University of California, Berkeley in 1919 (Anson & Marchesani, 1991; Johnson, 1972; Miranda et al., 2020; Muñoz & Guardia, 2009). On December 26, 1931, the two fraternities merged to form Phi Iota Alpha Fraternity, Incorporated (Baily, 1949; Fine, 2003; Kimbrough, 2003; Miranda & Martin de Figueroa, 2000; Torbenson, 2005).

The first Latina-based sorority in the continental United States was Lambda Theta Alpha Latin Sorority, Incorporated founded in December 1975 at Kean University (Bovell, 2009; Delgado-Guerrero, Cherniack, & Gloria, 2014; Miranda, 1999). There was substantial growth of Latinx/a/o-based sororities and fraternities "between 1975 and 1990, with the founding of 20 fraternities and sororities, including one co-ed Latino/a Greek-lettered organization" (Miranda et al., 2020, p. 179). As Latinx/a/o-based sororities and fraternities continued to flourish nationally there was still a missing piece; no national umbrella organization existed to represent these organizations.

Whereas many sororities and fraternities were nationally represented by the National Panhellenic Conference, North American Interfraternity Conference, or the National Pan-Hellenic Council, there was no such national council for Latinx/a/o-based sororities and fraternities. This left Latinx/a/o-based sororities and fraternities in a deficit: how would they be represented at the national level along their peers? As Muñoz and Guardia (2009) noted, "Although these councils can amend their bylaws to include LGLO [Latino/a Greek Lettered Organizations], none of these councils directly address the needs of LGLOs" (p. 115). The first Latinx/a/o-based sorority and fraternity council was created in 1991 at the University of Albany, SUNY by Phi Iota Alpha Fraternity, Inc. and Omega Phi Beta Sorority, Inc. (Miranda et al., 2020; Muñoz & Guardia, 2009). That initiative snowballed into a national movement that brought together Latinx/a/o-based sororities and fraternities in the creation of the National Latino Greek Council, also known as the Concilio Nacional de Hermandades Latinas (CNHL; Miranda et al., 2020). Similarly, the Western Regional Latino Greek Alliance had been in existence representing the interest of Latinx/a/o-based sororities and fraternities on the West Coast of the United States; those organizations would also be instrumental in creating the National Association of Latino Fraternal Organizations (NALFO). NALFO was established in 1988 to unify and improve communication amongst Latinx/a/o-based sororities and fraternities. For some time, the CNHL and NALFO coexisted and worked tirelessly to advocate for their respective organizations. In 2001, the CNHL dissolved and the NALFO member organizations continued to work to promote the mission and vision of Latinx/a/o-based sororities and fraternities. Currently, NALFO consists of 10 Latinx/a-based sororities, five Latinx/o-based fraternities, and one co-ed Latinx/a/o-based fraternal organization.

Juan's Viaje (Journey) of Joining a Latinx/o Fraternity

My journey into becoming a fraternity man was atypical. As an undergraduate student at Miami Dade College (then known as Miami-Dade Community College), a Hispanic-Serving Institution, they did not offer social sorority and fraternity involvement opportunities. When I transferred to Florida State University, a predominantly white institution, I had several friends who were members of sororities and fraternities, yet I did not see myself as a member of the SFL community. Namely, I did not see many Latinx/a/o peers who were affiliated members and, for me, that was an important aspect of student involvement. I did not even know then that Latinx/a/o-based fraternities were an option as there were none on campus at that time.

Fast forward to being in in my first higher education administrative position at George Mason University (GMU) as the Assistant Director of Hispanic/Latino Student Affairs in the Office of Diversity Programs and Services. In this role, I worked with the growing Hispanic/Latino community on campus and I learned there were two Latinx/a/o-based sororities and fraternities at GMU: the Mu chapter of Latinas Promoviendo Comunindad/Lambda Pi Chi Sorority, Inc. and the Alpha Delta chapter of La Unidad Latina/Lambda Upsilon Lambda Fraternity, Inc. I worked with members of both organizations through a variety of programs, in and out of their respective organizations and all the while, noticed their *orgullo* (pride) and commitment to the Latinx/a/o community, on- and off-campus, as affiliated members. It got me thinking: is it too late for me to join a Latinx/o-based fraternity?

When I began my doctoral program in higher education at Iowa State University, I contacted several Latinx/o-based fraternities to inquire about membership. Several did not offer any membership opportunities at the post-graduate level, but one did: Phi Iota Alpha Fraternity, Inc. After speaking with their national administration, I was told they had a graduate/professional process for men who had earned an undergraduate degree and/or were in graduate school. After further research, I found that the fraternity's mission and vision aligned with my morals, values, and goals; I submitted an application for membership.

I began the fraternity's graduate member process during the second year of my doctoral program in spring 2005. I was 31, a full-time student, worked as a graduate/teaching assistant, and married at the time. In addition, I was the only candidate (a solo)[2] going through the process. As such, it was a delicate balance

---

[2] A solo is one individual candidate completing the new member educational process in a Latinx/a/o-based sorority or fraternity.

of my personal, professional, and scholastic lives. Fortunately, I successfully completed the graduate process and "crossed"[3] into full membership into the fraternity.

My fraternity membership influenced what would become my dissertation topic. I was interested in researching Latinx/a/o students, ethnic identity development, and Hispanic-Serving Institutions. After meeting with my advisor, an affiliated sorority woman, and sharing my research interests with her, she advised that I could merge all three interests while looking at it from the lens of a Latino fraternity. As such, that led to my dissertation on the ethnic identity development of Latino fraternity members at a Hispanic-Serving Institution (Guardia, 2006) and later, a published journal article (Guardia & Evans, 2008).

My fraternity involvement provided me with several avenues of leadership and engagement, both within the organization and in the larger SFL community. I have volunteered my time at the regional and national level, including serving on the Board of Trustees, and even served as a co-trip leader for a service immersion trip with brothers to Peru. On a national level, I served as a facilitator for the Undergraduate Interfraternity Institute, sponsored by the North American Interfraternity Conference, and facilitated at the Interfraternity Institute for fraternity and sorority professionals and national staff. In addition, I served on the NALFO board as Vice Chair and, subsequently, Chair. Moreover, my fraternal and professional administrative experiences have allowed me to serve as a consultant to assess and evaluate colleges and universities' sorority and fraternity communities. Such opportunities would not have been afforded to me had it not been for my initial involvement with my fraternity.

I shared my fraternal journey because it is an important part of who I am and how it contributes to this chapter. Yet, my other various identities also inform my work as a scholar-practitioner: Cuban-American, Latinx/o, hijo/hermano/primo/tío, first-generation college student, gay, cisgender, temporarily able-bodied, fraternity man, freemason, and spiritual. All of these identities I hold contribute to my lens, professionally and personally, and show up in the work I do, including this chapter. Finally, as a scholar-practitioner and fraternity man, it is my privilege and responsibility to give back to the academy and the higher education literature so Latinx/a/o-based sororities and fraternities are continually represented and supported.

---

[3] Crossing refers to the final ceremony and successful completion of the new member educational process in a Latinx/a/o-based sorority or fraternity.

Strengths of Latinx/a/o-Based Sororities and Fraternities

Above and beyond the involvement opportunities provided by Latinx/a/o-based sororities and fraternities, members also gain a variety of important attributes, such as ethnic identity development and cultural empowerment, leadership development, and positive affirmation for their sexual orientation and gender identity. Each of these items will be discussed individually.

Ethnic Identity Development and Cultural Empowerment

Various researchers have explored ethnic identity development (Casas & Pytluk, 1995; Felix-Ortiz de la Garza, Newcomb, & Myers, 1995; Ferdman & Gallegos, 2001; Phinney, 1993), yet, Vasti Torres' research significantly contributed to the higher education literature on the ethnic identity development of Latinx/a/o college students (Torres, 1999, 2003, 2004; Torres & Delgado-Romero, 2008; Torres & Hernandez, 2007; Torres, Hernandez, & Martinez, 2019; Torres & Magolda, 2004). Her research has been an invaluable foundation for scholars connecting ethnic identity development to Latinx/a/o college students and Latinx/a/o-based sorority and fraternity members.

For members of Latinx/a/o-based sororities and fraternities, research has demonstrated how members' ethnic identity development has been enhanced and validated as a direct result of their membership. J. C. Hernandez (2000) described how Latinx/a/o college students involved in Latinx/a/o student organizations "stay[ed] culturally grounded" and how involvement in such organizations "nurture[ed] one's sense of ethnic identity" (p. 583). Castro (2004) observed that Latinx/a/o-based sororities and fraternities "provide support as well as a cultural education to individuals who are still defining the many aspects of their identity" (p. 1). Nuñez (2004) discovered how Latina sorority women gained a heightened sense of their ethnic identity, growth, and development as a direct result of their sorority membership. Finally, Guardia and Evans (2008) found that members' ethnic identity was enhanced and validated as a direct result of their fraternity affiliation. As such, Latinx/a/o-based sororities and fraternities empower, affirm, and enhance their members' ethnic identity.

The cultural empowerment embedded in Latinx/a/o-based sororities and fraternities cannot be understated. Miranda and Martin de Figueroa (2000) described how these organizations adopted four Latinx/a/o culture primary purposes: (a) advance Latinx/a/o cultural awareness, (b) continually advocate for Latinx/a/o goals, (c) provide a familial atmosphere during college and beyond, and

(d) solidify and continually add to the Latinx/a/o population. In addition, the Spanish language is an important part of Latinx/a/o-based sororities and fraternities. Members refer to one another as *hermanas* (sisters) and *hermanos* (brothers) and describe their organizations as *hermandades* (brotherhoods and sisterhoods; Kimbrough 2003; Rodriguez, 1995).

How Latinx/a/o-based sorority and fraternity members make meaning making of their affiliation also contributes to members' ethnic identity development and cultural empowerment. Miranda (2020) conducted a study on the experiences of undergraduate Latina students involved in Latina-based sororities and the meaning they made from their experiences. Several participants shared how they were empowered by aspects of their culture and these "were affirmations of identity that offered these participants comfort and pride in their individual and community cultural identity" (Miranda, 2020, p. 113). In addition, participants described how their Latina sorority membership directly empowered and/or affirmed their Latina identity. It is clear that Latinx/a/o-based sororities and fraternities aid and enhance members' ethnic identity development and cultural empowerment, yet membership in such organizations also contribute to members' leadership development.

Leadership Development

Of importance is how Latinx/a/o-based sorority and fraternity members embody Latinx/a/o cultural values as part of their leadership roles. Bordas' (2013) inclusive model of leadership incorporates Latinx/a/o cultural values such as *confianza* (trustworthiness), *familismo* (family), *personalismo* (value of each person), *respeto* (respect), and *honesto* (being honest), which Latinx/a/o-based sorority and fraternity members embrace as part of their leadership identities. Guardia (2019) found that Latinx/a/o-based sorority and fraternity members incorporated various Latinx/a/o cultural values in their leadership philosophies when working with their peers. Students shared how chapter meetings invoked a *familismo* atmosphere and members were always *honesto* and treated with *respeto* as they engaged in collaborative dialogue. In addition, members continuously provided *confianza* to their peers when planning programs and *personalismo* in affirming their importance to the chapter and organization overall.

Latinx/a/o-based sororities and fraternities provide various leadership opportunities for its members within their organizations and in the greater campus community. Within their organizations, members can serve as president, treasurer, and new member educators, to name a few. Such roles open doors for their involvement at a larger level across campus, including student government association, resident assistants, orientation leaders, and admissions ambassadors. Delgado-Guerrero and colleagues (2014) found that some Latina sorority members were attracted to joining their Latina-based sororities because of the leadership roles the members held across campus. As one participant shared, "All of the sisters ... were involved in executive board positions on campus suggesting strong leadership roles" (Delgado-Guerrero et al., 2014, p. 50). Guardia and Evans' (2008) study of Latino fraternity members at a Hispanic-serving institution demonstrated how being involved was an important part of their collegiate experience: "If it wasn't for the fraternity, I probably won't be involved in any extracurricular activities" (p. 175). The leadership development opportunities offered in Latinx/a/o-based sororities and fraternities contribute greatly to member's personal and professional development. Next, I will discuss how Latinx/a/o-based sororities and fraternities incorporate sexual orientation and gender inclusivity within their organizations.

Sexual Orientation and Gender Inclusivity

Although Latinx/a/o-based sororities and fraternities have always had members who have identified as Lesbian, Gay, Bisexual, Transgender, and Queer (LGBTQ), in the last 10 years, they have more directly demonstrated their commitment to these members. In May 2014, La Unidad Latina/Lambda Upsilon Lambda (LUL) Fraternity, Inc. hosted its first LUL Out retreat which served as a safe and supportive environment for their gay, bisexual, and questioning brothers to bond and ensure an inclusive *hermandad*. Established in 2015, Omega Phi Beta Sorority, Inc.'s Spectrum Committee focuses on policies and makes recommendations on gender identity, organizational sensitivity, promotion of inclusivity while also serving as a safe, affirming space for their LGBTQ sorority sisters. Several Latinx/a/o-based sororities and fraternities also have similar affirmative spaces for their LGBTQ members within their organizations.

Gender inclusive policies have also been enacted, namely by Latinx/a-based sororities, to demonstrate their commitment to current and prospective members. In 2016, Latinas Promoviendo Comunidad/Lambda Pi Chi Sorority, Inc. became the first trans-inclusive sorority at North Carolina State University. Gabrielle Diaz, chapter president at the time shared, "I'm hoping that us being the first sorority to become trans-inclusive this will encourage other fraternities and sororities to follow the same path" (Nubian Message, 2016, para. 8). Another example of trans and gender inclusivity comes from Kappa Delta Chi Sorority, Inc.'s (2017) National Diversity Policy. In it, their Statement on Title IX stated:

Federal and state law provides no clear and consistent definition of gender. Therefore, the Organization adopts the most expansive policy under present law in order to prevent exclusion and/or discharge of transgender members regardless of legal gender designation. This policy is not intended to change the all-female character of the Organization nor to waive the Organization's rights under Title IX. (para. 3)

In August 2018, Omega Phi Beta Sorority, Inc.'s membership amended their national constitution to include new language in which membership in the sorority was open to "all self-identified women, regardless of any identities they held, hold, or will hold" (para. 1). At least one Latinx/o-based fraternity has also established a gender inclusive statement. In 2018, Lambda Theta Phi Latin Fraternity, Inc. adopted an inclusive membership policy:

Lambda Theta Phi is a single sex organization. For purposes of eligibility for membership, any student who identifies as male and who meets all other requirements of our National Constitution, Policies & Membership Standards, may seek membership in the fraternity. Lambda Theta Phi does not discriminate on the basis of ability status, race, color, religion, national origin, ethnicity, or sexual orientation. Any member who does not or no longer identifies as male post-induction would not result in termination of membership. (para. 1)

It is important to note that Lambda Theta Phi's inclusive membership policy focuses specifically on members and prospective members that identify as male, which is the biological sex a person is assigned at birth. Yet, this may possibly open the door for the fraternity to incorporate gender, a social construct and how an individual identifies, in future iterations of their inclusive membership policy. In conclusion, such gender inclusive statements by Latinx/a/o-based sororities and a fraternity are providing trans and other individuals the opportunity for membership which at one time may not have been possible.

Students' expression of their sexual orientation and gender identity has become more visual and powerful on campuses than ever before. Latinx/a/o-based sororities and fraternities are continually working to update their policies to advocate for their members and prospective members. Colleges and universities should do the same with campus spaces dedicated to sexual orientation and gender identity, including LGBTQ affinity spaces, LGBTQ offices, and women's centers. Such spaces assist students in their exploration of self, their identities, and empower students' to be their best selves. Student affairs administrators should know the importance and worth of such spaces cannot be understated. As such, opportunities to connect these spaces with academic counterparts such as LGBTQ and Women's Studies provides an invaluable growth opportunity for students, inside and outside of the classroom. Moreover, Latinx/a/o-based sororities and fraternities should consider collaborations with such offices and centers for knowledge and resource sharing and training programs to assist their organizations to continually demonstrate their inclusivity for not only their sexual and gender minoritized members, but educating their overall organization.

Insights for Practitioners

As administrators, we have a duty to provide an inclusive campus environment for all students and student organizations, including Latinx/a/o-based sororities and fraternities, and be cognizant of the challenges facing Latinx/a/o-based sororities and fraternities on college and university campuses. Some of those challenges include campus space and university recognition and expansion. These will be discussed in more detail and recommendations offered to not only SFL administrators but all student affairs professionals to consider the importance of such organizations on our campuses.

Campus Space

Space allocation on any college or university campus is always a premium commodity. As university administrators, we need to be cognizant of the spaces provided for engagement across our campuses, and for our Latinx/a/o-based sororities and fraternities, that may show up in a variety of ways. On many of our campuses, especially at predominantly white institutions, Latinx/a/o sorority and fraternity members may seek out Latinx/a/o culture centers and/or multicultural centers as a space that validate their lived experiences. Lozano (2010) stated,

> A culture center is often the only space on campus to offer a holistic learning experience allowing Latina/o students to explore racial/ethnic identity development and engage in social justice activism, political education, community outreach, academic mentorship and support, leadership development, social and professional networking, and alumni outreach. (p. 11)

Cultural centers, as important counterspaces on campuses, assist and enable students in their college transition "as well as provide instrumental information about how to become a successful college student" (Keels, 2019, p. 84).

On some campuses, such centers serve as the home for Latinx/a/o-based sorority and fraternity chapters and Latinx/a/o-based sorority and fraternity councils. Center administrators may also advise these organizations. If that is the case, such centers can strategically partner with their office of SFL to utilize the best of both worlds: cultural centers administrators that can relate to students' racial and ethnic identities and SFL administrators who advocate for the importance of sororities and fraternities on campus. In addition, SFL offices with professionals affiliated with Latinx/a/o-based sororities and fraternities validate their commitment and support to the Latinx/a/o-based sorority and fraternity community. Such partnerships between cultural centers, student activities, and offices of SFL demonstrate the importance Latinx/a/o-based sororities and fraternities bring to the campus.

The simple act of just having Latinx/a/o-based sororities and fraternities on college and university campuses show up as important counterspaces for their members. Keels (2019) described how for marginalized students, counterspaces provide social bonding, affirm students' racial/ethnic identities, challenge stereotypical narratives, mitigate feelings of isolation, and help them learn adaptive strategies. Latinx/a/o-based sororities and fraternities equip its members with all these attributes, which assist in students' retention and persistence to graduation.

Student affairs administrators know and understand that affirmative spaces on campus including Latinx/a/o Centers or Multicultural Centers provide students a home-away-from-home and serve as important, invaluable spaces that aide in students' retention. In the case of Latinx/a/o-based sororities and fraternities, these affirmative spaces serve as additional avenues that enhance and validate individuals' identities and empowers students culturally. Student affairs administrators, including SFL professionals, should advocate for these spaces on campuses. If such spaces are not currently offered at your institution, working with students from these communities to submit proposals for space allocation signals their importance as part of the university's tapestry.

College and University Expansion

An additional challenge facing Latinx/a/o-based sororities and fraternities is expansion. On most college and university campuses, expansions are facilitated by the office of sorority and fraternity life (OSFL). In most cases, the OSFL announces that the college/university is open for expansion and interested organizations may submit an application expressing their interest in establishing a chapter on that campus. OSFL administrators review organization applications and, depending on the organization, the pertaining SFL council in which they would be affiliated. Depending on the campus, Latinx/a/o-based sororities and fraternities may be affiliated with a Latinx/a/o Greek Council and/or a Multicultural Greek Council. Council members take into consideration what the organization has to offer, how they would fit on campus, and the council then votes whether or not they will be offered the opportunity to be affiliated on their campus. In most instances, this should be an equitable, smooth process. Unfortunately, that is not always the case.

College and university expansion was a major topic amongst Latinx/a/o-based sororities and fraternities within a proposal that was submitted by NALFO delegates at the 2009 bi-annual NALFO meeting. The proposal stated if there were current NALFO organizations on a college or university campus that was open for expansion and a NALFO organization(s) applied and successfully met all the college/university requirements, the NALFO organizations on campus may not vote "No" for the new organization(s). This proposal, although a contentious issue for some of the NALFO organizations because NALFO has never been a regulatory umbrella organization, was passed and approved in 2009. This legislation assisted "NALFO organizations in expanding to new campuses across the country, and in some cases, increased the enrollment of Latinx and others students wanting to join NALFO's Latinx fraternities and sororities" (Miranda et al., 2020, p. 42).

Expansion is a great opportunity for Latinx/a/o-based sororities and fraternities to join a campus community. When done well, and in a justified manner, it provides these organizations and its prospective members an additional avenue for involvement that may have not been previously offered. As administrators, we should advocate for these organizations to be on our campuses and have an opportunity to assist our students in understanding the importance of expansion and the value it provides current and future students. We have a responsibility to educate our students that strengthening the Latinx/a/o campus community is of greater value than the competition perceived by a few to be more important.

As more and more Latinx/a/o students arrive on our college campuses, some of these students may seek out Latinx/a/o-based sororities and fraternities. If there are no current Latinx/a/o-based sororities and fraternities on your campus, work with the university's sorority and fraternity office to connect with NALFO and other Latinx/a/o SFL organizations to offer a potential expansion opportunity. This gesture demonstrates goodwill towards inclusivity on campus. If your campus currently has Latinx/a/o-based sororities and fraternities, a continual assessment of their needs and further growth with the addition of other Latinx/a/o-based sororities and fraternities can meet the needs of a growing Latinx/a/o student population.

Conclusion

Latinx/a/o-based sororities and fraternities are vital and serve as important contributors within the campus community. These organizations assist in recruiting, retaining, and graduating predominantly Latinx/a/o students, while culturally empowering and validating members' ethnic identity development. As practitioners, we have a responsibility to assist these organizations and its members in finding their space on campus, connecting them with fellow administrators and faculty to ensure they graduate as well rounded, holistically developed members of society effectively prepared to enter a global workforce.

Student affairs administrators affiliated with Latinx/a/o-based sororities and fraternities have an additional opportunity to assist as they may see themselves reflected in the students they serve. These affiliated staff understand the commitment they made while enduring and completing the new member education process, while balancing scholastic, familial, and work responsibilities. That balance demonstrates perseverance, and as administrators who have had similar experiences, we can serve as role models and mentors to these students and ultimately show it is possible to achieve academic excellence and meet our personal and professional responsibilities.

Questions for Reflection

Finally, I offer the following questions for administrators to consider when working with Latinx/a/o-based sororities and fraternities:

- If your campus has Latinx/a/o-based sororities and fraternities, what have you done to learn more about these organizations? When were they established? What need was there for them to be on campus?
- Does your campus have a substantial growth of Latinx/a/o identified students? If so, are there expansion requests/need for additional Latinx/a/o-based sororities and fraternities?
- What are the retention and graduation rates for Latinx/a/o identified students at your institution? How can Latinx/a/o-based sororities and fraternities on campus assist with student success?
- What resources does your campus and/or division offer to empower Latinx/a/o-based sorority and fraternity members' ethnic identity development? How can we educate and stress the importance to community members that Latinx/a/o-based sororities and fraternities play an important role in members' holistic development?
- What leadership opportunities, above and beyond those currently found within Latinx/a/o-based sorority and fraternity chapters, are available to these students? How can we stress the importance to these students that additional opportunities exist and that they are strongly encouraged to apply?

References

Anson, J. L. & Marchesani, R. F. (Eds.). (1991). *Baird's manual of American college fraternities* (20th ed.). Indianapolis, IN: Baird's Manual Foundation.

Baily, H. J. (Ed.). (1949). *Baird's manual of American college fraternities* (15th ed.). Menasha, WI: Banta.

Bernal, M. E., Knight, G. P., Ocampo, K. A., Garza, C. A., & Cota, M. K. (1993). Development of Mexican American identity. In M. E. Bernal & G. P. Knight (Eds.), *Ethnic identity: Formation and transmission among Hispanics and other minorities* (pp. 31–46). Albany, NY: State University of New York Press.

Bordas J. (2013). *The power of Latino leadership: Culture, inclusion, and contribution.* Oakland, CA: Berrett-Koehler.

Bovell, L. S. (2009). *The empowerment of Latin sorority women: Gender perceptions in Latin sororities* (Unpublished master's thesis, University of Florida, Gainesville, FL).

Casas, J. M., & Pytluk, S. D. (1995). Hispanic identity development: Implications for research and practice. In J. G. Ponterotto, J. M. Casas, L. A. Suzuki, & C. M. Alexander (Eds.), *Handbook of multicultural counseling* (pp. 155–180). Thousand Oaks, CA: Sage.

Castro, M. (2004, April). *The growth of multicultural organizations.* Paper presented at the meeting of the Association of Fraternity Advisors, Hollywood, CA.

Delgado-Guerrero, M., Cherniack, M. A., & Gloria, A. M. (2014). Family away from home: Factors influencing undergraduate Women of Color's decisions to join a cultural-specific sorority. *Journal of Diversity in Higher Education, 7*(1), 45–57.

Felix-Ortiz de la Garza, M., Newcomb, M. D. & Myers, H. F. (1995). A multidimensional measure of cultural identity for Latino and Latina adolescents. In A. M. Padilla (Ed.), *Hispanic psychology critical issues in theory and research* (pp. 26–42). Thousand Oaks, CA: Sage.

Ferdman, B. M., & Gallegos, P. I. (2001). Racial identity development and Latinos in the United States. In C. L. Wijeyesinghe & B. W. Jackson III (Eds.), *New perspectives on racial identity development: A theoretical and practical anthology* (pp. 32–66). New York, NY: University Press.

Fine, E. C. (2003). *Soulstepping: African American step shows.* Champaign, IL: University of Illinois Press.

Fry, R., & Lopez, M. H. (2012). *Hispanic student enrollments reach new heights in 2011.* Pew Research Center. https://www.pewresearch.org/hispanic/2012/08/20/hispanic-student-enrollments-reach-new-highs-in-2011/

Fry, R., & Taylor, P. (2013). *Hispanic high school graduates pass whites in rate of college enrollment.* Pew Research Center. https://www.pewresearch.org/hispanic/2013/05/09/hispanic-high-school-graduates-pass-whites-in-rate-of-college-enrollment/

Guardia, J. R. (2006). *Nuestra identidad y experiencas (Our identity and experiences): Ethnic identity development of Latino fraternity members at a Hispanic-Serving Institution* [Unpublished doctoral dissertation, Iowa State University, Ames, IA).

Guardia, J. R. (2019, June 21). *Líderes en Acción* (Leaders in action): The importance of Latinx/o/a leadership development for Latino/a fraternity & sorority members. *International Leadership Association—Membership Connector*. https://intersections.ilamembers.org/member-benefit-access/interface/new-item3/06-21-2019

Guardia, J. R., & Evans, N. J. (2008). Factors influencing the ethnic identity development of Latino fraternity members at a Hispanic serving institution. *Journal of College Student Development, 49*(3), 163–181.

Hernandez, J. C. (2000). Understanding the retention of Latino college students. *Journal of College Student Development, 41*(6), 575–588.

Johnson, C. S. (1972). *Fraternities in our colleges*. New York, NY: National Interfraternity Foundation.

Kappa Delta Chi Sorority, Inc. (2017). *National diversity policy*. Kappa Delta Chi Constitution.

Kimbrough, W. M. (2003). *Black Greek 101*. Vancouver, British Columbia, Canada: Fairleigh Dickinson University Press.

Keels, M. (2019). *Campus counter spaces: Black and Latinx students' search for community at historically white universities*. Ithaca, NY: Cornell University Press.

Lambda Theta Phi Latin Fraternity, Inc. (2018, September). *Lambda adopts inclusive membership policy*. Parsippany, NJ: Lambda Theta Phi Latin Fraternity, Inc.

Lozano, A. (2010). Latina/o culture centers: Providing a sense of belonging and promoting student success. In L. D. Patton (Ed.), *Culture centers in higher education: Perspectives on identity, theory, and practice* (pp. 3–22). Sterling, VA: Stylus.

Miranda, M. L. (1999). Greek life … with a little sazon: Fraternities and sororities get a Latino twist. *The World and I Magazine*, 190–197.

Miranda, M. L. (2020). *Nuestras voces: A qualitative exploration of the experiences of undergraduate Latinas in Latina sororities* (Unpublished doctoral dissertation, The University of Rochester, Rochester, NY).

Miranda, M. L., Garcia, K. D., & Guardia, J. R. (2020). NALFO: A retrospective y hacia adelante. In P. A. Sasso, J. P. Biddix, & M. L. Miranda (Eds.), *Foundations, research, and assessment of fraternities and sororities: Retrospective and future considerations* (pp. 39–46). Gorham, ME: Myers Educational Press.

Miranda, M. L., & Martin de Figueroa, M. (2000, Summer). *Adelante hacia el futuro!* (Forward to the future) Latino/Latina students: Past, present, and future. *Perspectives*, 6–8.

Miranda, M. L., Salinas, C., & Del Real, M. (2020). Latino/a fraternities & sororities: Historia y familia. In P. A. Sasso, J. P. Biddix, & M. L. Miranda (Eds.), *Supporting fraternities and sororities in the contemporary era: Advancement in practice* (pp. 177–187). Gorham, ME: Myers Education Press.

Muñoz, S. M. & Guardia, J. R. (2009). Nuestra historia y futuro (Our history and future): Latino/a fraternities and sororities. In G. S. Parks & C. Torbenson (Eds.), *Brothers and sisters: Diversity within college fraternities and sororities* (pp. 104–132). Madison, NJ: Fairleigh Dickinson Press.

National Center for Education Statistics. (2018). *Digest of education statistics: 2018.* https://nces.ed.gov/programs/digest/current_tables.asp

Nubian Message. (2016, March). *Lambda Pi Chi becomes first Trans-inclusive sorority at NC State.* https://www.thenubianmessage.com/2016/03/16/lambda-pi-chi-becomes-first-trans-inclusive-sorority/

Nuñez, A. M. (2014). Employing multilevel intersectionality in educational research: Latino identities, contexts, and college access. *Educational Researcher, 43*(2), 85–92.

Nuñez, J. G. (2004). The empowerment of Latina university students: A phenomenological study of ethnic identity development through involvement in a Latina-based sorority. Unpublished master's thesis, Iowa State University, Ames, IA.

Omega Phi Beta Sorority, Inc. (2018, November). *Trans day of resilience 2018 and a commitment to action.* https://www.omegaphibeta.org/trans-day-of-resilience-and-opbsis-commitment-to-action/.

Phinney, J. S. (1993). A three-stage model of ethnic identity development in adolescence. In M. E. Bernal & G. P. Knight (Eds.), *Ethnic identity: Formation and transmission among Hispanics and other minorities* (pp. 61–79). Albany, NY: State University of New York Press.

Rodriguez, R. (1995). *Hermandades* on campus: Elite Latino secret societies and fraternities of the past give way to today's brotherhoods and sisterhoods. *Black Issues in Higher Education, 12*(21), 26–29.

Suro, R. (2005). *Hispanics: A people in motion.* Washington, SC: Pew Research Center.

Torbenson, C. L. (2005). The origin and evolution of college fraternities and sororities. In T. Brown, G. S. Parks, & C. M. Phillips (Eds.), *African American fraternities and sororities: The legacy and the vision* (pp. 37–66). Lexington, KY: University Press of Kentucky.

Torres, V. (1999). Validation of a bicultural orientation model for Hispanic college students. *Journal of College Student Development, 40*(3), 285–298.

Torres, V. (2003). Influences on ethnic identity development of Latino college students in the first two years of college. *Journal of College Student Development, 44*(4), 532–547.

Torres, V. (2004). Familial influences on the identity development of Latino first-year students. *Journal of College Student Development, 45*(4), 457–469.

Torres, V. & Delgado-Romero, E. (2008). Defining Latina/o identity through adolescent development. In K. L. Kraus (Ed.), *Lifespan development theories in action: A case study approach for counseling professionals* (pp. 363–388). Boston, MA: Lashaka Press.

Torres, V. & Hernandez, E. (2007). The influence of ethnic identity on self-authorship: A longitudinal study of Latino/a college students. *Journal of College Student Development, 48*(5), 558–573.

Torres, V., Hernandez, E., & Martinez, S. (2019). *Understanding the Latinx experience: Developmental and contextual influences.* Sterling, VA: Stylus.

Torres, V. & Magolda, M. B. (2004). Reconstructing Latino identity: The influence of cognitive development on the ethnic identity process of Latino students. *Journal of College Student Development, 45*(3), 333–347.

U.S. Census Bureau. (2020). *QuickFacts: United States.* https://www.census.gov/quickfacts/fact/table/US/RHI725218#qf-headnote-b

Member Vignette: LGBTQ-Interest Sororities and Fraternities

AVERY WILLIS

My name is Avery, I use they/them or he/him pronouns, and I have been a brother of the Gamma Epsilon Chapter of Delta Lambda Phi at Georgia State University since the spring of 2017. My original interest in DLP stemmed from the person who is now my big. I met them at the beginning of the school year in the dining hall and we hit it off! They were in the recruitment process for DLP in the fall and after they crossed began introducing me to brothers. I had never considered sorority and fraternity life (SFL) in any format—being a trans person is already difficult enough in the South and the idea of being around who I assumed were a bunch of "dude bros" was horrifying to me. But in meeting with the people who are now my chapter brothers I was introduced to what I believe to be the true purpose of fraternities, which is camaraderie and a family unlike any other. The family that I have created with my brothers is something that uplifts me and supports me through anything and everything. My understanding of my gender identity, sexuality, what I want to do in my life—those have all been fluid and changing. My brothers have stood by me and talked me through some of my best and worst days. I wouldn't be where I am today without them.

The summer after I crossed into brotherhood, I decided to go to the fraternity Convention. That year it was in Ottowa, Ontario (Canada!) and somehow, my chapter brothers and I decided that driving there from Atlanta was a great idea. It took 23 and a half hours to get there, and 27 to get back home. But that Convention was a turning point for me. Being part of the business meeting, even though it's a very long process, was a lot of fun for me and I wanted to do it again. I became close friends with a brother from Michigan who encouraged me to continue being involved on the international level. He was my nominator for my Active-at-Large position on the Board of Directors and I am eternally grateful to him. In my 2-year tenure in that position, I was able to make connections with actives and alumni from all around the country and in Canada that are dear to my heart. I have been able to bring new perspectives into conversation and to find the voices needed to make the force for change heard. Being a part of a brotherhood formed mostly of queer brothers has given me the space to learn, grow, and to uplift others.

On a chapter level, however, things aren't always so magical. As a culturally-based fraternity in the Interfraternity Council, we are often left out or forgotten. The brothers and potential new members that we attract are generally not those interested in typical university SFL activities like parties or tailgating. In fact, as a chapter, our closest bonds are with sororities in other councils rather than the fraternities within our own. Georgia State University is by no means an unsafe place for queer people but SFL is a specific subset of the population that does not quite align with the goals of our members. But to me that is what makes DLP so special and so important. Gamma Epsilon Chapter brothers like to call ourselves the "freaks and geeks" fraternity. We prefer game nights to parties, brotherhood dinners to tailgating, Smash Brothers tournaments to sports games. There is no other fraternity on campus where you could find multiple trans members, many of whom are non-binary. Though SFL everywhere is changing and becoming more accepting of queer members, DLP has been standing on the right side for quite some time. You can go many places to be accepted, even to be liked. But with Delta Lambda Phi, you will find love, celebration, and a family that you can never lose.

CHAPTER SIX

Queering Greek Life: LGBTQ-Interest Sororities and Fraternities

Douglas N. Case

Sororities and fraternities oriented toward lesbian, gay, bisexual, transgender, and queer/questioning (LGBTQ) students have emerged in recent decades. This growth mirrors the trend for other culturally-based sororities and fraternities discussed in this text. This chapter will explore the history of LGBTQ-interest sororities and fraternities, the membership policies of the organizations, how they fit within sorority and fraternity life (SFL) communities, and how student affairs professionals can support the organizations. This chapter examines only collegiate LGBTQ-interest sororities and fraternities. Important to note, there are about 20–30 non-collegiate community and/or professional LGBTQ-interest sororities and fraternities. Most of these have primarily African American or multicultural memberships and have traditions similar to National Pan-Hellenic Council (NPHC) organizations.

History of LGBTQ-Interest Sororities and Fraternities

The first LGBTQ-interest fraternal organization, Delta Lambda Phi Social Fraternity, was established in 1986 in Washington, DC as a community-based fraternity for gay, bisexual and "progressive" men. The founder, Vernon L. Strickland, III, was a Georgetown University law student, who had been active in a fraternity as an undergraduate at the University of Florida. When he became aware of a student at George Washington University who was denied admission into a fraternity because he was presumed to be gay, he became motivated to start a fraternity open to all men regardless of their sexual orientation (Strickland, 2016). Since its founding the fraternity has chartered 72 chapters, but as of spring 2020, only 18 chapters and 2 provisional chapters remained active.

The first lesbian-based sorority, Lambda Delta Lambda, was founded in 1988 at the University of California, Los Angeles (Gordon, 1988). The sorority grew to five chapters, but after 2005, the only remaining chapter was the University of California, Davis. The national organization cited a lack of support among lesbian students due to a negative impression of sororities and fraternities, together with the belief that sororities were superficial and exclusive as reasons for the organization's decline (Windmeyer, 2000).

Gamma Rho Lambda National Sorority founded in 2003, however, has continued to grow and prosper. As of spring 2020, the sorority has 18 active chapters and 2 provisional chapters, located throughout the United States. Originally founded as a "social support system for lesbian, bisexual, transgender, and alternative lifestyle-friendly female students," the organization expanded membership to become a "support system for multicultural cis and trans women, trans men, and gender-variant students of all sexualities, as well as LGBTQIA+ ally female students" (Gamma Rho Lambda, 2020, para. 1).

In 2006, a group of students at the University of California, Santa Cruz established Delta Lambda Psi as the "world's first queer gender neutral frarority." Delta Lambda Phi Fraternity sued the organization claiming trademark infringement for using a similar name (Perry, 2012, para. 1–2). After a settlement, Delta Lambda Psi changed its name to Theta Pi Sigma. The organization dropped the term "frarority" due to its gender binary connotation and now refers to itself as "the first all gendered Greek organization" (Theta Pi Sigma, 2020, header). The organization expanded to include 6 chapters, with 4 active as of spring 2020.

As shown in Table 6.1, of the nine LGBTQ-interest sororities and fraternities that have been established, only Delta Lambda Phi, Gamma Rho Lambda and Theta Pi Sigma are currently active national/international organizations. Two others operate as local chapters on a single campus.

Table 6.1. LGBTQ-Interest Sororities and Fraternities in the United States and Canada

Organization	Type	Founding	Active and Provisional Chapters, Spring 2020
Delta Lambda Phi	Fraternity	1986—Washington, DC	20
Lambda Delta Lambda [1]	Sorority	1988—University of California, Los Angeles	0
Alpha Lambda Tau	Fraternity	1999—University of Nevada, Las Vegas	0
Sigma Phi Beta	Fraternity	2003—Arizona State University	0
Gamma Rho Lambda	Sorority	2003—Arizona State University	20
Theta Pi Sigma [2]	All Gender Inclusive	2006—University of California, Santa Cruz	4
Sigma Epsilon Omega	Fraternity	2007—University of California, Berkeley	1
Lambda Psi Omega	All Gender Inclusive[3]	2013—Illinois State University	0
Lambda Alpha Lambda	All Gender Inclusive[4]	2018—Florida Atlantic University	1

1 Most chapters changed their name to Lambda Delta Omega to avoid confusion with an existing fraternity named Lambda Delta Lambda.
2 Originally named Delta Lambda Psi.
3 Used the term "Frarority" to identify itself (Vidette Online, 2014).
4 Uses the term "Diaternity" to identify itself, which means transcending boundaries (Florida Atlantic University, 2020, para. 2).

Gender Inclusion Policies within Sororities and Fraternities

Sororities and fraternities have traditionally been single-sex organizations. Unlike other college organizations that were required to open their membership to people of different genders, social sororities and fraternities were granted an exemption from Title IX of the Higher Education Act of 1972. In recent years, many national and international sororities and fraternities have clarified or expanded their membership criteria to include all those who identify as women or men respectively. To date, however, relatively few non-LGBTQ sororities and fraternities have adopted polices inclusive of non-binary students. There are some exceptions. For example, Delta Phi Epsilon, an international sorority and National Panhellenic Conference (NPC) member organization, announced in 2017 a membership policy inclusive of trans-women and gender non-binary individuals (Delta Phi Epsilon, 2020). In April 2021, the NPC postponed consideration of a policy that would have allowed its 26 member organizations to change their definition of "women" in order to be more inclusive of non-binary members, citing a need to research the implications of such a change (Anderson, 2021). Of course, there are non-binary members within other organizations. In some cases, the members have not been public with their identity and in others the chapter has decided on a flexible interpretation of the national or international organization's membership policies.

On the other hand, LGBTQ sororities and fraternities have been more inclusive of transgender, non-binary and gender non-conforming (one whose behavior and/or expression deviates from societal or cultural gender norms) students. Theta Pi Sigma was originally established to be inclusive of all genders and sexualities; the policies of other groups have evolved over time. Gamma Rho Lambda developed more inclusive policies between 2008 and 2010, making membership open to all except those who identify as cisgender men. At their 2020 convention a resolution was adopted to offer membership to persons of all genders who support the organization's purpose. At its convention in 2015, Delta Lambda Phi established a committee to examine whether it should eliminate gender requirements for membership. The committee found that there was a strong sentiment to remain a fraternity for men. Consequently, membership eligibility was clarified as open to those assigned male at birth and those who identify as men at the time of their induction. That policy excluded certain non-binary individuals, and at its convention in 2020, the membership policy was amended so that anyone who is not a cisgender woman at the time of induction is eligible to join. Sigma Epsilon Omega was originally founded as a men's fraternity but is now open to all genders. Today, most LGBTQ-interest sororities have a wide diversity of sexual orientations and gender identities included in their membership, sometimes even including straight cis allies. Additionally, the groups tend to be reflective of the racial and ethnic diversity of their campus.

Literature Review

A search of the academic literature resulted in only two articles that deal specifically with LGBTQ-interest sororities or fraternities, and both articles were different analyses of the data from a single study regarding one fraternity (Yeung &

Stombler, 2000; Yeung, Stombler, & Wharton, 2006). There are however articles on related topics which may be instructive in advising LGBTQ-interest sororities and fraternities. Students often join these organizations because they do not feel welcome in traditional sororities and fraternities or because the traditional organizations do not meet their needs. This review will include two related studies that examine the experiences of LGBTQ students in traditional sororities and fraternities and a study of Queer Men of Color in culturally-based fraternities. Finally, brief summaries are provided of three studies that examine the perceptions of campus climate among LGBTQ students, which have clear implications for advising LGBTQ student groups.

Experiences in an LGBTQ Fraternity

A qualitative study of the culture of Delta Lambda Phi Social Fraternity (DLP) was conducted through 42 in-depth open-ended interviews with fraternity members from various chapters, observation over 2 years of a newly formed chapter, and attendance at a national convention of the fraternity. Two analyses were made of the data. One (Yeung & Stombler, 2000) examined how members negotiated their identity as both gay and Greek, and the second (Yeung et al., 2006) examined how the members negotiated the dimensions of hegemonic masculinity inherent within the traditional fraternity institution.

In the first analysis, Yeung and Stombler (2000) explored how self-identified gay men both emulated and sought to change the predominately straight heterosexist institution of the college fraternity. They found that while the DLP adopted most of the structure and traditions of the college fraternity model, DLP also challenged the model by rejecting practices such as hazing and race, religion, and class homogeneity. They stated, "the secure environment that DLP fostered allowed members to identify, reaffirm, and celebrate their sexual identity as gay men, incorporating them into the larger gay community" (Yeung & Stombler, 2000, p. 138). One of the identity paradoxes they discovered is that while the fraternity encouraged expressions of femininity within the private space of the fraternity, flamboyant feminine behavior and expression were discouraged in public, especially during interfraternity activities. In another attempt at mainstreaming, the fraternity promoted a goal of desexualizing. This included strict enforcement of a policy prohibiting sexual activity between active members and pledges and discouraging casual sex and in-group dating. Although some chapters were successfully immersed in both the gay community and the Greek community, in most cases assimilation goals fell short.

Researchers have found that college fraternity culture is an example of hegemonic masculinity, a set of gender practices that reinforces men's dominant position in society, justifies the subordination of women, and marginalizes feminine or gay men (Bird, 1996). Yeung et al. (2006) examined how gay DLP members negotiated their stigmatized status among other men (internal dimension of hegemonic masculinity) and how the gay men related to women (external dimension). They questioned to what extent a gay fraternity would challenge or succumb to an entrenched fraternity culture. They found that DLP tended to embrace feminine expression by its members and encouraged members to be themselves. The fraternity also supported qualities often associated with femininity such as asexual intimacy and emotion expression within the brotherhood. In order to gain acceptance within the fraternity community, however, members were asked to tone down feminine expression when interacting with predominately straight fraternities. The researchers found that the membership of DLP chapters tended to be ethnically diverse and inclusive of men on the gender expression continuum—from "queeny" members to straight-acting members. Some chapters even had straight brothers. With regard to their relations with women, while chapters often enjoyed social interactions with sorority women, fraternity members were adamant in their conviction that women, whether straight or lesbian, should be excluded from membership.

The studies of Delta Lambda Phi were completed in 1998, and there have been significant changes in the organization and its policies since that time. For example, the organization has become more inclusive of transgender and non-binary members. Additionally, sorority and fraternity communities have evolved with regard to LGBTQ acceptance, so there would likely be some differences in the results if these studies were replicated today, especially with regard to interactions within the SFL community.

Experiences of LGBTQ members in Non-LGBTQ-Interest Sororities and Fraternities

In the first major study of gay, lesbian and bisexual members of sororities and fraternities (Case, Hesp, & Eberly, 2005), over 500 individuals responded to a survey between 1992 and 1995. The study was initially for fraternity men only but was expanded to include sorority women, so approximately 90% of the respondents were men. The respondents included a geographical cross section and a wide diversity of age (range of 19- to 59-years old). Only eight were from culturally-based sororities and fraternities.

The study found that members joined for similar reasons as heterosexual members, namely, for friendship or camaraderie, to enhance their social life, to have a support group and sense of belonging and for leadership opportunities. The respondents tended to remain in the closet during their undergraduate years, with 75% of the men and 81% of the women indicating they believed that no members of the chapter were aware of their sexual orientation. There was a distinct generational difference with only 12% of the respondents who graduated prior to 1980 indicating that they revealed their sexual orientation to one or more chapter members while in college, while 39% of those who joined after 1980 had done so. Despite their fears, most members received personally supportive responses from fellow members when they came out. On the other hand, over 70% reported that they had encountered homophobic or heterosexist behavior within their chapter, with derogatory remarks about LGBTQ individuals being the most prevalent example. In their narrative accounts, several respondents described accounts of students being denied an invitation to join because of their perceived sexual orientation. Over 80% indicated they were satisfied with their overall sorority/fraternity membership. The most common factors that detracted from their membership experience were a felt need to hide part of their identity making it difficult to develop close bonds, social events geared toward heterosexual couples, and intimidation from homophobic remarks and attitudes.

Case's study was replicated in a similar follow-up online survey in 2007 under the auspices of Campus Pride's Lambda 10 Project (Rankin, Hesp, & Weber, 2013). The most significant findings of the 2007 study were the generational differences with regard to the age when the participants self-identified as lesbian, gay or bisexual; the age at which they "came out" to others; the degree to which they were "out" in college, and the level of acceptance within their organizations. To analyze this, the male participants were aggregated into three segments: those who joined before 1990, those who joined during the 1990s, and those who joined after 2000. The sample sizes of the female participants precluded a valid generational analysis.

For the 2000s cohort, over three-fourths self-identified as gay or bisexual at the time they were initiated and another 15% were questioning their sexual orientation. By contrast, of those in the pre-2000s cohorts, only about a quarter self-identified as gay or bisexual at the time they were initiated, although about 40% were questioning their sexual orientation. Another dramatic generational difference was the age when the male participants "came out" to fellow members. For the 2000s cohort, 26% were already "out" when they participated in recruitment, but only 2% of the pre-2000 cohorts were "out" when they joined. At the time they graduated from college, about three-fourths of the 2000s cohort were "out" to fellow members, but only one-third of the 1990s cohort and less than a quarter of the pre-1990s cohort had "come out" to any other chapter members prior to graduation. For the 2000s cohort, almost two-thirds rated the LGBTQ climate in their chapter as friendly or somewhat friendly, but only about a third of the 1990s cohort and only 7% of the pre-1990s cohort reported a relatively friendly climate. The data indicated significant regional differences with regard to chapter climate, with the Northwest being the most accepting and the Southeast being most homophobic. It is likely, given the societal changes with regard to LGBTQ acceptance that have occurred in the past 15 years, that if a similar survey were to be conducted today, it would find that non-LGBTQ-interest sororities and fraternities have become even more welcoming to LGBTQ students.

A recent narrative inquiry studied the experiences Queer Men of Color in culturally-based fraternities (Garcia & Duran, 2020). Eight alumni from NPHC (historically African American) or multicultural Greek organizations across the country were interviewed. All identified as Black/African American, Latino, or Afro-Latinx. The participants were drawn to their organizations because they wanted to connect with other Men of Color. While their racial identities were affirmed, their sexual identities and gender expressions were marginalized. Half of the participants felt the need to develop strategies to navigate and conceal their sexuality, forcing them to hide part of themselves to affirm another.

A commonality of all three of these studies is that despite generational improvements, a significant number of LGBTQ members of non-LGBTQ sororities and fraternities feel a need to hide part of their identity in order to fit in. Even in those chapters where their sexual orientation was accepted, LGBQ students often did not feel they were able to express themselves openly and fully. An LGBTQ-interest fraternity may be more likely to support their personal development.

LGBTQ Campus Climate

The most comprehensive national research study to date of LGBTQ campus climate issues (Rankin, Weber, Blumenfeld, & Frazer, 2010) included survey responses from over 5,000 students, faculty, staff and administrators. The study found that although there has been substantial progress with regard to LGBTQ visibility and resources, LGBTQ respondents still report a variety of negative experiences. For example, the incidence of experiencing harassment for LGBQ respondents (23%) was twice that of their heterosexual counterparts (12%). Over a third of transgender or gender non-conforming respondents experienced harassment. Almost two-thirds of those who identify as gay were targets of derogatory remarks, while over half lesbian-identified students reported being deliberately ignored or excluded. Overall, LGBTQ respondents had more negative perceptions of campus climate than their non-LGBTQ counterparts.

Within the last decade, several of the higher education research centers have begun to incorporate sexual orientation and gender identity demographic variables in their respective instruments. The Rutgers Tyler Clementi Center analyzed the data available from seven of these national surveys (Greathouse et al., 2018). Recognizing complexities of the language used to describe sexual and gender identities, their analyses looked at students along the queer-spectrum (those who do not identify as heterosexual) and along the trans-spectrum (those who do not identify as cisgender). They found several troubling disparities with regard to student health and engagement. The 2016 Undergraduate Student Research in the Research (SERU) Survey reported that only 43% of students on the queer-spectrum felt that their campus was safe and secure, compared to 57% of heterosexual students. Slightly less than half of the students on the queer-spectrum felt that their sexual orientation was respected on campus. The SERU survey found that only a third of trans-spectrum students felt their campus was safe and secure, compared to 55% of cisgender students. Only 31% of trans-spectrum students felt that students of their gender identity were respected on campus, compared to 65% of cisgender students. The 2016 National College Health Assessment (NCHA) conducted by the American College Health Association found that 59% of the queer-spectrum students and 56% of trans-spectrum students felt so depressed that it was difficult to function in the past 12 months, compared to 34% of heterosexual students and 37% of cisgender students. The NCHA survey also found that 3.5% of queer-spectrum students and 5.2% of trans-spectrum students had attempted suicide within the last 12 months, compared to 1.1% of heterosexual students and 1.4% of cisgender students.

There is however indication that over time the campus climate has been improving for LGBTQ students. Using data from the National LGBT Alumni Survey, Garvey, Sanders, and Flint (2017) examined generational perspectives of campus climate for over 3,000 students who graduated over a 70-year period, from 1944 to 2013. They noted clear evidence of generational progress, with improved perceptions of campus climate accelerating in mid-1990s and continuing to the present. Open-ended responses indicated that the Stonewall uprising in New York, the death of Matthew Shepard in Wyoming, media coverage of LGBTQ issues, the gradual societal acceptance and affirmation of LGBTQ people, increased LGBTQ visibility on campus and the emergence of campus LGBTQ resource centers have all contributed to the more positive perceptions.

These studies of LGBTQ campus climate demonstrate that despite progress, the college environment remains challenging and unwelcoming for many LGBTQ students. LGBTQ-interest sororities and fraternities may provide a strong mutual support group to help students navigate these challenges. Further, the mental health data for LGBTQ students should be alarming to student affairs professionals and should be taken into consideration by SFL staff as they work to support LGBTQ organizations.

My Positionality

I have personal experiences with two LGBTQ organizations, Delta Lambda Phi and Gamma Rho Lambda, and many of my observations and recommendations are based on those experiences. From 1992 to 2020, I served as the chapter advisor for the Alpha Delta chapter of Delta Lambda Phi, a multi-campus chapter with members primarily from San Diego State University and the University of California, San Diego. I also have served on the fraternity's international volunteer staff since 2007 with responsibilities for risk management and university relations. From 1979 to 2015, I served professionally on the SFL staff at San Diego State University, where I worked with the Beta chapter of Gamma Rho Lambda, established in 2008. I also serve as the Coordinator of the Lambda 10 Project, a national clearinghouse for information, research and policies regarding sexual orientation and gender identity issues related to sororities and fraternities. The Lambda 10 Project, an initiative of the non-profit organization Campus Pride, also develops programs to promote inclusion, visibility and acceptance of LGBTQ members within sorority and fraternity communities.

Discussion and Innovations in Practice

The Need for LGBTQ Sororities and Fraternities

Increased LGBTQ visibility and acceptance on college campuses provide both challenges and opportunities for LGBTQ-interest sororities and fraternities. LGBTQ sororities and fraternities were established because the doors of predominately straight, cisgender sororities and fraternities were generally closed to queer students, and those who chose to join often found a need to hide deeply in the closet. As the acceptance and understanding of LGBTQ people increases, those organizations are beginning to be more willing to accept sexual minorities. From my perspective, many more LGBTQ students are now able to join and express themselves freely and excel within the organizations. This creates competition for LGBTQ-interest sororities and fraternities, which often are already struggling with a small membership.

On the other hand, with more inclusive campus climates, the SFL community has become more welcoming of non-traditional organizations. Though the generally larger and more established mainstream SFL groups on campus may provide greater opportunities for leadership, networking, and social activities, LGBTQ-interest groups offer something different, unique, and special. One of the most frequent reasons that members of LGBTQ-interest organizations state for joining is the opportunity to provide self-affirming support and freedom to be themselves and not be judged by their displays of femininity or masculinity. Times are changing, but those with sexual orientations or gender identities and expressions that vary from what is considered the norm still face discrimination, isolation, and rejection. Having the opportunity to develop caring bonds with those who have traveled similar paths can be refreshing, life-changing, and in some cases life-saving. Particularly for those who are still questioning their sexual or gender identities, these organizations provide an outlet for exploration and self-discovery without judgment. Further the organizations provide opportunities to celebrate the queer culture and become immersed within the LGBTQ community. Another advantage over other organizations is that the dues for LGBTQ-interest sororities and fraternities tend to be substantially less.

While inclusion of gay, lesbian and bisexual members within traditional sororities and fraternities is becoming more common, it is rare for a transgender or gender non-binary student to join these organizations, even when the national membership policy does not discriminate. The dramatic recent increase in the number of youths openly affirming a more fluid gender identity amplifies the need for LGBTQ-interest sororities and fraternities.

Nationally, only about 30 campuses currently have one or more LGBTQ-interest sororities and fraternities. SFL professionals should assess whether their campus would benefit from such an organization and if so, contact the national organizations to determine the feasibility of establishing an interest group. When a Greek council is considering expansion (inviting new organizations to establish), SFL professionals should encourage students and other decision makers to examine the diversity of the existing SFL community and consider inviting organizations that cater to underrepresented populations, including LGBTQ-interest sororities and fraternities. SFL professionals should also ensure that LGBTQ student leaders and resource center staff are aware of the opportunity to form an LGBTQ-interest sorority or fraternity on campus.

Organizational and Community Issues

Greek council affiliation of LGBTQ-interest sororities and fraternities vary by campus. The most common affiliation is with the Multicultural Greek Council. On campuses where there are fewer Greek organizations, they may be a member of the All-Greek Council. A few are not affiliated with any Greek council or are part of an independent Greek council. As a member organization of the North American Interfraternity Conference (NIC), Delta Lambda Phi chapters can join the Interfraternity Council (IFC) on their campus. Only about half of Delta Lambda Phi chapters, however, affiliate with the IFC. In the past, some Gamma Rho Lambda chapters have been associate members of the National Panhellenic Council on their campus. In most cases, the decision of which council to join is at the discretion of the chapter, in cooperation with student leaders and SFL staff. One reason often given for chapters to join the IFC or NPC on their campus is that they want to avoid being marginalized. IFC and NPC communities tend to be more prominent on campus, partially due to their population size, resources and existence of chapter houses. Reasons given for membership in other councils relate to having more in common with the members of those councils, in terms of being focused on a specific population, chapter size, recruitment process, lower council dues and operating without a chapter house. It is rare for an LGBTQ-interest sorority or fraternity to operate an official chapter house.

Most of the chapters affiliated with a council participate in the council's recruitment process (except that NPC formal recruitment is limited to National Panhellenic Conference organizations); however, most LGBTQ-interest organizations rely on informal recruitment. Participating in a Greek council's formal recruitment process, where prospective members are required or expected to attend events of all of the organizations in the council during the recruitment period, is problematic. Students with a particular interest in joining an LGBTQ organization may not want to visit other organizations where they do not feel welcome. Likewise, many prospective members who do not identify as LGBTQ may find it awkward to attend a recruitment event for an LGBTQ-interest organization. Accordingly, Greek councils should be willing to excuse LGBTQ-interest organizations from participation in the formal recruitment process if that is what the organization prefers.

SFL professionals should ensure that all campus communications and activities promoting membership recruitment give equal attention to all Greek councils and chapters. Regardless of whether an LGBTQ-interest chapter exists on campus, recruitment efforts should include outreach to the campus LGBTQ community.

With few exceptions, the LGBTQ-interest chapters have been well-received within the interfraternal community, and participate in community events and activities such as Greek Week, Homecoming, council leadership and, less frequently, intramural sports. Although there may be some resistance at first, once the chapters begin interacting within the Greek community, their acceptance usually grows. When there is a lack of involvement or participation by a chapter, it is often attributed to a small membership size rather than feeling unwelcome. Some organizations, however, have experienced homophobic/transphobic incidents (such as shouted or whispered insults about their appearance or sexual preferences), but often the perpetrators have been outside of the Greek community.

Most of the chapters also have good relationships with other campus LGBTQ organizations and the local LGBTQ community, although there have occasionally been tensions. Other campus LGBTQ organizations may reject association with an institution with a history of heteronormativity or simply resent the competition. This tension can be mitigated by community service projects implemented by the chapters to benefit local LGBTQ organizations, especially those aimed toward youth (homeless shelters, suicide prevention program, HIV-prevention programs, queer proms, etc.) and by chapter involvement with programs sponsored by other LGBTQ student organizations.

Some chapters have also actively reached out to the SFL community to invite them to participate in their community service events, anti-bullying awareness activities, drag shows, and educational programs on LGBTQ issues for other sororities and fraternities. Panel presentations about the experiences and challenges of being an openly LGBTQ student on campus and within the SFL community can be especially effective, since students tend relate better to fellow SFL students than other presenters.

Ways to Support LGBTQ-Interest Organizations

Please note: The final paragraph of this section includes a reference to suicide, which may be a sensitve topic for some readers.

SFL professionals and other campus officials who work with LGBTQ-interest sororities and fraternities, or who are on campuses interested in bringing such groups to their campus, should become familiar the LGBTQ resources available on campus, participate in campus Safe Zones/Allies programs and other trainings, attend campus and community LGBTQ events, and demonstrate by word and action that they are allies. It is especially important to learn and properly use the pronouns chosen by the LGBTQ students with whom the staff interacts. For campuses that have LGBTQ resource centers, SFL staff should consider a collaborative partnership approach in providing advising services to LGBTQ organizations. For example, a chapter can be assigned an advisor from both the LGBTQ resource center and the SFL office.

When a new LGBTQ-interest chapter is established on campus, SFL advisors should prepare the Greek student leaders with basic LGBTQ education, sensitivity training and group discussions on strategies for supporting the organization. Student leaders can form a Greek Allies program (for resources go to www.campuspride.org/greekally). Although the organizations usually assign mentors to interest groups and provisional chapters, SFL staff can be helpful by helping them to find campus mentors (e.g., an officer of a Greek council or a campus LGBTQ resource center staff member) to help the new group during its formative period. Since the LGBTQ-interest chapters often do not have the alumni and national resources comparable to those available to other organizations, they may require some extra attention and support. It may be useful to contact LGBTQ faculty and staff association members to recruit campus advisors for the group.

Additionally, recruitment processes, publications and electronic communication, and programmatic activities should be scrutinized for heterocentricity and non-inclusive language. For example, an educational speaker on positive dating relationships and sexual assault should be instructed to specifically make references to same-genders partners. Greek council activities such as Greek Week should not organize teams based on gender. Instead of giving out awards for Greek Man and Woman of the Year, consider Greek Leader of the Year. Publications and documents should include gender-neutral language (e.g., "siblinghood" instead of "sisterhood" and "brotherhood" and use gender-neutral pronouns). Student leaders and others need to be confronted when they use inappropriate language (e.g., "that's so gay") or misgender other students.

SFL and Greek council policies should include flexibility for chapters with small numbers. The average chapter size for LGBTQ-interest sororities and fraternities is 10–20, although it's not uncommon for chapters to drop to only a handful of members. Helping struggling chapters can minimize attrition, which has historically been a problem for LGBTQ-based sororities and fraternities.

Since the national or international organizations do not have paid staff and physical headquarters, the best way to contact them is through electronic communications. Each organization has its own procedures and criteria for establishing interest groups and provisional chapters, but each has a specific officer charged with expansion activities. SFL staff should keep in mind that the groups don't have the resources available to larger and more established organizations.

Finally, on a sober note, it is important to realize that the LGBTQ-interest organizations have memberships that are more vulnerable than most all other campus organizations, as indicated by some of the national research assessments data previously cited regarding harassment, discrimination, and emotional and mental health. When I was advising the chapter of Delta Lambda Phi, the chapter held a bonding retreat for each pledge/new member class. One activity was a round-robin sharing of personal information the members felt comfortable sharing. It was common to hear heart-wrenching stories of family rejection, suicide attempts, depression, substance abuse, sexual assault, and other detrimental experiences that occurred because of their sexual orientation or gender identity. During the 28 years I served as the chapter advisor, four members died by suicide. The last was an 18-year-old international transgender student who jumped off the Golden Gate Bridge because his parents were from a culture that could not accept his gender identity. It is important for SFL staff to make sure that LGBTQ organizations are connected to the counseling center and to provide regular workshops and trainings on mental health issues for the entire SFL community. Further, all instances of harassment and discrimination should be promptly reported to the appropriate campus authority.

Conclusion

Attitudes related to sexual orientation and gender identity have transformed college campus environments, changing the nature of LGBTQ-interest sororities and fraternities. The value of these organizations remains high, and practitioners can help guide the students they advise to create more welcoming campus environments for all. As indicated in the literature review, there is very limited research on LGBTQ-interest sororities and fraternities. Opportunities for further research might include studying how involvement in an LGBTQ-interest sorority or fraternity contributes to the personal growth of the members. Each SFL community is unique, but as you examine the role of LGBTQ organizations on your campus, the following questions can guide you in developing a strategy as a student affairs professional to help such groups grow and thrive on your campus.

Questions for Reflection

1. Given the greater acceptance of LGBTQ students on campus, what is the best niche for LGBTQ-interest sororities and fraternities? What are the advantages of a student joining an LGBTQ-interest sorority or fraternity rather than a non-LGBTQ-interest sorority or fraternity?

2. How do students who identify as non-binary or gender fluid fit into a fraternal system that is based the assumption of a gender binary?
3. How can practitioners enhance the effectiveness of LGBTQ-interest sororities and fraternities within the sorority and fraternity community, within the campus LGBTQ community, and within the broader campus community?

References

Anderson, G. (2021, April 20). Sororities delay vote on inclusion of nonbinary members. *Inside Higher Ed.* https://www.insidehighered.com/quicktakes/2021/04/20/sororities-delay-vote-inclusion-nonbinary-members

Bird, S. R. (1996). Welcome to the men's club: Homosociability and the maintenance of hegemonic masculinity. *Gender & Society, 10*(2), 120–132.

Case, D. N., Hesp, G. A., & Eberly, C. G. (2005). An exploratory study of the experiences of gay, lesbian and bisexual fraternity and sorority members revisited. *Oracle: The Research Journal of the Association of Fraternity Advisors, 1*(1), 15–31.

Delta Phi Epsilon. (2020). *Delta Phi Epsilon announces policy on trans and non-binary inclusion.* https://dphie.org/delta-phi-epsilon-announces-policy-on-trans-and-non-binary-inclusion

Florida Atlantic University. (2020). *Lambda Alpha Lambda.* https://fau.campuslabs.com/engage/organization/lambdaalphalambda

Gamma Rho Lambda. (2020). *Frequently asked questions.* https://www.gammarholambda.org/FAQ

Garcia, C. E., & Duran, A. (2020). "In my letters, but I was still myself": Highlighting the experiences of Queer Men of Color in culturally based fraternities. *Journal of Diversity in Higher Education.* Advance online publication. https://doi.org/10.1037/dhe0000167

Garvey, J., Sanders, L., & Flint, M. (2017). Generational perceptions of campus climate among LGBTQ undergraduates. *Journal of College Student Development, 58*(6), 795–817.

Gordon, L. (1988, February 4). UCLA accepts first sorority in U.S. formed by lesbians. *Los Angeles Times.* https://www.latimes.com/archives/la-xpm-1988-02-24-me-11690-story.html

Greathouse, M., BrckaLorenz, A., Hoban, M., Huesman, R., Jr., Rankin, S., & Stolzenberg, E. B. (2018). *Queer-spectrum and trans-spectrum student experiences in American higher education—The analyses of national survey findings.* New Brunswick, NJ: Rutgers Tyler Clementi Center.

Perry, G. (2012, November 12). *UCSD's Delta Lambda Psi sued by gay fraternity.* https://www.santacruz.com/news/ucscs_delta_lambda_psi_sued_by_gay_fraternity.html

Rankin, S. R., Hesp, G., & Weber, G. N. (2013). Experiences and perceptions of gay and bisexual fraternity members from 1960 to 2007: A cohort analysis. *Journal of College Student Development, 54*(6), 570–590.

Rankin, S., Weber, G., Blumenfeld, W., & Frazer, S. (2010). *2010 State of higher education for lesbian, gay, bisexual and transgender people*. Charlotte, NC: Campus Pride.

Strickland, V. L., III. (2016). *Strong the Circle We – A Delta Lambda Phi Chronicle* (1986–1992), 1–22.

Theta Pi Sigma. (2020). *Home*. https:wwwthetapisigma.org

Vidette Online. (2014, April 2). *New "frarority" places unique spin on Greek life*. https://www.videtteonline.com/new-frarority-places-unique-spin-on-greek-life/article_dd980445-f328-54fb-b1f4-29f7ca2e8f0f.html

Windmeyer, S. L. (2000). Gay, lesbian & bisexual sensitive fraternities: A house with no closets. *Perspectives: Association of Fraternity Advisors, 27*(2), 10–11.

Yeung, K-T, & Stombler, M. (2000). Gay and Greek: The identity paradox of gay fraternities. *Social Problems, 47*(1), 134–52.

Yeung, K-T, Stombler, M., & Wharton, R. (2006). Making men in gay fraternities: Resisting and reproducing multiple dimensions of hegemonic masculinity. *Gender and Society, 20*(1), 5–31.

Member Vignette: Multicultural Sororities and Fraternities

JAVIER MENA AND JESSICA SNELL

My journey into joining an NMGC organization was well thought out and contemplated. While transitioning from a 2-year college into a 4-year institution, my deciding factor was which college campus had a thriving Greek community. I was looking for an experience that was unlike any other; a sense of belonging among a community was particularly what drew me to Greek Life. I searched all Greek organizations and came across multicultural organizations, which piqued my interest as I am biracial and felt drawn to something much more diverse than the world around me. My knowledge of Greek life was growing as I attended events with friends at other colleges and universities. My first introduction to Lambda Tau Omega Sorority, Inc. was unforgettable; the womyn were kind, provided a comforting atmosphere, and it was as if I knew these members my whole life. Their pillars of multiculturalism, womyn empowerment, and welfare of womyn and children drew me in as I looked for something bigger than myself.

Since joining my organization, I've been fortunate enough to hold many leadership opportunities, make meaningful connections, and find a passion for helping and advocating for others. My career in higher education was heavily influenced by my experience with my sorority as I worked closely with advisors as an undergraduate member, worked with undergraduate members as an alumnae, and wanted to share the advocacy and support that was given to me to others that needed that experience.

- Jessica Snell, Member Lambda Tau Omega Sorority, Inc.

As someone who transitioned from a 2-year college into a 4-year institution, my experience was different than others. I was involved with the New Jersey DREAM Act Coalition (NJDAC) at the time when I transferred. Two of the leaders in the organization recommended that I look into the organization that they joined together as undergraduate students—Psi Sigma Phi Multicultural Fraternity, Inc. They mentioned how as undocumented college students they were able to have a lot of support from the fraternity in their leadership development and in navigating an institution that was not designed to help them succeed. At the same time I explored other Greek life organizations on campus. Naturally, as a Latino man I first gravitated to a Latino fraternity. I attended a club and organization fair in the beginning of the semester. Something just did not feel right about any organizations that I came across. I then decided to reach out to the brothers who I worked with through NJDAC. They recommended me to meet with some of the brothers on campus, specifically the chapter president. There was something unique about them. They had a diverse group of men who came from all walks of life. There were brothers who identified themselves as biracial/BIPOC and/or of a variety of sexual orientations. The president of the chapter sat down with me and talked to me about the organization and what they could offer me. They also welcomed me with open arms and made me feel like family. I still kept my options open in the beginning, but ultimately the difference was the potential of the organization to make an impact on the campus, myself, and the community. The principles of the organization of multiculturalism, brotherhood, academic excellence and service to the community were all aspects that I felt were important to me.

As the only multicultural fraternity on campus it opened my eyes to something bigger than myself. Attending a predominantly white institution, our organization was able to be part of the solution in helping bridge the gap between the white, BIPOC, and LGBTQ+ communities, which were socially segregated on campus. There were several conversations that came up throughout the years of both blatant and systemic racism. We continued to break social fears and ignorance throughout the years. We were even invited to be part of a focus group to express those concerns that many people had in the community.

Over the years I stayed involved in the organization through all levels of leadership. I left a career in sales to go into higher education because of the impact my organization left on me. Our fraternity president throughout my years was a higher education professional. His mentorship helped create a passion in me to be a leader, especially as a Latino male in higher education. I continue to push to become an executive leader in higher education to help create policy that will end racism on all levels. I hope to inspire others to become as driven as I am to fight for justice and equity.

- Javier Mena, Member Psi Sigma Phi Multicultural Fraternity, Inc.

CHAPTER SEVEN

Building Solidarity: A Guide for Supporting Multicultural Sororities and Fraternities

JESSICA PEÑARANDA AND JESSICA SNELL

As National Executive Board leaders in the National Multicultural Greek Council (NMGC), we recognize that though we are speaking as leaders of our national council there are many nuances that we won't be able to capture about our members, their organizations, and the varied diverse and unique dynamics of each. Our goals throughout this chapter are to deepen awareness of our multicultural community, the challenges we face, and the tensions present in being members of multicultural Greek organizations. Additionally, we acknowledge that our national council is not the only multicultural community and that there are many other multicultural organizations that exist outside of our council. It is our collective goal that all sorority and fraternity life (SFL) professionals and those in power to bring systemic change within the higher education system center support, advocacy, and awareness of all culturally-based sororities and fraternities equally.

Our aim with this chapter is to provide some basic information about multicultural organizations in the NMGC, to discuss some of the challenges and policies and practices that disproportionately impact our organizations, and to provide recommendations and a call to action in support of the multicultural sorority and fraternity movement.

Historical Context of Multicultural Sororities and Fraternities

Multicultural sororities and fraternities began to emerge on college campuses in the 1980s and 1990s (Association of Fraternity/Sorority Advisors, 2009). Their establishment was attributed to an increasingly diverse student body that resulted from the success of the civil rights movement and new waves of immigration. Although other culturally-based sororities and fraternities such as those for Asian Pacific Islander Desi Americans, Black, Latinx/a/o, Lesbian, Gay, Bisexual, Transgender, and Queer (LGBTQ), and Native American individuals already existed or were forming, multicultural sororities and fraternities emerged as an avenue to affirm cultural identities more broadly. As detailed by Jefferson et al. (2007):

> Multicultural fraternal organizations, like the fraternal organizations before them, exist to address a need that had yet to be addressed by prior organizations. While most, if not all, organizations have diverse membership, there is still a cultural concentration and focus, and that concentration may take precedence over other cultures represented in that organization. Founders of Multicultural fraternal organizations did not want to prioritize one aspect of a person's cultural identity over another and, thus, established organizations that taught its members to respect and embrace each individual as an individual – "the foundation of unity." (para. 4)

As organizations formed to center the concept of multiculturalism, the umbrella association, the National Multicultural Greek Council, was established in 1998 to provide support to these organizations. As shared by the association:

> The purpose of NMGC is to provide a forum that allows for the free exchange of ideas, programs, and services between its constituent fraternities and sororities; to promote the awareness of multicultural diversity within collegiate institutions, their surrounding communities, and the greater community-at-large, and to support and promote the works of its member organizations. (NMGC, n.d.a, para. 1)

Although the NMGC is a relatively young association in the sorority and fraternity realm, its presence has already made notable contributions to SFL, which will be described in more detail in the following section.

Unique Dynamics of Multicultural Sororities and Fraternities

The NMGC is currently made up of 10 organizations, eight sororities and two fraternities alphabetically listed as follows: Delta Xi Nu Sorority, Inc.; Delta

Xi Phi Multicultural Sorority, Inc.; Gamma Eta Sorority, Inc.; Lambda Sigma Gamma Sorority, Inc.; Lambda Tau Omega Sorority, Inc.; Mu Sigma Upsilon Sorority, Inc.; Omega Phi Chi Multicultural Sorority, Inc.; Phi Sigma Chi Multicultural Fraternity, Inc.; Psi Sigma Phi Multicultural Fraternity, Inc.; Theta Nu Xi Multicultural Sorority, Inc. (NMGC, n.d.b). What brings us together is our shared value of multiculturalism:

> NMGC defines multiculturalism as not only diversity of membership, but a concrete commitment to acknowledge and celebrate all cultures equally through its programming, public service outreach efforts, and community education. (NMGC, n.d.a, para. 7)

This commitment and mission existed since the beginning of each of our organizations' founding.

Our sororities and fraternities are unique, in that we have a shared commitment and mission to actively practice intersectional multiculturalism. We recognize the responsibility of multiculturalism as a powerful tool to not only celebrate diversity, but to truly model within our organizations the importance of building equitable communities. We do so while also emphasizing a human rights practice against the backdrop of living in a country that is deeply rooted in historically oppressive systems. Our organizations in NMGC anchor our value of multiculturalism through an active practice of justice and equity.

Community building is a cornerstone of our organizations. As smaller sized national organizations, we value the importance of relationships and support leadership development and lifelong commitment to the mission of our organizations. All of our organizations are volunteer led by alumni members; for many of us, most active membership goes beyond the collegiate experience. Our organizations live out their mission of multiculturalism by taking active political stances and organizing their members to be advocates for social justice. They do so through programming, community service, values they live by in their personal life, promoting diversity and equity in programming and recruitment, and by being gender inclusive organizations. Additionally, members of the NMGC organizations engage in year-long multicultural and diversity programming as part of their national organizational standards.

Another unique dimension of our organizations is our ability to evolve and be responsive to emerging social justice issues impacting their members as well as building solidarity across social movements. Our organizations empower their members to exist and live in their multiple identities and actively work to meet the needs of their diverse membership. Importantly, although we have shared experiences, we are also not a monolith. We center and value recruiting members from different cultural and social groups to widen our community reach and strengthen our ability to mobilize for change on our campuses and communities.

Challenges Multicultural Sororities and Fraternities Face

Our organizations face similar challenges that other culturally-based sororities and fraternities experience. Most common amongst these challenges are that our organizations experience advising from a model that centers and caters to the needs of National Panhellenic Conference (NPC) and North American Interfraternity Conference (NIC) groups (historically white organizations). As a result, we are held to institutional standards that impact our success on college campuses. Some of the policies that have negative impacts on multicultural organizations have been minimum membership requirements enforced by campus policies. Historically, our organizations are typically smaller in numbers and pride ourselves on personable, close relationships with interested members that become new members. Because of the difference in recruitment styles further detailed below, comparable to their historically white organizational counterparts, multicultural sororities and fraternities continue to struggle with retention and recruitment.

A barrier to meeting minimum member requirements also stems from the lack of institutional priorities to actively recruit and retain a diverse student body that is representative of our broader society, particularly on predominantly white college campuses. If institutions are not actively committed to recruiting a broad spectrum of communities, then policies such as minimum member requirements for our organizations will continue to be a structural barrier for us to thrive and remain active on college campuses. These policies also create additional opportunities for increased stigma and invisibilizing of our practices and processes. As a result, chapters struggle with not meeting requirements such as minimum numbers to remain active and many of our chapters experience dormancy with limited ability to return to recharter their chapters. Our members recruit through a model that emphasizes getting to know prospective members one-on-one and learning whether interested individuals are a good fit to make the lifelong commitment to our organizations. We aim to recruit quality members and recognize that having larger numbers does not equate committed leaders and future members that will support the sustainability of chapters. Too often we hear firsthand reports of sorority and fraternity professionals being misinformed and uneducated about our discrete and relational community building model of recruitment. Campus-based professionals can support our members by not holding us to these advising standards and models and work one-on-one with chapters and national organizations to meet them where they are by providing them with resources for recruitment, retention, and sustainability.

An additional challenge NMGC groups face is that multicultural organizations, among other culturally-based sororities and fraternities, experience hyper-policing and profiling of our members and our organizations on campus. For example, we often hear from our council members that they are required to have police/campus safety present for events that draw larger crowds and have to pay for police/campus safety presence while their NPC and NIC counterparts are not upheld to the same standard nor required to follow this policy. The underlying causes of this disparate practice and policy towards our organizations are rooted in bias against our members and our cultural events. These policies do no not take into account the personal experiences our members have encountered with police or other authorities that may trigger students while also requiring that organizations with already limited financial resources pay to have their events policed and profiled.

Furthermore, campus-based professionals often tokenize our members as a performative tool to showcase the diversity of their campuses. Campus administrators may not be familiar with multicultural organizations and have no idea how to build rapport, support, and/or advocate for their success and overall well-being. Oftentimes, their lack of rapport or understanding of chapters may hinder their ability to be attuned to and understand that members of chapters may be balancing multiple leadership and personal responsibilities from institutions and headquarter standards and requirements while also trying to manage the demands of their overall education. These same students are often asked to serve on panels, tabling events, and to educate others to amplify their voices.

Finally, the ever-evolving nature of our value of multiculturalism and the tension of organizations now calling themselves multicultural presents challenges for NMGC organizations. Many organizations are lumped together in a "multicultural" Greek council of sorts on campuses. Particularly for MGC, it is difficult to advocate that the campus provides inclusivity and designated spaces for growth and dedicated resources to each culturally-based sorority and fraternity when Asian Pacific Islander Desi American, Black, Latinx/a/o, LGBTQ, Native American, Multicultural, and other identity-based organizations are labeled as multicultural; in doing so our identities are conflated and our needs are generalized. While there is a desire to reimagine the shared spaces that can provide support for these organizations, we have experienced instances where some campus administrations confuse an MGC as NMGC when searching for support for multicultural organizations due to the overwhelming pattern of grouping all culturally-based groups into one. This practice is yet another barrier and a function of white supremacy that sees all non-white social groups or mixed racial groups as "other" and delegitimizes the lived experiences and unique and important needs of all of our culturally-based sororities and fraternities. While we recognize that we may have shared lived experiences, challenges, and even histories, by lumping us all into one group it creates a system by which our needs are not equitably addressed. Instead, we need resources to meet each of our needs while also supporting our joint efforts and partnerships as culturally-based organizations.

While we recognize the larger systemic challenges found within higher education, we also acknowledge the tensions and challenges within multicultural organizations. We are uniquely aware that because our organizations are a microcosm of our society at large we must contend with the ways that implicit bias and structural oppression exists within our organizations. Our sororities and fraternities work towards striking a balance between honoring and respecting multiple identities and experiences while also holding true to centering our most marginalized members including our Black, Indigenous, and People of Color (BIPOC) members. With this in mind, we continuously navigate and interrogate the following questions as we hold ourselves accountable and lean into our value and practice of intersectional multiculturalism. How do we imagine multiculturalism as being borderless, beyond limits, beyond a framework that limits our understanding of multiculturalism as we perpetuate and hold onto a concept of only race, ethnicity and culturally-based diversity?

Suggestions for Practice and Research

Multicultural sororities and fraternities have been forced to assimilate to the dominant culture, particularly at predominantly white institutions, that favor the SFL model and structure for NPC/NIC organizations. Some do so by even forcing NMGC organizations to fall under these councils, making the organization adapt to the rules and policies that follow these larger council structures. These structures were not designed to be inclusive of the multicultural organizations, let alone any culturally-based sorority or fraternity. This is not conducive to the overall growth and retention of identity-based organizations. The lack of education on multicultural organizations and NMGC, has fallen through the cracks from campus-based professionals, larger SFL communities, chapter members, and their (inter)national organization leadership. Through a lack of education and knowledge of these organizations and their history, NMGC and multicultural organizations have been overlooked or looked to as the catchall for unidentified organizations that are locally on campus.

Often, campus-based professionals will apply intersectionality as it relates to theory but may not feel comfortable in applying it to practice when advising multicultural organizations. We offer the following recommendations to consider in campus-based policies for culturally-based organizations, and NMGC sororities and fraternities specifically:

Strengthen Relationships with Our Organizations

- Relationships Strengthen Solidarity: Get in the right relationship with our organizations, confer power, and invest resources (financial and otherwise).
- Resist the urge to intervene from a place of saviorship, paternalism, and tokenizing our communities.
- Practice mutual accountability towards our communities.
- Adopt a political strategy that includes the issues that are impacting and important to our diverse communities.

Advocacy/Policy Changes

- Policing and profiling of non-white students on campus: we recommend that campus administrators waive the requirement for police/campus safety presence at culturally-based sorority and fraternity events and programming.
- Move beyond allyship to active accomplices demanding structural changes. One key recommendation is for institutions to begin by waiving the minimum membership requirement for chapters.
- Rename your local "MGC" councils to help alleviate the conflation between the NMGC and other culturally-based fraternal organizations.
- Adopt an anti-oppression and cultural humility practice through your lifelong commitment to learning about our communities and members.
- Adopt Transformative Justice models (see TransformHarm.org., 2020) to respond to violations of policy and student behaviors that go beyond restorative justice practices that do not address the root causes of harm, abuse, and community accountability.

Campus-based professionals are encouraged to re-evaluate their relationships with our organizations and ask how they could best be utilized as a resource. Invest resources and support, financial and otherwise, as they are helpful for chapters that have been deemed smaller and have a lack of resources provided to them. This will help strengthen the relationships between NMGC groups and campuses and provide solidarity when the foundation of support is laid. Resist the urge to intervene from a place of saviorship, paternalism, and tokenizing our communities. Our organizations are called on as our members wear many hats and already have a number of responsibilities at hand.

When advocating for multicultural organizations, demand for structural changes and re-evaluate practices and policies in place that have oppressed or hindered the overall success of these chapters. Adopt Transformative Justice models to respond to violations of policy/students' behaviors. These models go beyond restorative justice practices that do not address the root causes of harm, abuse, and community accountability. Do not be afraid to be the larger voice for the community when questions come in place such as, are chapters aware of policies and their reasoning behind them? Are there guidelines in place that may be outdated or since dissolved throughout the shifting and evolution of SFL?

Conclusion

> If you have come here to help me, you are wasting your time. But if you have come because your liberation is bound up with mine, then let us work together. ~Lilla Watson

We hope this chapter has not only helped to deepen your understanding of multicultural sororities and fraternities within the NMGC, but brings you closer to recognizing that it is time to be in active solidarity and resistance with our members, our leaders, and our communities. Since the emergence of culturally-based sororities and fraternities, our communities have had to endure and struggle against the very systems of oppression that exist in higher education that simultaneously tell us they are here to support and help us. What we demand is for your praxis to match your theory, for your curiosity and lack of understanding about us to no longer be used as an excuse to continue to further isolate and marginalize us.

Questions for Reflection

- Can you recognize your complicity in upholding the policies, practices, and institutional biases towards multicultural sororities and fraternities as a function of white dominant/supremacist culture? Can you recognize the harms these cause to students and their communities?
- What daily commitment will you make to advocate, agitate, resist, and be in solidarity with multicultural sororities and fraternities?

- How will you be accountable to multicultural sororities and fraternities and the larger communities they are a part of?
- What concrete material resources will you, your institution, your organization invest towards multicultural sororities and fraternities?

References

Association of Fraternity/Sorority Advisors. (2009). *NMGC resource guide.* http://nationalmgc.org/wp-content/uploads/2008/12/NMGC-Resource-Guide.pdf

Jefferson, G., Pipersburg, D., Paige, J., Soto, E., Medrano, C., Pagan, M., & Martell, L. (2007). *National Multicultural Greek Council statement on multiculturalism.* Presidential Documents.

National Multicultural Greek Council. (n.d.a). *About.* https://nationalmgc.org/about/

National Multicultural Greek Council. (n.d.b). *Member organizations.* https://nationalmgc.org/about/member-organizations/

TransformHarm.org. (2020). *Transformative justice.* https://transformharm.org/transformative-justice/

Member Vignette: Historically Native American Fraternities and Sororities

HEATHER MCMILLAN NAKAI

I have been a member of Alpha Pi Omega Sorority, Inc. since 2000, but I have benefited from and was bolstered by the organization for several years before that. As a student, Alpha Pi Omega was both a refuge and a mechanism for my voice in the world surrounding me in the college environment. As a result, Alpha Pi Omega became a building block in my career; it taught me the skills I needed to navigate, first a system, and later a larger world that was never meant to sustain or support my existence. Reflecting on that experience, I gained far more from my college education than I would have without Alpha Pi Omega because bringing Alpha Pi Omega to my campus required me to push the boundaries of institutional structure, participating in Alpha Pi Omega facilitated my growth as a community leader, and experiencing Alpha Pi Omega gave me a deeper sense of purpose than I would have had as an unaffiliated student.

As a high school student in my tribal homelands, a place I lovingly refer to as Lumbee Land, I knew I was expected to go to college. I'm fortunate in that respect, because I've since learned that other Native high school students don't often benefit from the same expectations. My community expected that I'd consider the schools across North Carolina and I did. I made visits to local colleges, most notably a visit to UNC Chapel Hill. There I was hosted by a group of students including several women who were sisters of Alpha Pi Omega Sorority. This was not my first visit to a college but it was the first time I deeply considered how I, as a Native woman, would make a new place my home. Watching the Alpha Pi Omega women during that visit, several who were also from Lumbee land,

I left with a clear impression that these women had a place at UNC Chapel Hill. I didn't choose a college in North Carolina and instead, I made the monumental choice to attend a college in faraway small-town New England where I was sure I'd find my place.

My college was a world away from Lumbee Land. I had spent 18 years preparing for the academic rigor that lay ahead of me and I was excited about the possibilities that a residential college experience would offer me. In the days leading up to my departure, my community busied itself both preparing me for the coming relocation and expressing concern that I would lose myself in this new world. I assured them that I wouldn't allow that to happen—a youthful assurance without any awareness of how profoundly different my college life would be from what I'd known. As a Native American, I was acutely aware that I was going to be far removed, both literally and figuratively from my tribal community. However, my college had arguably, the most comprehensive academic and social support system for Native students in the country. I falsely believed that would be the replacement for what I was losing in Lumbee land. Neither I, nor anyone in my existing support system, realized how necessary it would be for me to create a space for myself at the college which, despite its "comprehensive" support program, was not prepared to fully support me.

My college is known for its outstanding academic programs and residential programming, particularly its Greek Life system. Located in a very rural place, these residential programs were more important than they typically are for residential colleges, which developed, in form and substance, over the college's history. Older than the United States, the college developed along the same lines as the country, from colony to country, slowly integrating, first with Men of Color, and eventually women. As the college grew so did the campus' land base. The Greek organizations that had been there the longest had the most centralized land bases and because of both history and society, were predominantly white and contained more fraternities than sororities. In the first few weeks on campus, students quickly realize how important Greek life is to campus society. Greek organizations own and operate a substantial portion of the non-academic social space. If you wanted to engage in basic social interactions with large groups of your peers indoors, you mostly had to do so at the invitation of Greek organizations. Not coincidentally, it seemed that nearly every student either participated in Greek life or was opposed to it entirely, with nothing in between.

I'd always been a very active and well-rounded student and that continued in college. I was actively involved in programs and activities across campus and, like other students, I considered Greek life. However, I never felt overwhelmingly welcomed in any Greek organization on my campus. Yet I appreciated the value that Greek organizations had at the college and my prior experience with Alpha Pi Omega informed my opinion that while I hadn't found a place in Greek life yet, there were options available that I wanted to consider. I was also aware that there were fiscal resources and influence that weren't accessible to those outside of the Greek system. I saw no reason to accept that limitation to my college experience and set out to establish Alpha Pi Omega at my college.

To bring Alpha Pi Omega to my campus I tested, and then pushed, the boundaries of a system not designed with Alpha Pi Omega or similar organizations in mind. At the outset, I was confronted with a moratorium on expansion due to campus fraternities' misbehavior, which I considered a challenge of my personal sovereignty. I joined Alpha Pi Omega during a term I was not in school at another campus. It took over a year for the moratorium to be lifted, and we were then confronted with barriers, particularly the financial requirements, to "colonization." It took over 4 years of networking, civil disobedience, occasional blatant defiance, and ultimately legal negotiations to get Alpha Pi Omega recognized on campus.

Today, one of the most significant victories of my legal career was negotiating the reduction of insurance requirements for non-residential Greek letter organizations by the office of Greek life. I am now a practicing attorney and the alumni advisor to my former undergraduate chapter. My understanding of the resources available to Greek organizations and not available to other organizations are reaffirmed as an alumna. I have witnessed the significant level of influence that Greek-affiliated alumni have on the institution and, as an undergraduate chapter advisor, have access to information and resources I'd be ignorant to otherwise. A less tenacious person would have given up; it took 7 years, including three post-graduation, to firmly establish Alpha Pi Omega on campus. As a first-generation college student, from a minoritized underserved community, I spent too much time and energy simply trying to achieve equal access to the resources available to other mainstream organizations.

CHAPTER EIGHT

Confronting Colonization: Moving Forward to Remove Barriers for Historically Native American Fraternities and Sororities

SYMPHONY OXENDINE AND DEREK OXENDINE

> In order to decolonize the system, institutions and practitioners must closely examine their infrastructure and confront the policies, processes, practices, procedures, and their own beliefs that are based in colonizing systems. (Oxendine, 2017, p. 3)

Higher education, and the United States, is founded upon and continues to operate in ongoing settler colonialism and imperialism that together are "a multidimensional force underwritten by Western Christianity, defined by White supremacy, and fueled by global capitalism" (Grande, 2015, p. 180). It is imperative to understand the history of the Indigenous peoples of this country, and how the United States government forced cultural assimilation upon them through various educational policies and practices. For centuries, the United States government used education as the vehicle to obliterate Indigenous Knowledge Systems (IKS; see Kovach, 2010; Salis Reyes & Tauala, 2019; Waterman & Bazemore-James, 2019) by assimilating, marginalizing, colonizing Native Americans. *Colonization* refers to "the idea that European American thought, knowledge, economic structures, and power structures dominate and frame present-day society in the United States" (Brayboy, 2013, p. 92). Tribal Critical Race Theory (TribalCrit; Brayboy, 2005) addresses the needs of Native Americans in education, and its central tenet argues that colonization is endemic to society.

As Indigenous Student Affairs practitioners and members of Historically Native American Fraternities and Sororities (HNAFS; Jahansouz & Oxendine, 2008), this chapter will situate the experiences of HNAFS, using TribalCrit (Brayboy, 2005). We hope to bring attention to the policies, processes, practices, procedures, and beliefs in sorority and fraternity life (SFL) as a system rooted in colonization. Additionally, we provide implications for policy and innovative practice to build capacity for transforming institutions into places of equity and culturally revitalizing support systems for students who are members of HNAFS.

The Emergence of Native American Fraternities and Sororities

Historically Native American Fraternities and Sororities are places of survivance within the higher education system for Native students. Survivance connects resistance and survival (Brayboy, 2008; Vizenor, 1999). The founders of HNAFS resisted colonization and assimilation into an institutional environment that was not created for them, by rooting IKS into every aspect of their creation. The existence of HNAFS shows survival by claiming space within a system that was not created for them: "As Indigenous people, we have been taught that when we forget who we are, the struggles we have come through and the struggles that we have yet to go through, we cease to remain our authentic selves" (Oxendine & Oxendine, 2012, p. 1).

On September 1, 1994, Alpha Pi Omega Sorority, Inc. was founded on the campus of the University of North Carolina at Chapel Hill, making it the first Native American Greek Organization and birthed the Historically Native American Fraternities and Sororities (Jahansouz & Oxendine, 2008) movement. In a little over a decade, seven additional HNAFS were founded across the country: Phi Sigma Nu Fraternity, Inc. at Pembroke State University (now the University of North Carolina at Pembroke, 1996); Epsilon Chi Nu Fraternity, Inc. (East Carolina University, 1996); Sigma Omicron Epsilon Sorority, Inc. (East Carolina University, 1997); Beta Sigma Epsilon Fraternity (University of Arizona, 2001); Gamma Delta Pi, Inc. (University of Oklahoma, 2001); Sigma Nu Alpha Gamma, Inc. (University of Oklahoma, 2004); and the now defunct Omega Delta Psi Sorority (University of Northern Colorado, 2006).

Each individual HNAFS was founded at a non-Native college and university (NNCU; Shotton, Lowe, & Waterman, 2013) in response to the unique needs of Native college students. The founding members of HNAFS "recognized the importance of retention and support of Native students, a need for cultural awareness, and an opportunity to expand and promote the Native community on their respective campuses" (Oxendine, Oxendine, & Minthorn, 2013, p. 69). Though these NNCUs had some iteration of a Native American Student Association (NASA) and/or a chapter of the American Indian Science & Engineering Society (AISES), HNAFS served as a more intimate way to preserve and cultivate students' cultural beliefs by supporting the ethnic and cultural identity development of its members, because HNAFS have woven elements of tribal culture and the importance of ceremony into the fabric of their organizations (Oxendine et al., 2013). Additionally, the founders of HNAFS were fascinated by the leadership development taking place amongst their peers whom were affiliated with sororities and fraternities, viewed the sorority and fraternity system as a way to emerge as leaders on their respective campuses, and thought being a part of the sorority and fraternity system would provide a greater voice to highlight the needs of Native American Students (Oxendine et al., 2013). The scholarship surrounding HNAFS is sparse, yet growing. For an in-depth overview on the history, foundations, and challenges of HNAFS, see Oxendine et al. (2013), Minthorn and Youngbull (2020 and Still and Farris (2019).

Situating the Context: Problematizing the Interfraternal System

Sororities and fraternities operated as single entities for over a century before the emergence of the first national interfraternal organizations, which organized multiple individual organizations into a collective, also referred to as umbrella organizations or umbrella councils (Johansen & Slantcheva-Durst, 2018). These umbrella organizations are described as "the councils governing the diverse collegiate fraternal organizations" (Hevel & Bureau, 2014, p. 23). The affiliation of sororities and fraternities into collective umbrella organizations not only provided increased resources and collaboration, but was also instrumental in streamlining and regulating the fraternal system (Johansen & Slantcheva-Durst, 2018). At the macro-level of the fraternal system, that is to say the (inter)national level, the following umbrella organizations currently exist: the National Pan-Hellenic Council, Inc. (NPHC), the National Association of Latino Fraternal Organizations (NALFO), the National Asian Pacific Islander Desi American Panhellenic Association (NAPA), the National Multicultural Greek Council (NMGC), the National Panhellenic Conference (NPC), and the North American Interfraternity Conference (NIC).

The main professional association for the sorority/fraternity advising profession, the Association of Fraternity/Sorority Advisors (AFA), considers itself the "catalytic force in aligning the fraternity/sorority experience with the changing dynamics and enduring principles of higher education" (AFA, n.d.). The origins of AFA and its organizational culture are particularly "intertwined with the relationship between campus professionals and staff and volunteers from (inter) national organizations [including umbrella organizations]" (Bureau, 2019, p. 1). Given the intertwined relationship between umbrella organizations, AFA, and campus professionals as described by Bureau (2019), it is no surprise that institutional (micro-level) sorority and fraternity policies, practices, and procedures are proper subsets of the macro-level. These relationships are problematic as the broader fraternal system is situated in a hierarchy of power and privilege that provides access to social, cultural, and economic capital, and assigns value and legitimacy to affiliation in an umbrella organization, and/or other (inter)national fraternal associations.

Throughout the rest of this chapter we will expose some of these systemic policies, practices, and procedures and how they impact HNAFS. As TribalCrit scholars, we believe that "there is little room for abstract ideas in real communities" (Brayboy, 2005, p. 440). Therefore, we will also provide recommendations for transforming practice and ideas for how to begin the process of decolonizing sorority and fraternity communities at the institution level.

Innovations in Practice: Opportunities and Challenges for HNAFS

Woven throughout the rest of this chapter, we cite literature to provide SFL professionals with an understanding of Native worldviews, epistemology, and Indigenous Knowledge Systems. We also encourage all professionals to seek out additional scholarship to be more knowledgeable about and inclusive of Native students. Below, we outline opportunities and challenges HNAFS currently face in SFL.

4 R's (Respect, Relevance, Reciprocity & Responsibility)

In 1991, "Kirkness and Barnhart put forward the four Rs as a way to change the discussion about how we think about supporting Indigenous students" (Waterman, 2020, p. 69).

These four Rs of respect, relevance, reciprocity, and responsibility are intended to provide Native students with "an education that respects them for who they are, that is relevant to their view of the world, that offers reciprocity in their relationships with others, and that helps them exercise responsibility over their own lives" (Kirkness & Barnhardt, 1991, p. 10). When HNAFS members engage on campus, they do so from the perspective of their own Indigenous epistemologies and lived experiences (Still & Faris, 2019) and it is imperative that those working with HNAFS are situating themselves in inclusive, equitable, and socially/racially just practices and frameworks.

There is a pervasive underlying "fraternal" experience (i.e., patterns of behaviors, ways of thinking, values, beliefs, etc.) that perpetuates a particular world-view and thus marginalizes those whose realities are different or do not conform to that standard. Cultural integrity is essential for Native students and culture is tied to place and community; therefore, students are going to need to go home for ceremonies and to support their family and kin. These home-going practices can often be difficult for practitioners to understand given that ceremonies vary and are not congruent with traditional IHE calendars (Still & Farris, 2019; Waterman, 2020). This lack of comprehension on the behalf of practitioners often causes conflict for HNAFS members especially when there are mandatory events to maintain chapter status or within standards programs. To put it another way, SFL professionals do not schedule mandatory events on Easter. Similarly, respecting the ceremonies of Native students means not scheduling mandatory events when Native students need to be at their traditional ceremonies or offering alternative accommodations if you find out that there is a conflict.

Increasing Sense of Belonging

Sense of belonging is an important component of HNAFS. The definition of sense of belonging within the collegiate experience is best represented as "an individual's sense of identification or positioning in relation to a group, which frequently results in an affective response" (Tovar & Simon, 2010, p. 201). In other words, students gain a feeling of comfort and come to believe they "fit in" or have a place within the campus community. In particular, Native student's sense of belonging is contingent on support and validation of their cultural identity, beliefs, customs, values, language, and philosophies within the institution (Oxendine, 2015; Tachine, Cabrera, & Yellow Bird, 2017). Membership in HNAFS provides students with a familial group that is rooted in IKS, cultural practices, tribal symbolism, and tribal ceremonies. HNAFS provide a cultural anchor within the campus community that affirms and validates their IKS and worldviews. However, given the diversity of Native peoples, HNAFS cannot and do not replace specific cultural needs that individual Native students may have.

Connections and relationality, or relationships, for Indigenous peoples is the heart of Indigenous paradigms (Salis Reyes & Tauala, 2019). The importance of connection and a need for social bonds emerged in the late 1960s from psychological research and has characterized "sense of belonging" as one of the most important social needs for individuals (Maslow, 1968). From an Indigenous perspective, however, there is not only an interpersonal element to belonging or relationships:

> In other words, from the perspective of Indigenous paradigms, we are, we know, and we do through our relationships with not only other people but also the natural and spiritual worlds. Our relationships root us and provide us with direction for growth. (Salis Reyes & Tauala, 2019, p. 47)

The relationships with land and place are sacred for Indigenous peoples: the land of our ancestors, the land of our present-day communities, and the lands in our creation stories (Cajete, 2005; Waterman & Bazemore-James, 2019; Weber-Pillwax, 2004). For example, higher education literature associates increased student engagement with persistence. In practice, there is a significant push for engaging students *on campus* to increase socialization and integration while implicitly conveying that family and external campus connections are detractors (Bowman, Jang, Jarratt, & Bono, 2019; Waterman, 2012; Wright & Shotton; 2020). However, for Native students, "home-going" is one strategy that helps with persistence because of the importance of community, place, and relationships (Waterman, 2012).

In their text examining belonging for minoritized populations, Quaye and Harper (2014) asserted, "Far too often, the onus is put on students to assimilate to predominantly White cultural norms and divorce their cultures and identities from learning processes" (p. 15). Though HNAFS provide a sense of belonging for individuals within the respective organizations, this may not equate to a sense of belonging within the sorority and fraternity community or institution. SFL professionals can increase sense of belonging for Native students through the following:

- Providing a communal space for organizations to meet, fellowship, and perform ceremonies
- Promoting home-going (Still & Farris, 2019; Waterman, 2012)
- Ensuring that policies allow for ceremonies that include smudging which is the "burning of cedar, sage, or sweet grass (or other medicine) by an elder

to purify and protect a student or a living community incorporating prayer" (Minthorn, 2014a, p. 156)
- Affirming various terminology used by HNAFS that is intricately linked with tribal and cultural traditions (Minthorn & Youngbull, 2020; Oxendine et al., 2013)
- Developing intentional and meaningful relationships (Marroquín, 2020; Oxendine, 2015)

Critical Action to Create Change

Whether intentionally or not, the SFL community has benefited from and continues to reinforce policies, practices, and procedures rooted in power, privilege, oppression, and assimilation. As TribalCrit scholars, we are calling for *critical action*, as a measure to decolonize the sorority and fraternity system. Critical action is the ability to "take action against oppressive forces in society" (Freire, 2000, p. 35). There is a responsibility for professionals within higher education as well as in the broader SFL community to review policies and procedures to disrupt assimilation, power, and legitimacy inherent in the system to better account for HNAFS. However, we want to be clear that reviewing policies is not enough. There needs to be action for transformation. In this section, we examine some examples of changes that should be made to support HNAFS on campus and within the broader SFL community including expansion policies, chapter size requirements, standards programs, grade point average (GPA) requirements, and multicultural competency and training.

Expansion

Higher education as a structure, has not willingly provided access or been welcoming and required legislation and policies to be accessible for marginalized groups (Waterman, Lowe, & Shotton, 2018). It is highly problematic that many IHE mandate affiliation with an umbrella council to expand/be recognized. In other words, if a sorority or fraternity is not nationally affiliated with NPHC, NALFA, NAPA, NMGC, NPC, or NIC, then the campus will not allow the organization to create a chapter even if there is student interest. This is often attributed to the dominant narrative that if an organization is not affiliated, there will not be "resources from national headquarters, supervision from national consultants, and professional staff members to guide chapters" (Johansen & Slantcheva-Durst, 2018, p. 6).

Our combined experience of 30 years as higher education practitioners and executive board officers of HNAFS has illustrated many times how campus-based professionals have been unwilling to build partnerships with HNAFS as they discriminate based on the prejudice that not belonging to a national umbrella organization assumes certain realities. To provide an example, this is a response from South College (name has been changed) in regards to our request to know the institution's expansion policy that we received from a Native American student at the institution through our national website:

Alpha Pi Omega will not be considered for expansion based upon the following:

1. Alpha Pi Omega is not a member of a national governing body.
2. New single-sex student organizations must be created in accordance to the Student Organization Affiliation Policy.
3. No South College students have expressed interest in creating a Native American sorority.

> I understand that Alpha Pi Omega does not traditionally fall under the National Panhellenic Conference, National Association of Latino Fraternal Organization, Inc. or National Pan-Hellenic Councils, Inc. on college campuses. At South College, these [NPC and NPHC] are the only two sorority governing bodies represented based on the current sororities we have on campus. South College strongly believes in the value of the undergraduate Greek experience. We recognize the necessity of national support for these organizations to be successful. (personal communication, 2005)

As readers can see, there is a pervasive delegitimization of HNAFS within the sorority and fraternity community. Even when there are councils on a particular campus that are for culturally-based organizations, another interesting phenomenon that we have encountered is not only with the institution's policies creating a barrier for expansion, but also campus-based councils. At East University (name has been changed), Alpha Pi Omega was asked to work directly with an undergraduate student serving as a council president: "Currently, we do have a Native American Sorority, Nu Delta Nu (name has been changed) as we do value and promote diversity and inclusion. The Multicultural Greek Council is discussing expansion plans for the future and how they will select expansion organizations" (personal communication, June 22, 2016). Then upon following up with the East University two months later, we received the following response: "At this time we are not looking to expand our Multicultural Greek Council. We already have one Native American Sorority on our campus" (personal communication, August 31, 2016).

There are several issues that we would like to call attention to from this institution's response. First, SFL professionals should consider the unintended consequences from the power structure that is created by having campus-based councils vote whether to expand or not. Council-based decision making is also problematic given that college students are still developing cognitively and may not be able to challenge their own internalized oppression (Duran & Jones, 2020). There should be minimum standards for expansion within a campus community. SFL professionals should ensure that if council-based decisions are part of the process that students' decisions are based upon standards and not one of limiting competition. Second, the "one-size-fits-all" mentality is pervasive in student engagement within higher education (Quaye, Harper, & Pendakur, 2020). In the instance above, the reasoning is since there already exists *ONE* Native sorority, then why do we need another one? If we translated this to any other group, there certainly would be a backlash on how wildly unreasonable it would sound. The population size of Native students, as well as stereotypes that all Native peoples are one monolithic group, has been and continues to be used as a way for IHE to "argue against prioritizing" and treating Natives as "an aside in discussion of educational practices, conditions, and subsequent attainment" (Faircloth & Tippeconnic, 2015, p. 130). Campuses should have a structured open expansion policy at all IHE that is situated from a shared governance model between the councils and professional staff to ensure inclusive and equitable expansion policies and practices.

Chapter Size Requirements

Many IHE have policies that place restrictions on minimum membership requirements for chartering new chapters or maintaining chapters (Oxendine, 2017; Oxendine & Oxendine, 2012; Oxendine et al., 2013). There is generally no rationale for how these minimum numbers are decided upon except that it is "policy" and so these arbitrarily contrived standards are creating barriers for HNAFS. An across the board minimum chapter size requirement disproportionately disadvantages smaller populations on campus, especially those with membership that is composed mainly from smaller student sub-populations. These minimum requirements are often hard to reach for HNAFS. For instance, at a large campus with 19,200 enrolled undergraduates there are only 90 Native undergraduates enrolled (based on actual enrollment data at one institution) which comprise approximately .4% of the total undergraduate population. Therefore, if a chapter was required to have 8 members that is 8.89% of the total Native students enrolled. If we applied that standard with the total number of students enrolled, then that would equate to 1,706 members to meet the 8.89% proportion.

The overarching question is how do these requirements support or hinder what a quality SFL experience is for HNAFS? HNAFS nationally set their own policies for minimum chapter size requirements and IHE should respect that these are based on their expert knowledge of what is needed to maintain chapter functions and their population of students.

Standards Programs

There has been little research within the SFL community that has critically examined how institutions have sought to review, assess and set standards for campus SFL communities (Sasso, 2012). For over 35 years, the existence of campus-based standards and evaluation programs had the "initial intent of fraternity/sorority standards programs was to exert control as an intervention or response against negative behaviors scourging the student experience and causing significant institutional liability" (Sasso, 2012, p. 33). Yet, this core premise has not changed as these types of programs have evolved on campuses. Standards/assessment programs are based on expectations of traditionally white sororities and fraternities which are implemented by individuals with "little or no professional preparation ... the majority of advisors draw from their undergraduate experience to inform their advising of chapters" (Sasso, 2012, pp. 1–2). The chapter size for HNAFS tend to be smaller and these types of programs are problematic especially when they require a specific percentage of the chapter to attend events. This is especially relevant for HNAFS because their members are often student leaders who are committed and dedicated to making their communities better, on campus and in their communities. These students often wear many hats, are tokenized and expected to speak on behalf of all "their people," and feel that they must work harder to meet expectations to prove they belong (Brayboy, Solyom, & Castagno, 2015; Minthorn, 2014b; Moon, 2003; Shotton, 2008; Shotton, Oosahwe, & Cintrón, 2007; Shotton et al., 2013).

Grade Point Average Requirements

If you ask any campus-based professional working with sororities and fraternities, they will tout "scholarship" as one of the common basic principles that organizations were founded upon (Komives et al., 2003). In fact, many campus-based policies require organizations to maintain a minimum GPA in order to maintain recognition. A prevalent required practice by SFL departments is for sororities to meet or exceed the institutional all women's GPA and fraternities to meet or exceed the institutional all men's GPA each semester. For HNAFS, this has been problematic as chapters have been placed on probation and suspended, thus losing official recognition from the institution, even when they exceeded standards set forth by the governing bodies of their organizations. To provide an example, one semester a Phi Sigma Nu chapter (7 men) at a NNCU was facing losing official recognition due to its cumulative chapter GPA of 2.85. The all men's GPA was 3.03 (12,450 men) and the institution's policy stated the minimum acceptable GPA is 0.10 below the average of the all men's GPA. Unfortunately, Phi Sigma Nu fell at 0.18 below the all men's average for that semester. Let us be clear, the average GPA of seven Native American men was compared to the average GPA of 12,450 undergraduate men, mostly white men. These seven men totaled .056% of the entire population they were being compared to. Though a campus-based professional may think this practice is equitable due to following policy, it does not take into account educational gaps, locked-in inequality, and racial and ethnic differences in college achievement (Fletcher & Tienda, 2010; Gilborn, 2008). A more just and fair comparison would have been to compare Phi Sigma Nu to their peers by using the institutional all Native American GPA or the institutional all Native American men's GPA, instead of comparing it to the institutional all men's GPA, consisting of mostly white undergraduate men.

Multicultural Competency, Cultural Relevancy, and Training

Multicultural competency and cultural relevancy is essential for working with HNAFS. Indeed, within the ACPA/NASPA professional competencies, the two leading professional associations for student affairs have identified that multicultural, social justice, and inclusion are essential competencies for student affairs professionals (ACPA/NASPA, 2015). Pope et al. (2019) identified multicultural competency as:

> ... an expectation that student affairs practitioners consistently challenge themselves to increase their awareness and knowledge of self, of others, and of the relationship between the two; understand systems of oppression and inequities to create a deeper understanding of structural barriers within higher education; and develop the advocacy and action skills essential to eradicate the structural barriers, eliminate the inequities, and create multicultural change on campus and in society. (p. 6)

Furthermore, AFA, the association for sorority/fraternity professionals, has created the AFA Core Competencies. AFA's Competency model identifies two domains that competencies are categorized into, Foundational Knowledge and Professional Skills. The competency of "Working across Differences" is listed under the domain of Professional skills and includes three sub-competencies: embracing our differences; facilitating interactions across differences; and advocating for inclusive policies, practices, and learning environments (AFA, 2018, p. 25).

Professionals working with HNAFS need to educate themselves on the diversity of Native/Indigenous people and the sororities/fraternities that they join. For example, there is a significant unique aspect of identity for Native people especially within the United States:

> ... the complicated relationship between American Indians and the United States federal government and begin to make sense of American Indians' liminality as both racial and legal/political groups and individuals. It is this liminal space that accounts for both the political/legal nature of our relationship with the U.S. government as American Indians and with our embodiment as racialized beings. (Brayboy, 2005, p. 427)

Professionals working with HNAFS should also familiarize themselves on the scholarship surrounding Native American students in higher education. There has been a plethora of literature cited in this chapter. However, for a starting point we recommend *Postsecondary Education for American Indians and Alaska Natives: Higher Education for Nation Building and Self-Determination* (Brayboy et al., 2012) and *Beyond the Asterisk: Understanding Native Students in Higher Education* (Shotton et al., 2013).

Conclusion

> ... for Indigenous people(s), narratives and stories are an important form of theorizing and imparting important ancestral knowledge ... when we share stories, we create and share theory. (Brayboy, 2013, p. 92)

Our stories define who we are as a people (Brayboy, 2005). As Indigenous Student Affairs practitioners and members of Historically Native American Fraternities and Sororities, we have shared the experiences of HNAFS, through this chapter. The time for change is long overdue and there is now a recognition that systemic oppression and racism are inherent within higher education and the sorority and fraternity community:

> This time we asked you to reflect on what it would look like to dismantle systemic oppression within the fraternity and sorority experience. Regarding race, what would a truly antiracist professional industry and member experience look like ... one that moves beyond mere inclusion to establishing a true sense of belonging and equity for all [Question B]? ("What's Your Perspective", 2020, p. 7)

We hope that by reading this chapter, SFL professionals acknowledge that colonization is also a persistent problem, so that they can "begin moving toward constructing measures to directly confront and dampen the effects of colonization" (Brayboy, 2013, p. 93). For this to happen, we need SFL professionals to not only "hear" our story, but to "get it" as well. We must own the responsibility to acknowledge the historical and present-day contexts in which our institutions exist and we work (Lee & Ahtone, 2020). By telling our story, we hope it serves as a catalyst to decolonize the sorority and fraternity system.

Questions for Reflection

1. What ways are HNAFS included or not in the sorority and fraternity community on campus? What kind of assumptions underlie the various ways that other sorority and fraternity organizations seek out partnering with HNAFS?
2. How does the language and terminology used within sorority and fraternity communities (e.g., colony, membership intake) marginalize particular types of organizations?
3. What opportunities can be created to provide education about Native or Indigenous culture, identity, or issues? Inviting students to share their stories will create relationships but the burden of educating professionals should not be placed on the students.
4. What ways are campuses inherently reinforcing the perceived legitimacy of particular organizations via resources such as dedicated professional staff rather than Graduate Assistants, a focus on housing/property, marketing and publicity for formal recruitment?

References

ACPA–College Student Educators International & NASPA–Student Affairs Administrators in Higher Education. (2015). *ACPA/NASPA professional competency areas for student affairs educators.* https://www.myacpa.org/professional-competency-areas-student-affairs-practitioners

Association of Fraternity/Sorority Advisors. (AFA). (n.d.). *Get to know AFA.* https://www.afa1976.org/page/AboutAFA

Association of Fraternity/Sorority Advisors. (2018). *AFA core competencies manual.* https://www.afa1976.org/page/CoreCompetenciesBartlett, L., & Brayboy, B. M. J. (2005). Race and schooling: Theories and ethnographies. *The Urban Review, 37*(5), 361–374.

Bowman, N. A., Jang, N., Jarratt, L., & Bono, T. (2019). The process of college adjustment: Weekly changes and racial differences. *Journal of Student Affairs Research and Practice, 56*(4), 423–437. https://doi.org/10.1080/19496591.2019.1614935

Brayboy, B. M. J. (2005). Toward a tribal critical race theory in education. *The Urban Review, 37*(5), 425–446. https://doi.org/10.1007/s11256-005-0018-y

Brayboy, B. M. J. (2008). "Yakkity yak" and "talking back": An examination of sites of survivance in Indigenous knowledge. In M. Villegas, S. R. Neugebauer, & K. R. Venegas (Eds.), *Indigenous knowledge and education: Sites of struggle, strength, and survivance* (pp. 339–346). Cambridge, MA: Harvard Educational Review.

Brayboy, B. M. J. (2013). Tribal critical race theory: An origin story and future directions. In M. Lynn & A. D. Dixson (Eds.), *Handbook of critical race theory in education* (pp. 88–100). Oxfordshire, UK: Routledge.

Brayboy, B. M. J., Solyom, J. A., & Castagno, A. E. (2015). Indigenous Peoples in higher education. *Journal of American Indian Education, 54*(1), 154–186. http://www.jstor.org/stable/10.5749/jamerindieduc.54.1.0154

Bureau, D. A. (2019). Does history dictate AFA's future? *Essentials, H*(07).

Cajete, G. A. (2005). American Indian epistemologies. In M. J. Tippeconnic Fox, S. C. Lowe, & G. S. McClellan (Eds.), *Serving Native American students* (New Directions for Student Services, no. 109, pp. 69–78). Hoboken, NJ: Jossey-Bass. https://doi.org/10.1002/ss.155

Duran, A., & Jones, S. R. (2020). Complicating identity exploration: An intersectional grounded theory centering Queer Students of Color at historically white institutions. *Journal of College Student Development, 61*(3), 281–298.

Faircloth, S. C., & Tippeconnic III, J. W. (2015). Leadership development for schools serving American Indian students: Implications for research, policy, and practice. *Journal of American Indian Education, 54*(1), 127–153.

Fletcher, J., & Tienda, M. (2010). Race and ethnic differences in college achievement: Does high school attended matter? *The Annals of the American Academy of Political and Social Science, 627*(1), 144–166.

Freire, P. (2000/1970). *Pedagogy of the oppressed.* New York, NY: Continuum.

Gillborn, D. (2008). *Racism and education: Coincidence or conspiracy?* Oxfordshire, UK: Routledge.

Grande, S. (2015). *Red pedagogy: Native American social and political thought.* Lanham, MD: Rowman & Littlefield.

Hevel, M. S., & Bureau, D. A. (2014). Research-driven practice in fraternity and sorority Life. In G. L. Martin & M. S. Hevel (Eds.), *Research-driven practice in student affairs: Implications from the Wabash national study of liberal arts education* (New Directions for Student Services, no. 147, pp. 23–36). Hoboken, NJ: Jossey-Bass. https://doi.org/10.1002/ss.20098

Jahansouz, S., & Oxendine, S. D. (2008, Spring). The Native American fraternal values movement: Past, present, & future. *Perspectives,* 14.

Johansen, A., & Slantcheva-Durst, S. (2018). Governing councils and their defining role in the development of campus Greek communities: The case of the University of Toledo, 1945-2006. *American Educational History Journal, 45*(2), 1–17.

Kirkness, V. J., & Barnhardt, R. (1991). First Nations and higher education- the four R's—respect, relevance, reciprocity, responsibility. *Journal of American Indian Education, 30(3),* 1–15.

Komives, S. R., & Woodard, D. B., Jr. (2003). *Student services: A handbook for the profession* (4th ed.). Hoboken, NJ: Jossey-Bass.

Kovach, M. (2010). *Indigenous methodologies: Characteristics, conversations, and contexts.* Toronto, Ontario, Canada: University of Toronto Press.

Lee, R., & Ahtone, T. (2020, March 30). Land-grab universities. *High Country News, 52*(4). https://www.hcn.org/issues/52.4/indigenous-affairs-education-land-grab-universities

Marroquín, C. (2020). The validation of the North American Indigenous College Students Inventory (NAICSI). *Journal of American Indian Education, 59*(1), 73–97.

Maslow, A. H. (1968). *Towards a psychology of being.* New York, NY: D. Van Nostrand Company.

Minthorn, R. (2014a). Accommodating the spiritual and cultural practices of Native American college and university students. *Journal of College & University Student Housing, 41*(1), 154–163.

Minthorn, R. (2014b). Perspectives and values of leadership for Native American college students in non-Native colleges and universities. *Journal of Leadership Education, 13*(2), 67–95.

Minthorn, R., & Youngbull, N. (2020). Reclaiming and asserting our nations through the growth of historically Native American fraternities and sororities (HNAFS). In P. Sasso, J. P. Biddix, & M. L. Miranda (Eds.), *Supporting fraternities and sororities in the contemporary era: Advancements in practice* (pp. 189–197). Sterling, VA: Stylus.

Moon, N. L. (2003). *Warriors in graduate school: Using rorschach and interviews to identify strengths in Native American graduate students* (Doctoral dissertation, Alliant International University, San Diego, CA). ProQuest Dissertations and Theses Global.

Norman, E. M., & Biddix, J. P. (2019). (Re)Establishing a fraternal community. In P. Sasso, J. P. Biddix, & M. L. Miranda (Eds.), *Supporting fraternities and sororities in the contemporary era: Advancements in practice* (pp. 85–96). Sterling, VA: Stylus.

Oxendine, D. R., & Oxendine, S. D. (2012). From the margins with no reservations. *Essentials*, (May). http://www.afa1976.org/Publications/Essentials/May2012Essentials2.aspx

Oxendine, D. R., Oxendine, S. D., & Minthorn, R. W. (2013). The historically Native American fraternity and sorority movement. In S. C. Lowe, H. Shotton, & S. Waterman (Eds.), *Beyond the asterisk: Understanding Native students in higher education* (pp. 67–81). Sterling, VA: Stylus.

Oxendine, S. D. (2015). *Examining the impact of institutional integration and cultural integrity on sense of belonging to predict intention to persist for Native American students at non-Native colleges and universities* (Doctoral Dissertation, University of North Carolina at Greensboro, Greensboro, NC). ProQuest Dissertations and Theses Global.

Oxendine, S. D. (2017, October). A call to action: Disrupting assimilation and colonization in fraternity and sorority life. *Essentials, F*(08).

Pope, R. L., Reynolds, A. L., & Mueller, J. A. (2019). *Multicultural competence in student affairs: Advancing social justice and inclusion.* Hoboken, NJ: John Wiley & Sons.

Quaye, S. J., & Harper, S. R. (2014). *Student engagement in higher education: Theoretical perspectives and practical approaches for diverse populations* (2nd ed.). Oxfordshire, UK: Routledge.

Quaye, S. J., Harper, S. R., & Pendakur, S. L. (2020). *Student engagement in higher education: Theoretical perspectives and practical approaches for diverse populations* (3rd ed.). Oxfordshire, UK: Routledge.

Salis Reyes, N. A., & Tauala, M. (2019). Indigenous paradigms: Decolonizing college student development theory through centering relationality. In E. S. Abes, S. R. Jones, & D. L. Stewart (Eds.), *Rethinking college student development theory using critical frameworks* (pp. 45–54). Sterling, VA: Stylus.

Sasso, P. A. (2012). Towards a typology of fraternity/sorority programs: A content analysis. *Oracle, 7*(1), 22–41. Shotton, H. J. (2008). *Pathway to the Ph. D.: Experiences of high-achieving American Indian females* (Doctoral dissertation, The University of Oklahoma, Norman, OK]. ProQuest Dissertations and Theses Global.

Shotton, H. J., Lowe, S. C., & Waterman, S. J. (2013). Introduction. In H. J. Shotton, S. C. Lowe, & S. J. Waterman (Eds.), *Beyond the asterisk: Understanding Native students in higher education* (pp. 1–24). Sterling, VA: Stylus.

Shotton, H. J., Oosahwe, E. S. L., & Cintrón, R. (2007). Stories of success: Experiences of American Indian students in a peer-mentoring retention program. *Review of Higher Education, 31*(1), 81–107.

Still, C. M., & Faris, B. R. (2019). Understanding and supporting historically Native American fraternities and sororities. In K. E. Gillon, C. C. Beatty, & C. Salinas Jr. (Eds.), *Critical considerations of race, ethnicity, and culture in fraternity & sorority life* (New Directions for Student Services, no. 165, pp. 51–59). Hoboken, NJ: Jossey-Bass. https://doi.org/10.1002/ss.20293

Tachine, A. R., Cabrera, N. L., & Yellow Bird, E. (2017). Home away from home: Native American students' sense of belonging during their first year in college. *The Journal of Higher Education, 88*(5), 785–807. https://doi.org/10.1080/00221546.2016.1257322

Vizenor, G. (1999). *Manifest manners: Narratives on postindian survivance*. Lincoln, NE: Nebraska University Press.

Waterman, S. J. (2012). Home-going as a strategy for success among Haudenosaunee college and university students. *Journal of Student Affairs Research and Practice, 49*(2), 193–209.

Waterman, S. J. (2020). A holistic approach to support adult Indigenous students. *Explorations in Adult Higher Education, Winter*(6), 68–77.

Waterman, S. J., & Bazemore-James, C. M. (2019). It's more than us. In E. S. Abes, S. R. Jones, & D. L. Stewart (Eds.), *Rethinking college student development theory using critical frameworks* (pp. 158–170). Sterling, VA: Stylus.

Waterman, S. J., Lowe, S. C., & Shotton, H. J. (2018). *Beyond access: Indigenizing programs for Native student success*. Sterling, VA: Stylus.

Weber-Pillwax, C. (2004). Indigenous researchers and Indigenous research methods: Cultural influences or cultural determinants of research methods. *Pimatisiwin: A Journal of Aboriginal & Indigenous Community Health, 2*(1), 77–90.

What's your perspective? (2020). *Perspectives*, *1*(1), 7. https://issuu.com/afa1976/docs/afa-2020-perpectives-issue1-v1-final

Wright, E. K., & Shotton, H. J. (2019). Engaging Indigenous students. In S. J. Quaye, S. R. Harper, & S. L. Pendakur (Eds.), *Student engagement in higher education: Theoretical perspectives and practical approaches for diverse populations* (3rd ed., pp. 69–88). Oxfordshire, UK: Routledge.

SECTION 3

INNOVATIONS IN PRACTICE: ISSUES IN THE BROADER LANDSCAPE OF CULTURALLY-BASED SORORITIES AND FRATERNITIES

CHAPTER NINE

Attending to Intersecting Identities in Culturally-Based Sororities and Fraternities

KEITH D. GARCIA

At the time of writing this chapter in 2020, the sociopolitical climate within which higher education professionals are having this dialogue around supporting culturally-based sororities and fraternities cannot be overstated. As the United States grappled with civil unrest in the wake of the murders of Breonna Taylor, Tony McDade, Ahmaud Arberry, George Floyd, and countless other Black community members, the nation's foundation of white supremacy has been laid bare. This chapter itself transgresses prescriptions from government leadership which paint critical discourse as "divisive" (Vought, 2020, p. 1). Therefore, it would be irresponsible of me to attend to intersecting forms of oppression without first acknowledging this context and affirming that Black Lives Matter.

Within this chapter, I hope to broaden the understanding practitioners have about the implications of identity within culturally-based sororities and fraternities as well as the ways in which attending to identities can enhance the membership experience. It is important to me to acknowledge that the identities held by membership are never one-dimensional. In explicitly focusing on identities which are not centered in the constitution of culturally-based sororities and fraternities, I wish to illuminate gaps in our knowledge and raise our consciousness in service of transformative praxis. I am explicitly centering minoritized identities and addressing the compounded nature of marginalization at the intersections.

In this chapter, I will attempt to provide an understanding of nuances between intersecting identities and intersectionality for those working with culturally-based sororities and fraternities. Though these concepts are often used interchangeably, they are not the same. Each concept is valuable as part of the framework I'll use to interrogate culturally-based sororities and fraternities' approaches to inclusion. I believe practitioners must embrace the difficult work of attending to intersecting identities so that sororities and fraternities can move beyond empty rhetoric. In offering strategies for effective leadership in this area, I hope to advance our collective work to this end.

My Positionality

For the purpose of this chapter I situate myself, sororities, and fraternities in the racialized, gendered, and other societally constructed contexts within which we exist. It is important to me that I acknowledge the identities I hold and experiences I have had as they impact my lens on this work. I am Afro-Latino/Black, gay, and a cisgender man. I am Puertorriqueño and a United States citizen. I live with both visible and invisible disabilities. I was raised in a low-income household and am currently considered middle-class. I grew up in a Christian household and hold a complex relationship to religion. I carry forward my parents' hopes having been a first-generation college student and obtaining a master's degree. My fraternal affiliation is within a Latinx/o men's fraternity: La Unidad Latina, Lambda Upsilon Lambda Fraternity, Inc. I share these identities, experiences, and affiliations in an effort to contextualize my words.

I acknowledge the limitations there are in my ability to account for all identities in this chapter. I have made a conscious decision to discuss race, gender, sexuality, socioeconomic status, ability, age, familial status, documented status/U.S. citizenship, and first-generation college students. Certainly there are identities beyond the aforementioned that are worthy of discourse and consideration in practice. Seeing these limitations as gaps, I ask anyone utilizing this text to inform their practice to acknowledge and interrogate the ways in which culturally-based sorority and fraternity life (SFL) can perpetuate marginalization of these and other identities.

Defining Identity and Intersectionality

In order to attend to identities in the context of culturally-based sororities and fraternities, it is important to first develop an understanding of the various concepts that inform the dialogue. Clarity surrounding these ideas and defining the language practitioners utilize enhances our ability to effectively communicate. What do we mean when we say identity? How are identities constructed and contextualized? What is the difference between intersecting identities and intersectionality? There is also value in recognizing the contributions of membership in culturally-based sororities and fraternities to identity development. What might the impact of someone joining a historically Black or Latinx/a sorority be on their sense of Blackness or Latinidad? Why is it important to have this dialogue in the context of culturally-based sororities and fraternities at all?

When discussing identity in this chapter, I am referring to socially constructed identities. Socially constructed identity is defined as "one's sense of self and beliefs about one's own social group as well as others are constructed through interactions with the broader social context in which dominant values dictate norms and expectations" (Torres, Jones, & Renn, 2009, p. 577). Being explicit about this matters to me because of the nature in which discourse around identity can be harmful absent this framing. Socially constructed identities interface with society and all of its systems where some identities are deemed as superior and are privileged in society and others are recognized as inferior and are treated as such. And so as we navigate the world around us systems shape and impact our identities. I also must be clear with respect to the fact that while everyone holds multiple social identities and that those identities do intersect, acknowledging these is not the equivalent of intersectionality. The concept of intersectionality was first introduced into the academy by Kimberlé Crenshaw in 1989. Crenshaw (1989) offered a Black feminist critique of the "tendency to treat race and gender as mutually exclusive categories of experience and analysis" (p. 139). In doing so, Crenshaw illuminated the ways in which marginalization of identities was compounded at the intersection. Crenshaw (1991) also made plain the role of systems in rendering compounded marginalization invisible. As the discourse around intersectionality has continued, this theoretical framework has been used to broaden the understanding of intersections across various marginalized identities.

I exist at the intersection of both privileged and marginalized identities. The collection of my identities and how I make meaning of the experiences are explored in the Model of Multiple Dimensions of Identity (Jones & McEwen, 2000) and Reconceptualized Model of Multiple Dimensions of Identity (Abes, Jones, & McEwen, 2007). They help me to understand how my identities intersect because they provide clarity around how identities might become more or less salient based on context as well as the ability to make meaning through my capacities to filter contextual influence. For example, my sexual identity was heavily influenced by dominant societal norms until I developed a greater capacity to make meaning of my experiences and limit the role of dominant influences on my self-perceptions about sexuality.

When discussing intersecting identities, because these are socially constructed, we must always account for the society and systems within which those identities exist. Perhaps when we label those identities as privileged or marginalized we get closer to acknowledging the reality about how these identities impact our lives and still we must interrogate further. When discussing the intersection of identities I could readily address my identities as cisgender and gay or Afro-Latino/Black and a man. This would be appropriate as I experience the world at the intersections of these identities. However, I often made the mistake of conflating the intersections of my identity with the concept of intersectionality; to be clear, these concepts are not the same thing. Intersectionality is not simply the overlap of the various identities one holds. Rather, it is an interrogation of individuals' experiences at the intersections of their marginalized identities and the systems that compound their marginalization at those intersections. So a more appropriate view of my identities as it relates to intersectionality would require me to consider how systems of power disproportionately create barriers for my Afro-Latinidad/Blackness.

Identity in the Culturally-Based Sorority and Fraternity Context

The implications of issues related to racism, patriarchal systems, and other forms of oppression in sorority and fraternity are tied, in part, to the environments within which the organizations were developed. White supremacy served as the foundation of institutions of higher education and informed attitudes that still remain pervasive in the U.S. (Museus, Ledesma, & Parker 2015). The first historically/predominantly white sororities and fraternities were established in all-white environments (Garcia & Shirley, 2019). And while race was often the central identity in the spaces within which these groups developed so too were gender, socioeconomic status, religion, as well as countless other societally prescribed identities. Institutions of higher education in the United States were explicit about their practices of exclusion and commitments to Eurocentric ideals (Wright, 1988). The advent of culturally-based sororities and fraternities was often a response to the overt racism which excluded non-white people from fraternal organizations.

As we explore concepts related to identity we also delve into the ways in which membership within culturally-based sororities and fraternities contribute to identity development. Guardia and Evans (2008) shared the factors influencing ethnic identity development of Latino identified members of Latino fraternities at a Hispanic Serving Institution. Their research concluded that membership enhanced members' ethnic identity. With culturally-based sororities and fraternities impacting member identity development in this way, it is critical that those supporting these organizations whether as volunteers, advisors, and/or staff cultivate experiences that acknowledge the whole person and who they are as they arrive in our contexts.

However, though these organizations were designed to serve minoritized communities, they are not without fault and can be complicit in marginalization at the intersections. Duran and Garcia's (2020) narratives of Queer Men of Color in culturally-based fraternities shed light on the role of organizations in creating hostile environments for queer people and the resultant forms of resistance members participate in. In a study about attitudes toward queer women in Black sororities, Literte and Hodge (2012) noted that while their participants weren't "virulently homophobic" and either "tacitly or fully embraced gays and lesbians" there was a "pervasive silence about the subject of homosexuality, not only within [Black] sororities, but within the [Black] community at large" (p. 695). It is important to consider how these toxic environments and participation in resistance inform queer identity development in the culturally-based sorority and fraternity context. The experiences of queer people in culturally-based sororities and fraternities is just one example of the ways in which failure to attend to intersecting identities can create challenge for membership. In my personal experience, I have navigated the harms of homophobia and hegemonic masculinity within the context of the Latinx/o fraternity of which I am a member. Even still I am here committed to enhancing this experience and a commitment to equitable experiences for members yet to join. And while we do this work we must also remain diligent about the ways in which we racialize homophobia – implicitly or otherwise – so as to not replicate the harms of whiteness (Connell, 2016).

Toward Attending to Intersecting Identities

I believe that culturally-based sororities and fraternities have the ability to serve as powerful affinity spaces for students and community members. Their ability to connect people through shared values and lived experiences has been a hallmark of their existence (Garcia, 2020). That said, I have witnessed these organizations struggle with meeting the needs of their membership whose identities are not explicitly centered. When attending to identities within culturally-based sororities and fraternities, intersectionality can establish an incredibly powerful framework. In her keynote at the Association of College Personnel Administrators (ACPA) Convention in Nashville, TN, in 2020, Crenshaw provided institutions of higher education a way toward intersectional institutions which I believe to be valuable for culturally-based sororities and fraternities invested in doing the challenging work of transformation. Her recommendations include performing an intersectional audit, doing an intersectional assessment of "inclusionary" practices, incentivizing more robust inclusion, and building out from oversights of power (Ardoin, 2020b). To show how these can transform culturally-based sororities and fraternities, I will demonstrate these recommendations' application to these organizations.

Intersectional Audits

As part of Crenshaw's call for organizations to perform an intersectional audit, I recommend that organizations first acknowledge the identities they explicitly center in their existence and work. For instance, the gendered nature of sororities and fraternities can serve as a starting point when explicitly addressing identity in organizations. As an organizational leader, identify whether your organization maintains a clause for membership based on gender, recognize this fact and then begin to interrogate the ways in which the maintenance of this clause impacts current and prospective members. A campus professional should consider what an organization's policies on gender mean within their campus context. Then, they can facilitate a document review for implicit and explicit references to identity. A working assumption can be made that most, if not all, culturally-based sororities and fraternities center at least one marginalized or targeted identity; perhaps it is race, ethnicity, religion, or sexuality. And though surely there are dominant identities that might exist within their context as well, centering marginalization and the impact of systemic oppression on those targeted identities creates pathways for attending to intersecting identities with intersectionality as a frame.

For instance, I am a member of a historically Latinx/o men's fraternity. Identifying as a man is explicitly centered in our context. Latinidad is also central to the organization's identity. However, there is a lot of room to work through the experiences of hermanos who might identify outside of the confines of the fraternity's limited prescriptions of Latinidad and what it means to be a man. For instance, I think about notions of Latinidad which do not account for racial identification, tying Latinidad to one's ability to speak Spanish, or expectations of masculine performativity to identify as a man. Similarly, NPHC women can consider what messages chapters center around what it means to be a Black woman.

A NAPA chapter might consider ways chapters may reinforce heteronormativity, causing queer Asian people to feel unwelcome within that space. As part of an intersectional audit, naming the centrality of these identities within the organization's context can serve as the launching point to consider how to both expand our conceptions of racial/ethnic identity, gender, and sexuality among others while unearthing identities which are consciously or subconsciously made invisible.

In another organization's case, where Latinidad might also be central, one could examine the role of race. Exploring race in the organization, perhaps existing as Black and Latinx/a/o, could further consciousness about the extent to which an organization does or does not attend to these intersecting identities. Examine the ways in which messaging about your organization's identity as Latinx/a/o erases or affirms Afro-Latinidad. You can facilitate a census of sorts within your membership to learn how they identify. If you value a sense of belonging and community within your organization, knowing how members identify could enhance your capacity to impact that sense of belonging and cultivation of community. As much as knowing how members identify within organizations is important, it is also incredibly important to identify who isn't involved as a member and how organizations' ways of being might be read as unwelcoming to particular identities. Just because certain identities aren't currently represented in membership, that does not mean they are not worthy of attention in this work.

Facilitating this work could very well be a collaborative effort. There may already be practices identified about how to shift narratives around Latinidad. Partners in this work for my office at Northwestern University include colleagues from Campus Inclusion & Community: Multicultural Student Affairs, Social Justice Education, and Student Enrichment Services—an office dedicated to serving first-generation, low income, and undocumented students. These offices, and offices like them, exist to advance students' feelings of safety and sense of belonging and can be powerful partners in facilitating these types of audits. Crenshaw (1989) has provided us with the prism of intersectionality through which practitioners can be asking these questions. Pursuing answers is just the beginning of interrogating how systems of oppression might reify harm, such as examining and treating Latinidad and Blackness as not existing alongside one another.

Intersectional Assessments of Inclusionary Practices

Part of an intersectional audit might include identifying ways in which organizations work toward inclusion. Answer the questions: What have we done? What are we doing? And what do we need to do? Organizations that center racial or ethnic identity may well have done some of the previously mentioned work, specifically exploring intersections of race and ethnicity. They might have also expanded their efforts to include interventions meant to foster broader inclusion. Crenshaw called on us to assess those practices. Let us explicitly center gender. We can identify whether trans-inclusive membership policies exist and assess whether or not they lend themselves to the recruitment, retention, and satisfaction of trans siblings. In a conversation I had with Alex C. Lange, a scholar whose work focuses on transgender communities in higher education, I sought their perspective on Crenshaw's keynote and its implications for the discourse within this book chapter. Something that stood out to me from our conversation was how trans-inclusive policies within the sorority and fraternity context still come with explicit and implicit expectations about gender expression and performance. It forced me to critically consider the progress we've made in a system which is still shaped by the gender binary. As a campus-based practitioner I want to know how trans members of the community I serve are experiencing these attempts at inclusion and create opportunities for them to inform my work.

The gendered nature of sororities and fraternities also exists alongside societal prescriptions of heteronormativity. McCready and Radimer (2019) addressed the role of gender performativity in sororities and fraternities, specifically addressing hegemonic masculinity and femininity. And so individuals who exist in ways that do not conform to these expectations can often be lost within the fraternal context. What does it mean when a fraternity's—read historically cishet (cisgender and heterosexual) men's organization—ways of being revolve around heteronormative expectations? I can recall countless examples from my fraternal experience where the expectations for co-sponsoring social events included co-hosting with women groups or sororities. Co-hosting parties or mixers with men's organizations or co-ed organizations was often discouraged if not outright derided. In my opinion, these perspectives are not unknown to practitioners supporting and leading culturally-based sororities and fraternities. And so the proactive work of addressing these attitudes and their manifestation within chapters can begin today. Scholars have already spoken to these experiences in their research (Duran & Garcia, 2020). There may also be an opportunity to hear directly from members who are impacted.

Consideration must be given to the labor expended by marginalized communities and an open invitation to offer perspective should be available, providing agency to members who identify across the universe of sexualities to inform their experiences. Practitioners can ask them what their social experiences have been within the context of the organization. Membership can then do the work to change cultural norms within their chapters to be more welcoming to potential queer members, allowing them to engage in events and environments that are affirming of their whole selves. This may well create other opportunities for partnership. Campus professionals can create connections for their offices, sororities, and fraternities to their institution's gender and sexuality resources. Organizations can and should explore intra-organizational affinity spaces that can provide safe-haven for members within the context of sororities and fraternities. In my experience, the existence of LULOut—my fraternity's affinity space for GBQ members—created opportunity for hermanos to discuss the ways in which membership is different as queer people. Campuses can foster inter-organizational affinity spaces for queer students to engage about their experiences as well.

Consider facilitating a climate study of your organization or community that explores the experiences of identities that haven't been explicitly acknowledged in your context. And utilize the information learned from these studies to do something. Though the results of these studies may very well yield data that speaks to painful experiences of marginalization amongst membership, they also can provide a foundation upon which truly inclusive practices can be built. Additionally, dialogues from within these spaces can, with consent, permeate the fraternal movement through shared knowledge, research, and presentations aimed at ways to improve the member experience.

Incentivizing Inclusion

Sororities and fraternities are part of an inherently exclusionary system. Membership requisites are often presented as necessary in order to ensure alignment with organizational purpose. I often question whether requisites actually advance an organization's aims. Practitioners must confront these realities and devise opportunities to incentivize more inclusive communities within sororities and fraternities. Perhaps the area with the greatest opportunity for change are "single-sex" or single gender policies. To be clear, my position is that there is a place for organizations meant to serve as affinity spaces built around gender. However, sororities and fraternities must investigate their current understanding of gender and commitments to dated conceptions of gender as tools of oppression. Gender is not a binary and this is perhaps one of the greatest flaws of how sorority and fraternity is conceptualized. As mentioned previously, policy changes around gender identity have quite slowly progressed and made organizations more inclusive, but there is still so much more to be done as it relates to gender diversity. This is especially important as culturally-based sororities and fraternities stand to gain so much from broadening their understanding around gender. Situating this dialogue in a different context might help individuals consider the opportunities. Discourse around the value of diversity in educational spaces are plentiful. I think of the realm of possibility where organizations can re-examine their commitments to cisgender membership and serve as incredible advocates intra-community for our trans, gender non-conforming, and non-binary siblings.

Barriers to entry are another significant area for opportunity within culturally-based sororities and fraternities. In the years that I have been a member and have advised sororities and fraternities professionally, I have lost track of the number of students whose desire to find community with peers who look and experience the world like them is shattered because of the cost of membership. First-generation and socioeconomic status is something we cannot continue to ignore. Based on my experiences, first-generation students often arrive at campuses with little conception of what the sorority and fraternity experience could afford them. A cultural aversion for recruitment within corners of the culturally-based sorority and fraternity community serve as unnecessary barriers to entry. Organizations must position themselves so that students know who they are and how to access the opportunities associated with membership. Identifying campus offices that provide support to first-generation students and partnering to provide not only access to membership but also programming and communal support is a strategy for culturally-based sororities and fraternities to utilize.

Additionally, there are plenty of conversations to be had about the cost of membership. And when organizations have these dialogues it is unsurprising that they often center their bottom line on their ability to operate. However, ignoring the intersections of socioeconomic status alongside the identities organizations proclaim a commitment to is oppressive. Members who come from lower socioeconomic statuses are not to be viewed with a deficit lens but rather as having critical perspective to inform community-focused work. There is ample opportunity to revisit dues structures and consider the role cost plays in deterring individuals from seeking membership and staying engaged. Membership should not be a decision between the medical bills you might be juggling and national/chapter dues. I've witnessed students, for instance, grapple with a decision between tuition and convention attendance.

Campuses and organizations alike must reimagine the mechanisms for supporting barrier free engagement. Develop scholarship programs in partnership with the campus alumni association or fraternal foundation. Identify grant opportunities to help reduce the cost of delivering programming and ultimately minimizing the financial burden of members. Consider tying reduced dues or increased funding support to individuals who exemplify organizational or institutional values. Culturally-based sororities and fraternities already seek to provide space for historically and contemporarily marginalized communities. It is unfathomable to me that we would cause more harm by creating precarious financial situations for members. I do not believe the benefits of membership previously identified can be realized when members are unable to be full participants in the experience.

Incentivizing inclusion may well yield creative approaches to recruitment, retention, and engagement from individuals who might have viewed the membership experience as beyond their reach. For instance, culturally-based sororities and fraternities should consider the role accessibility plays in their members' experiences. And when I reference accessibility I want to be explicit in that I'm referencing the visible and invisible disabilities members live with. Decisions about locales and venues for programs and events must consider access. Build accessibility into your organization's expectations for planning at every level. The first time I ever confronted this issue was in 2009. One of the interested gentlemen for my fraternity was deaf. We rarely considered the role of accessibility at our events and programs and now we were in a position where we would need to adapt our new member process. The hermanos who were ultimately responsible for this new member's experience framed this as an opportunity for greater inclusion rather than a challenge to be overcome. We didn't get everything right and we worked through things as they arose. It would have been much better if our national organization had considered this question well before it arrived at our doorstep. I think about our recruitment practices and all the prospective members we lost throughout the years because of our failure to be responsive to varied identities and consider the possibilities of a broadened membership.

Retention and engagement may also benefit from an incentivization of inclusion. Creating access within recruitment and new member experiences is incredibly valuable. As previously stated, practitioners must ensure members can be full participants in the experience. Two anecdotes illustrate my thinking around the issues for individuals navigating undocumented status in the U.S. and familial status as a parent or caregiver. With respect to undocumented status, I recall a dialogue a few years ago amongst members of the Latinx/o fraternal community regarding a fraternity hosting their national convention in the Dominican Republic (D.R.). Most organizations had rarely if ever left the continental United States for these functions. There was much to be said about the beauty of hosting the event in a place like the D.R. and the value added for various constituents in the organization: alumni with families, brothers who hailed from the D.R., etc. And while all of this might have been true, there was also a parallel discussion about the impact on undocumented members who wouldn't be able to travel overseas for the conference. If you add the inordinate expense of international travel, then you're certainly excluding members from the experience. My recommendations are that organizations always consider various ways of engaging which meet members where they are. At the time of writing this chapter in 2020, we are navigating a public health crisis caused by COVID-19 which has forced institutions of higher education and culturally-based sororities and fraternities to think creatively about engagement. Take the lessons we've learned about digital engagement, access, and apply them in these contexts. Consider the decision to host a function that is inaccessible to some and think about why you might choose to do so. Center the humanity of your membership in those decisions to ensure they aren't further marginalized by your operation.

Considering familial status I think back to my undergraduate experience and the challenges faced by brothers who were parents and caregivers. It is not uncommon for practitioners to operate with traditional-aged college students who fit a particular social profile in mind. Often the experiences that are offered are geared toward traditional-aged college students, those who enroll immediately after high school, attend full-time, and maintain little to no responsibility outside of their academic experience. This leaves other students to wonder whether these experiences are available to them. Knowing the diversity of student bodies, it is a disservice to operate from this frame of mind. Being a parent can impose different demands on a student's time for engagement opportunities. Having to serve as a caregiver or provider within your household might also serve as a barrier to involvement. An area for development is the role that culturally-based sororities and fraternities can play in creating community for "non-traditional" students. If culturally-based sororities and fraternities are meant to serve as agents of community uplift, we need to examine who we're leaving out of the work that we're doing. Consider programs that partner members or alumni who have similar experiences. Create initiatives that specifically speak to the unique circumstances these members might be navigating. I recently participated in a program my fraternity hosted for members who have aging parents they are needing to care for. Participating in the event was a reminder of the value added of my membership and why I want to continue my engagement.

Building Out from Oversights of Power

It may seem overwhelming to think through how to provide support to every member and meet all of their needs. And that's the difficult work that's absolutely necessary to transform what culturally-based sororities, fraternities, and those who support them mean when we say we are about community. And we do not have to do this work in a vacuum. Our peers may have already done the work of attending to one identity while we focused on the other. What would a mutually beneficial partnership between my fraternity and Delta Lambda Phi look like, where Lambda Upsilon Lambda shared perspective on Latinidad and Delta Lambda Phi shared perspective on gender diversity and sexuality? Each organization can take ownership of their position and utilize their power to close the gap in knowledge.

Taking a cue from Crenshaw, who named the failures of the feminist and antiracist movements to account for the totality of Black women, thereby making them vulnerable and erasing their experiences at the intersection, culturally-based sororities and fraternities can make the effort to close the gaps. Culturally-based sororities, fraternities, and campuses can partner to sharpen each other's understanding of this work. A thorough examination of practices to identify how we might be actively contributing to marginalization would go a long way in illuminating transformative approaches to this work. And it's worth reminding folx that SFL often reinforces societal norms and marginalizations simply by maintaining the status quo. When volunteers, advisors, and staff assess their work they should take stock of where they can affect change (Martin & Garcia, 2020). You may not be in the position to dissolve an organization's commitment to a "single-sex" or single gender experience. That said, you can expand the universe for how the organization might define those things.

Conclusion

A professional regret of mine is having missed ACPA's 2020 Convention and the opportunity to hear from Kimberlé Crenshaw during the opening keynote for the convention. Though I was not able to attend there was so much I learned from colleagues who graciously shared what they were learning via Twitter and blogs post-convention, special thanks to Alex C. Lange and Dr. Sonja Ardoin specifically. What Crenshaw offered was a reeducation of sorts, the opportunity for folx to reorient themselves and their usage of intersectionality. It was a challenge to those within higher education who might have misappropriated intersectionality and reduced it to a buzzword in the spaces within which we utilized her concept. She reminded us that our identities interface with systems and power structures. She illuminated the vulnerabilities faced by Black women particularly when we fail to examine compounded marginalization. The summary that Crenshaw provided of her keynote was that "Intersectionality is … 1. prism for understanding 2. analysis for intervention 3. cautionary tale against intersectional failures"

(Ardoin, 2020a). It is incumbent upon culturally-based sororities, fraternities, and campus professionals who support them to apply her concepts in ways that advance the existence of intersectional institutions.

Questions for Reflection

- Consider the identities that have historically anchored your organization in its vision, mission, and operations. Utilize Crenshaw's recommendation of an intersectional audit to determine areas of opportunity for and growth towards inclusion.
- What would expert engagement and partnership toward assessment of equitable practices look like within your organization/institution?
- Where might your organization be able to leverage positional power/social capital to engage peers in this work?

References

Abes, E. S., Jones, S. R., & McEwen, M. K. (2007). Reconceptualizing the mode of multiple dimensions of identity: The role of meaning-making capacity in the construction of multiple identities. *Journal of College Student Development, 48*, 1–22.

Ardoin, S. [@SonjaArdoin]. (2020a, March 2). @sandylocks offers a summary of her keynote: Intersectionality is … 1. prism for understanding 2. analysis for intervention 3. cautionary tale against intersectional failures [Tweet]. Twitter. https://twitter.com/SonjaArdoin/status/1234619530632101892

Ardoin, S. [@SonjaArdoin]. (2020b, Mar 2). @sandylocks recommends #HigherEd institutions do the following: -Perform intersectional audit -Do an intersectional assessment of "inclusionary" practices -Incentivize more robust inclusion [Tweet]. Twitter. https://twitter.com/SonjaArdoin/status/1234620732623278080

Connell, C. (2016). Contesting racialized discourses of homophobia. *Sociological Forum, 31*(3), 599-618.

Crenshaw, K. (1989). Demarginalizing the intersection of race and sex: A Black feminist critique of antidiscrimination doctrine, feminist theory, and antiracist politics. *University of Chicago Legal Forum, 140*, 139–167.

Crenshaw, K. (1991). Mapping the margins: Intersectionality, identity politics, and violence against Women of Color. *Stanford Law Review, 43*, 1241–1299.

Duran, A. & Garcia, C. E. (2020). Post-undergraduate narratives of Queer Men of Color's resistance in culturally based fraternities. *Journal of Student Affairs Research and Practice*. Advance online publication. https://doi.org/10.1080/19496591.2020.1772083

Garcia, C. E. (2020). Belonging in a predominantly White institution: The role of membership in Latina/o sororities and fraternities. *Journal of Diversity in Higher Education, 13*(2), 181–193.

Garcia, C. E., & Shirley, Z. E. (2019). Race and privilege in fraternity and sorority life: Considerations for practice and research. In P. Sasso, P. Biddix, & M. Miranda (Eds.), *Foundations, research, and assessment of fraternities and sororities* (pp. 155–163). Sterling, VA: Stylus.

Guardia, J. R, & Evans, N. J. (2008). Factors influencing the ethnic identity development of Latino fraternity members at a Hispanic serving institution. *Journal of College Student Development, 49*(3), 163–181.

Jones, S. R., & McEwen, M. K. (2000). A conceptual model of multiple dimensions of identity. *Journal of College Student Development, 41*(4), 405–414.

Literte, P. E. & Hodge, C. (2012). Sisterhood and sexuality: Attitudes about homosexuality among members of historically Black sororities. *Journal of African American Studies, 16*(4), 674–699.

Martin, T. L., & Garcia, K. (2020, February 19). Dismantling systemic organizational oppression: Making institutional commitment to culturally based fraternities & sororities at predominantly white institutions. *Essentials E-Publication, I(01)*. https://cdn.ymaws.com/www.afa1976.org/resource/collection/BE790C86-9389-45C7-A4EC-85BC326E59F3/MartinGarcia_February2020.pdf.

McCready, A. & Radimer, S. (2019). Gender performativity in college social fraternities and sororities. In P. Sasso, P. Biddix, & M. Miranda (Eds.), *Supporting fraternities and sororities in the contemporary era* (pp. 151–160). Sterling, VA: Stylus.

Museus, S. D., Ledesma, M. C., & Parker, T. L. (2015). Racism and racial equity in higher education. *ASHE Higher Education Report, 42*(1), 1–112.

Torres, V., Jones, S. R., & Renn, K. A. (2009). Identity development theories in student affairs: Origins, current status, and new approaches. *Journal of College Student Development, 50*(6), 558–573.

Vought, R. T. (2020, September 28). *Ending employee trainings that use divisive propaganda to undermine the principle of fair and equal treatment for all*. https://www.whitehouse.gov/wp-content/uploads/2020/09/M-20-37.pdf

Wright, B. (1988). "For the children of the infidels"?: American Indian education in the colonial colleges. *American Indian Culture and Research Journal, 12*(3), 1–14.

CHAPTER TEN

Addressing Hazing Practices within Culturally-Based Sororities and Fraternities

JENNY NIRH AND MARCOS GUZMAN

Although hazing is a problem across all facets of educational institutions, and should be addressed widely, there is an opportunity to tailor anti-hazing work to have a larger impact on culturally-based sororities and fraternities. Hazing activities are against institutional policy at all higher education institutions, and depending on the state, there are additional laws or statutes surrounding hazing. Yet, hazing continues to be consistent on university campuses, and is pervasive in and detrimental to all sororities and fraternities (Allen & Madden, 2008). Culturally-based sororities and fraternities in particular exist to increase belonging, and encourage equality, unity, and the empowerment of members of their community (Giacalone, 2018). The presence of hazing activities within culturally-based sororities and fraternities have the opposite impact, as hazing creates unequal power dynamics, disenfranchises members, and can have a negative impact on both physical and mental health. To address hazing practices within these groups, it is important to understand the history and prevalence of hazing both in higher education and sororities and fraternities.

Sororities and fraternities have existed within higher education since 1776, as secret societies for students to gather outside of the classroom setting (Sasso & DeVitis, 2015). Beginning in the mid-19th century, institutions began to see the first instances of hazing within fraternities (Finkel, 2002). In English secondary schools, upperclassmen would force underclassmen to act as their servants, also known as "fagging," and in some cases newcomers would be placed in a dangerous and harmful situation (Finkel, 2002). One deadly incident occurred when a student was abandoned and forced to find his way back home, but tragically fell into a gorge and was killed (Finkel, 2002). As the sorority and fraternity community grew and developed to include culturally-based organizations, hazing within the community also grew in parallel. Though many culturally-based sororities and fraternities developed later than National Panhellenic Conference (NPC) and most North American Interfraternity Conference (NIC) groups, and individual chapters of the organizations are often smaller, there is still a significant hazing problem within the organizations.

Hazing has many forms, and can include a variety of activities along a spectrum, from embarrassing to life threatening. Hazing commonly consists of personal servitude, or more dangerous activities like forced consumption of alcohol or toxic substances, beatings, skin brandings, and simulated or real sex acts. Hazing activities regularly include physical and psychological traumas for participants (Allen & Madden, 2008; Finkel, 2002). Occasionally hazing activities escalate beyond harmful; there have been more than 100 deaths related to hazing from 1970 to present, and at least one per year from 1970 to 2019 (Nuwer, 2020).

In the past 20 years there has been increased focus on hazing prevention in the media and on college campuses (Pike, 2000). There are now multiple groups like Stophazing.org, and Hazingprevention.org that promote hazing education at a national level, and large-scale research on hazing has occurred. Programs dedicated to hazing prevention exist on college campuses and within national organizations; however, hazing education must continue to improve. This chapter will focus on hazing and hazing education with a specific focus on culturally-based organizations. We begin with a brief history of hazing, information on the intersection of hazing and identity, sense of belonging, and the Hazing Prevention Framework. Additionally, ideas are presented surrounding hazing education and reflection questions for practitioners.

Positionality Statement

We, the authors of this chapter, are members of an NPC and NIC group respectively. We acknowledge our viewpoints on the sorority and fraternity community were developed through the lens of our predominantly white organizations. We have worked at institutions within the Southwest United States with strong MGC communities, and have more than 25 years combined experience working with sororities and fraternities. Our experience and knowledge come from directly advising and supporting culturally-based organizations over those 25 years and participating in countless hazing investigations and organizational reviews. We each attended public higher education institutions in the states of New Mexico, Arizona, and Texas. We have been involved with our own organizations at both the campus and national organization level, and are passionate about hazing education and prevention.

Literature Review

This section will highlight the academic literature around the history of hazing, the intersections of hazing and social identity, and how hazing plays a role in a student's sense of belonging. This literature review will aid practitioners in understanding hazing as it specifically relates to culturally-based sororities and fraternities.

Definition of Hazing & Brief History

Joining a student organization can be one of the most exciting, yet scary, things to do as a college student. Individuals seek out various organizations, such as club sports, business and professional clubs, student government, marching band, sororities and fraternities, cultural groups, and more. A student joining a co-curricular campus organization is beneficial to the mission of the college or university, as it increases sense of belonging, retention, and persistence (Biddix, Singer, & Aslinger, 2018; Sims, Luebsen, & Guggiari-Peel, 2017). However, some students face interpersonal violence as they seek to attain that membership. Hazing, which is a form of interpersonal violence, is an all too real experience for some students (Allan & Madden, 2012). Many institutions have similar definitions of hazing, but the word is commonly defined as any activity that someone must do to gain membership that humiliates, degrades, or places them in a potentially harmful situation, regardless of their willingness to participate (Allan & Madden, 2012; Allan, Payne, & Kerschner, 2019). Hazing activities can lead to irreversible brain and organ damage, burns, suffocation or aspiration, emotional and psychological harm, sexual misconduct, and death (Finkel, 2002). Perpetrators of hazing generally use bullying tactics such as aggressive behavior, which is repeated over time, to frighten or cause discomfort (Allan & Madden, 2012).

However, the term "hazing" can have a different meaning to different people, especially perpetrators and victims of hazing. Student affairs professionals, such as a conduct officer, may define hazing differently than an individual being hazed (Salinas & Boettcher, 2018). Often, students can identify that they engaged in specific activities that would be considered hazing, but then do not recognize that they "were hazed" (Allan & Madden, 2012). The cognitive dissonance between participating in hazing activities but not ascribing to the label of hazing can be in part attributed to the word hazing to many different definitions (Allan & Madden, 2012). Usually students attribute hazing to more extreme practices such as being paddled and beaten or made to perform sexual acts (Allan & Madden, 2012). In that same context, you might hear hazing defined differently between culturally-based and historically white Greek organizations. It is important to establish a common language amongst students when talking about the definition of hazing.

Hazing is a term to describe certain actions that one person or group perpetrates against an individual trying to become a member in their group. The historical context of those actions can be traced back to the 1600s when first-year students of German Protestant universities were oppressed and tormented by elder students (Finkel, 2002). The term *Pennalism* was used to describe how underclassmen were maliciously groomed by upperclassmen and university administrators as a requirement for graduation (Finkel, 2002). Serious injuries and deaths occurred, during the 18th and 19th centuries, when upperclassmen would bully underclassmen into servitude. In the 20th century, no longer called *Pennalism* but instead hazing, incoming students had to earn respect to join a student organization (Finkel, 2002). Hazing has become a habit within organizations. Salinas and Boettcher (2018) began to use the phrase "hazing as a habit" rather than tradition. They posit that traditions are often steeped in history, are positive, and serve to enhance the organizations. Habits, on the other hand, do not have the same positive connotations as traditions.

In 1994, The *Chronicle of Higher Education* highlighted four major hazing cases involving Black Greek-Letter Organizations (BGLOs). After the death of Michael Davis, a first-year student who was pledging Kappa Alpha Psi Fraternity, Inc. at Southeast Missouri State, a number of Black students shared their experiences of being hazed at similar institutions (Shea, 1994). Despite bad press coverage, hazing continued in many BGLOs (Kimbrough, 2003). According to Shea (1994), BGLOs engaged in some of the most highly publicized hazing incidents for that time period; however, they were not alone. Lambda Theta Phi, a Latino fraternity, was removed the same year from Rutgers University for harming pledges. In 2017, the *New York Times* published the story of Michael Deng who died as a result of joining an Asian American fraternity (Kang, 2017). Additionally, in 2017, Hermandad de Sigma Iota Alpha, which is a Latina Greek-letter intercollegiate and independent sorority, was suspended from William & Mary for violating the university's hazing policy (Fearing, 2017). Sigma Delta Lambda, which was the first Latina-based sorority at Southwest Texas State, was suspended for 4 years after the organization was found responsible for hazing (Texas State University, 2020). We know hazing occurs across a wide range of student groups, and culturally-based organizations are not immune (Allan & Madden, 2008). There is limited data to show the prevalence and hazing rates within culturally-based sororities and fraternities (Hughey, 2010). Yet we know the same hazing practices of predominantly white Greek organizations are being reproduced in culturally-based organizations.

Hazing and Identity

Culturally-based sororities and fraternities are excellent organizations to recognize and value a student's minoritized identity and culture. Sisterhood/brotherhood/siblinghood is an invaluable experience that Greek-letter organizations provide. Garcia (2019) found during a study of membership and belonging in Latina/o sororities and fraternities that participant's sense of belonging was greatly tied to the sisterhood and brotherhood experience. Joining a sorority or fraternity is about building lifelong relationships that extend beyond ordinary friendships.

When working with students, it is necessary to reflect on their various social identities, and more specifically the identities of those in a culturally-based sorority or fraternity. Social identities such as race, sexual orientation, ethnicity, social class, and other salient identities inform how people view ourselves in relation to others (Turner & Oakes, 1986). In the book, *Brothers and Sisters: Diversity in College Fraternities and Sororities*, author King-To Yeung (2009) described how members of a Delta Lambda Phi chapter viewed hazing. Delta Lambda Phi is an international fraternity founded by gay men, for all men (Yeung, 2009). In the United States, gay men face violence and discrimination because of their sexual orientation. Due to this, members interviewed by Yeung (2009) indicated they felt hazing was inappropriate within any student group, but especially in a gay fraternity because gay men have been always been hazed by society. Similarly, Black students enrolled at predominantly white institutions have always faced institutional racism, disenfranchisement, and exclusion (Hughey, 2010; Person & Christensen, 1996). In 1906, Alpha Phi Alpha Fraternity, Inc. was founded at Cornell University and according to the organization's official website was "the first intercollegiate Greek-letter fraternity established for African American Men" (Alpha Phi Alpha, 2018, para. 1). Since then, eight additional historically Black Greek organizations within the National Pan-Hellenic Council (NPHC) have formed and persisted. About 10 years after the beginning of NPHC sororities and fraternities, hazing behaviors began to emerge within the organizations

(Kimbrough, 2003). NPHC organizations were founded to address issues of race and provide advocacy for the Black student community. These same organizations engaged in violent hazing rituals. It is important to understand minoritized populations have always experienced interpersonal violence from society, and to understand this connection between societal violence and discrimination and hazing.

Sense of Belonging & Hazing

Students often feel uncertain about their potential to succeed and their ability to belong in a university setting (Strayhorn, 2019). Research on sense of belonging can provide insight on the relationship between hazing and the need to belong, as well as how belonging might impact culturally-based sororities and fraternities. According to Strayhorn (2019):

> In terms of college, sense of belonging refers to students' perceived social support on campus, a feeling or sensation of connectedness, and the experience of mattering or feeling cared about, accepted, respected, valued by, and important to the campus community or others on campus such as faculty, staff, and peers. (p. 4)

Strayhorn (2015) emphasized that belonging is fluid, and can change at different stages or in different situations, and that belonging can determine behavior. Research also shows that belonging is a basic need (Maslow, 1943; Strayhorn, 2019), which is of increased importance in environments where certain individuals are less likely to feel welcomed, supported or valued. Students like People of Color and members of the Lesbian, Gay, Bisexual, Transgender, and Queer (LGBTQ) community feel less of a sense of belonging in the college environment.

The need to belong is a basic need that can drive actions and behaviors (Strayhorn, 2019). As students search for the need to belong, they can look to sororities and fraternities to satisfy that need. When practitioners consider the need for a sense of belonging, and how it can drive human behavior, it should be easier to understand why students are willing to participate in hazing activities in order to belong (Nuwer, 2018; Tingely et al., 2018). Culturally-based sororities and fraternities emerged because of the racist, discriminatory, or exclusionary practices of society, institutions of higher education, and historically white sororities and fraternities (Giacalone, 2018). Students of Color and other minoritized individuals were excluded from all facets of campus life including academic and social activities. Forming their own organizations based on their identities allowed them to create groups that would uplift their members, and create a safer environment within hostile institutions. Similarly, women's culturally-based organizations were formed to help women navigate both gender and racial oppression. Culturally-based organizations were created as groups that validated their members and helped them feel that they belonged in oppressive higher education institutions. Organizations served as a safe space for students as they worked to persevere in institutions that perpetuated systems of oppression such as racism, sexism, and heterosexism.

Joining a culturally-based sorority or fraternity can create a sense of belonging different and stronger than other campus organizations, but how does the need to create belonging impact hazing in those organizations? Research has shown that white students believe belonging is found in creating fun, social experiences, while Students of Color and LGBTQ individuals want to develop stronger, deeper relationships and desire to feel secure and safe to cultivate a sense of belonging (Giacalone, 2018). If LGTBQ students and Students of Color, who are likely the students joining culturally-based sororities and fraternities, need to feel safe and secure in order to belong, it directly harms sense of belonging to engage in hazing activities. Hazing practices do not empower, validate, or create safety and security for organizational members. Members may justify the actions by ascribing them to a larger good like earning respect, or showing pride, but they do not serve those purposes in reality (Allan, Kerschner, & Payne, 2019). Hazing practices continue to humiliate and degrade students who are already often marginalized by the institutions they attend.

The Hazing Prevention Framework

The Hazing Prevention Framework was developed by researchers associated with the Hazing Prevention Consortium. They recognized that a research-informed approach to hazing prevention was necessary to move the needle in terms of hazing on college campuses. To this point, hazing education is often reactionary. Education and prevention often fall completely within the realm of sorority and fraternity life (SFL), and hazing is one of many topics that is necessary for staff to address. There is also limited data on research-based approaches to hazing prevention (Allan et al., 2018), and more specifically little data highlights culturally-based organizations. To better understand hazing on college campuses, researchers formed the Hazing Prevention Coalition, a group of eight higher education institutions that committed to research on the topic over a period of 3 years. Their research, and research of others, showed that students believe that hazing can create group cohesion, but the data does not support that (Allan et al., 2019; Campo, Poulos, & Sipple, 2005). Additionally, the research conducted through the Hazing Prevention Coalition showed that there are differences in perception of hazing by race, while there are not statistically significant distinctions in frequency or prevalence of hazing by race. Students of Color were more likely than white students to agree with positive statements related to hazing prevention including:

- Hazing is not an effective way to create bonding.
- There is no good reason to haze new members of a group.
- Hazing is a problem on this campus.
- Hazing is not an effective way to initiate new members.
- I would be more likely to report hazing if I could do it anonymously.
- I would be more likely to report hazing if I thought it would make a difference. (Allan et al., 2019, p. 41)

Students of Color reported limiting interactions with others, drinking games, personal servitude, verbal abuse, and being awoken at night as the most common hazing activities they experienced (Allan et al., 2019). However, this research does not separate the experiences of students in MGC or NPHC groups from those in NPC and IFC. What the research does tell us is that Students of Color and LGBTQ students are exposed to a similar type and frequency of hazing activities and do need to engage in regular hazing education.

Innovations in Practice

The chapter has discussed what hazing is, and how hazing intersects with identity, belonging, oppression and exclusivity within the sorority and fraternity community. How can those frameworks be used to create hazing education and prevention that is centered in advancing culturally-based organizations? How can we examine and use the underlying causes of hazing, to create change within the community without focusing on the hazing acts? The following section will provide anti-hazing programmatic ideas, which include addressing traditional gender roles, focusing on identity/power/privilege, and using a research-based framework to plan prevention activities.

Traditional Gender Roles

Many hazing practices are reinforced through traditional gender roles (Johnson & Holman, 2009). For example, someone joining a fraternity must prove their masculinity by partaking in dangerous acts (Syrett, 2009), having multiple sexual relationships, or being willing to tolerate violence. Another example of hazing reinforced through traditional gender roles is when an individual joining a sorority is coerced to look a certain way (perhaps more feminine), expected to have a high social standing with fraternity men, or made to work out for an excessive amount of time. Individuals not complying with gender norms are embarrassed and demeaned in front of their peers. To focus on the root cause rather than solely the action can not only combat hazing but other toxic activities and ideals within the organization.

Hegemonic masculine behaviors, such as being dominant or forceful, fearless, strong and successful, are expectations taught by men and reinforced through society (Porter, 2017). This type of behavior is often prominent within fraternities (Seabrook, Ward, & Giaccardi, 2018). We have witnessed culturally-based fraternities rely heavily on traditional gender roles in their hazing practices. There is nothing wrong with having pride or being self-reliant, but if an organization is using hazing practices to create a sense of being "manly" then it becomes problematic. In many cultures, being manly means tolerating violence: "Be A Man!" "Don't Cry, Only Girls Cry." Take this mindset and flip it on its side. What does it mean to be a man? What does it mean to be a fraternity man? Or better, what does it mean to be an Asian/Hispanic/Black/Indigenous fraternity man? Do our actions towards ourselves and others create a world where all human beings are loving and respectful? Addressing traditional gender roles is a creative way of addressing hazing. Culturally-based sorority and fraternity members can benefit from a holistic approach to addressing traditional gender roles.

At the University of Arizona, the SFL Office partnered with a southern Arizona domestic violence non-profit and "A Call to Men," which is a violence prevention organization that addresses issues of manhood, male socialization, and prevention of violence against all women and girls. Together, they hosted a half-day interactive workshop with 100 fraternity men, which included culturally-based fraternities. The goal was simple: to educate fraternity men on the importance of living by the principles of healthy and respectful manhood. Though hazing prevention was not the goal, each participant addressed the growing interpersonal violence that occurs within the sorority and fraternity community. Participants discussed how men bully other men, especially during new member periods, and shared ideas of how to put a stop to it. This program was able to address men's issues while incorporating race, culture, and creed. Staff may consider partnering with other campus departments that already have masculinity initiatives in place (no need to recreate the wheel). How do your culturally-based SFL members fit in these initiatives? Initiatives can focus on the unique dynamics related to masculinities and how they intersect with other identities (e.g., race, first-generation status, and low-income backgrounds). Professional staff should focus on challenging normative gender roles at multiple levels of engagement.

The same deconstruction of traditional gender roles can be done for culturally-based sororities. Culturally-based sororities were created to empower Women of Color and women with other minoritized identities. These sororities, while rooted in feminism, have a mission of addressing and promoting women's rights and often issues of race, therefore it is counterproductive for these organizations to engage in hazing. In a personal blog titled "Nonsense & Shenanigans," Monica Snell (2017) shared her story of being hazed after she joined Sigma Lambda Gamma. Sigma Lambda Gamma is a multicultural sorority founded in 1990 by five collegiate women who wanted an organization to empower Latina women. During her new member process, Monica provided details about what she experienced during "beauty week." She was expected to wear all black, including undergarments, at a specific time of the day, and was not allowed to wash said clothes, wear jewelry, eat fast food, put on deodorant or perfume, or talk to men (Snell, 2017). So, how should SFL professionals address this type of behavior?

A one-day symposium, similar to the example above, could include a keynote speaker who is a Woman of Color on the topic of empowerment and small group sessions to discuss the importance of positive sisterhood relations. Participants could discuss the negative effects hazing has on the development of sisterhood and how cultural expectations of women play a role in their sorority experience. These types of initiatives can educate students about how sorority hazing replicates the same unequal power that exists between men, women, and those who identify with other genders. Today's college women, especially of Women of Color, are challenging existing gender inequalities, and culturally-based sororities should be used to perpetuate this movement. Hazing prevention needs to include addressing the root cause of the behavior. Traditional gender roles are the underlying issue of many hazing practices. Similar to pulling weeds in a yard, if you don't pull the entire root out of the ground, it will only be a matter of time before it reemerges.

Take the opportunity to address traditional gender roles and challenge your culturally-based groups to redefine what it means to be a culturally-based sorority or fraternity member. How does a student's view on traditional gender roles influence the way they treat each other?

Focus on Identity/Power/Privilege

Power and privilege operate in almost every aspect of a college student's life. A professor has power over their classroom. Student social circles are usually controlled by the ones who have the most privilege. Sororities and fraternities have systems in place that put certain students in positions of power, and a new member is less likely to have any power until they "prove" themselves worthy. So how do you begin to address these dynamics in culturally-based SFL organizations? Student affairs practitioners must help build systems of empowerment for those who hold less power and privilege and have accountability put in place for those that hold more (Parker, 2009).

Students must be reminded that power and privilege, among other things, were key elements to keeping Students of Color out of NPC sororities and IFC fraternities. Culturally-based sororities and fraternities, like historically white organizations, benefit from a historical understanding. Implement a new member education specifically for culturally-based organizations. Professionals should create educational experiences that cover the historical overview of race and racism in SFL and how the common elements of hazing in culturally-based Greek organizations are forms of power and privilege. Additionally, it is important to provide educational opportunities for new members to understand and recognize different forms of hazing. These opportunities can help students realize the systems of oppression they face in their everyday lives should not exist in the organization that was designed to build lifelong community. Students should also learn that hazing is a reproduction of oppression. Practitioners and advisors can ask students to identify ways they have been marginalized by a group, or the institution, and how they may be replicating those acts within the organization through their new member or intake processes.

Use a Research-Based Framework to Plan Prevention Activities

After completion of the research within the Hazing Prevention Coalition, Allan and colleagues (2018) created the Hazing Prevention Framework using their research along with additional public health prevention frameworks as guides. The themes of the Hazing Prevention Framework are: commitment, capacity, assessment, planning, evaluation, sustainability, cultural competence, and implementation (Allan et al., 2018). Staffing, time, and capacity are often limited for those who work with sororities and fraternities at both the campus and organization level. Those limitations may seem like a barrier to creating a strategic approach using the Hazing Prevention Framework, but many themes and strategies in the framework can increase capacity and institutionalize hazing prevention. Using the Hazing Prevention Framework can assist in creating an intentional, strategic hazing prevention effort that will impact campus hazing long-term.

Commitment

Hazing prevention should begin with clear policies and top down messaging from campus leaders and administrators regarding hazing. Hazing is a campus wide issue that can affect a student's sense of belonging, academics, and their retention or persistence at an institution, which means all prevention work should not only come from and rely on the SFL professionals. However, SFL professionals can take the lead and provide institutional administrative leadership with hazing information, data, research and information on campus initiatives. Depending on the campus, this could be campus health, student affairs, retention or student success focused staff. Through assessment, learn about student's connections to campus and work with those campus leaders to promote messaging around hazing. If students have strong connections to faith-based campus programs, cultural resource centers, specific academic departments, or identity-based groups, work with those groups to share the same messaging. After research showed that students believed that The University of Arizona staff and faculty knew about and condoned hazing behaviors, anti-hazing placards were created (Nirh & Ives, 2015). The placards, placed in staff and faculty offices displayed the institutional message on hazing, indicated the owner had participated in institutional hazing education and did not condone hazing. These placards were a visible signal to students that there was a campus commitment to hazing prevention and that they could report activities to these staff or faculty.

Capacity

Create sustained collaboration with areas on campus, and bring together a larger group that can discuss and work together to create change. This group should have members from cultural or identity centers, student government, student activities, band, and both club and NCAA athletics. As the focus here is on centering the experiences of culturally-based sororities and fraternities, include alumni from the culturally-based organizations, and staff representing cultural resource centers or organizations on campus if possible. However, we know that Staff of Color are often asked to engage in an unsustainable amount of service to higher education institutions (June, 2015; Social Sciences Feminist Network Research Interest Group, 2017). To show institutional commitment to hazing education and prevention, and to promote diverse voices within the group, offer some compensation to account for the time being asked of members.

Assessment and Planning

Create proactive, multi-faceted activities, and plans based on research and assessment in a way that allows for both understanding the big picture and a focus on culturally-based groups. Staff may be creating programming based on reactions to *known* hazing incidents on campus. Create assessments that look at what is happening, and determine what motivations for hazing may be in play. Assessment will also allow for programs tailored more toward the real needs of the culturally-based groups and help staff develop a real understanding of what the larger issues might be. Create proactive, multi-faceted activities, and plans based on research and assessment. It can be difficult for SFL professionals or organizational staff to find the time amidst all the other pieces demanding attention. Determine from research, assessment and personal experience how to best address hazing on the campus. After reviewing findings from participation in the first Hazing Prevention Consortium Cohort, The University of Arizona Hazing Prevention Coalition with leadership from the SFL staff created staff, faculty, and family outreach campaigns. The research showed that many staff, faculty, and family members knew about hazing activities on campus as they occurred. Appealing to staff and faculty as mandatory reporters, and to student support systems or parents, the hazing prevention coalition was able to create programming that increased the collective knowledge around hazing. Determine what works best for the group or campus, and where the most impact would occur instead of simply repeating past programs or activities. Hazing education needs to occur regularly each year, not only during National Hazing Prevention Week. Culturally-based organization intake or recruitment processes may not be occurring on the same timeline as Panhellenic or Interfraternity Council organizations, so education should be done during the new members cycles for all councils.

Evaluation, Implementation and Sustainability

Examine the effectiveness of programming. Determine whether learning outcomes are being met and if programming is resonating with the appropriate audience, in this case the culturally-based sorority and fraternity community. Advocate for hazing education each semester or quarter, and implement a multi-faceted approach that looks at different community members, alumni, cultural center staff, families and supporters as well as different modes of communication. For example, are anti-hazing materials for family or student supporters available in multiple languages? Create a collaborative group that can share education successes, evaluations and assessments across campus. Anti-hazing education and conversations need to occur outside of just hazing prevention week, and stay on the education and prevention agenda of the institution and within culturally-based organizations. Many students are only experiencing, at the most 4 years, within a sorority or fraternity; therefore, the groups can lose knowledge and adopt hazing practices very quickly.

Cultural Competence

Understand the landscape of the institution and the organizations and work toward being educated on issues impacting students in culturally-based organizations. It is important to acknowledge that campus-based staff, according to the Association of Fraternity/Sorority Advisors (AFA) are 73% white, and work in the field an average of 3.3 years (AFA, 2016). This means the same staff are likely not present to see students from their first semester through the entirety of their college experience. It may be challenging for offices with high turnover and predominately white staff to build and maintain the strong relationships and cultural competence needed to engage culturally-based groups on the topic of hazing. It takes time and trust to have productive conversations about topics like hazing which are often cloaked in secrecy. When using a framework that emphasizes greater cultural competence, hazing education needs to be centered around the experiences of culturally-based groups. Working with these students should consider and acknowledge how activities like personal servitude, verbal abuse, and limiting interactions with others, mimic racist and exclusionary behaviors. Gaining cultural competence can also help adequately address how hazing behaviors are impacted by the need to feel a sense of belonging in predominantly white institutions, or within the sorority and fraternity system.

Conclusion

Hazing in sororities and fraternities corrupts the purpose and value of the organizations. Through a research-based approach centered in the experiences of culturally-based sororities and fraternities, proactive and strategic education can create positive change. Utilizing frameworks related to identities, historical and contemporary forms of oppression, as well as exclusivity can provide a different lens to why hazing is antithetical to the mission of organizations. Strong, healthy, culturally-based sororities and fraternities serve an invaluable role in sense of belonging for students, can empower members, and help them succeed in higher education.

Questions for Reflection

- How can hazing prevention education be centered around the experiences of members of culturally-based organizations?
- Who can practitioners collaborate with to support hazing prevention and education?

- How can practitioners help culturally-based sororities and fraternities create a deeper sense of belonging within their membership?
- How does addressing hazing practices within culturally-based sororities and fraternities differ from Panhellenic or Interfraternity Council organizations? What does anti-hazing support look like for culturally-based sororities and fraternities?

References

Alpha Phi Alpha. (2018, September 24). *Our history.* https://apa1906.net/our-history/

Allan, E. J., Kerschner, D., & Payne, J. M. (2019). College student hazing experiences, attitudes, and perceptions: Implications for prevention. *Journal of Student Affairs Research and Practice, 56*(1), 32–48.

Allan, E. J., & Madden, M. (2008). *Hazing in view: College students at risk.* University of Maine, College of Education and Human Development. https://www.stophazing.org/wp-content/uploads/2014/06/hazing_in_view_web1.pdf

Allan, E. J., & Madden, M. (2012). The nature and extent of college student hazing. *International Journal of Adolescent Medicine and Health, 24*(1), 83–90.

Allan, E. J., Payne, J. M., & Kerschner, D. (2018). Transforming the culture of hazing: A research-based hazing prevention framework. *Journal of Student Affairs Research and Practice, 55*(4), 1–14.

Association of Fraternity/Sorority Advisors. (2016). *The Association of Fraternity/Sorority Advisors membership: What we know about our members and why it matters.* https://cdn.ymaws.com/www.afa1976.org/resource/resmgr/association_business/2016MembershipReport.pdf

Biddix, J. P., Singer, K. I., & Aslinger, E. (2018). First-year retention and National Panhellenic Conference sorority membership: A multi-institutional study. *Journal of College Student Retention: Research, Theory & Practice, 20*(2), 236–252.

Campo, S., Poulos, G., & Sipple, J. W. (2005). Prevalence and profiling: Hazing among college students and points of intervention. *American Journal of Health Behavior, 29*(2), 137–149.

Fearing, S. (2017, December 07). William & Mary sorority suspended for hazing, socially isolating new members. *Wydaily.* https://wydaily.com/local-news/2017/11/30/william-mary-sorority-suspended-for-hazing-socially-isolating-new-members-nws/

Finkel, M. (2002). Traumatic injuries caused by hazing practices. *American Journal of Emergency Medicine, 20*(3), 228–233.

Garcia, C. E. (2019). Belonging in a predominantly White institution: The role of membership in Latina/o sororities and fraternities. *Journal of Diversity in Higher Education.* Advance online publication. https://doi.org/10.1037/dhe0000126

Giacalone, M. D. (2018). A review of sense of belonging for LGB fraternity and sorority members: Recommendations for research and practice. *Journal of Student Affairs, 27,* 93–110

Hughey, M. W. (2010). A paradox of participation: Nonwhites in white sororities and fraternities. *Social Problems, 57*(4), 653–679.

Johnson, J., & Holman, M. (2009). Gender and hazing. *Journal of Physical Education, Recreation & Dance, 80*(5), 6–9.

June, A. W. (2015, November 8). The invisible labor of minority professors. *The Chronicle of Higher Education*. https://www.chronicle.com/article/the-invisible-labor-of-minority-professors/

Kang, J. C. (2017, August 9). What a fraternity hazing death revealed about the painful search for an Asian-American identity. *New York Times*. https://www.nytimes.com/2017/08/09/magazine/what-a-fraternity-hazing-death-revealed-about-the-painful-search-for-an-asian-american-identity.html

Kimbrough, W. M. (2003). *Black Greek 101: The culture, customs, and challenges of Black fraternities and sororities*. Vancouver, British Columbia, Canada: Fairleigh Dickinson University Press.

Maslow, A. H. (1943). A theory of human motivation. *Psychological Review, 50*(4), 370–396.

Nirh, J. & Ives. J. (2015, June 11–12). *The University of Arizona* [Conference Presentation]. The Hazing Prevention Consortium Summit. Orono, ME, United States.

Nuwer, H. (2018). *Hazing: Destroying young lives*. Bloomington, IN: Indiana University Press.

Nuwer, H. (2020). Hazing deaths database. *Hank Nuwer's Hazing Scholarship Site*. hanknuwer.com.

Parker, L. (2009). Disrupting power and privilege in couples therapy. *Clinical Social Work Journal, 37*, 248–255.

Person, D. R., & Christensen, M. C. (1996). Understanding Black student culture and Black student retention. *NASPA Journal, 34*(1), 47–56.

Pike, G. R. (2000). The influence of fraternity or sorority membership on students' college experiences and cognitive development. *Research in Higher Education, 41*(1), 117–139.

Porter, T. (2017, July 21). *What is the man box?* https://www.acalltomen.org/homepagefeatures-all/2017/7/21/what-is-the-man-box

Salinas, C., Jr., & Boettcher, M. L. (2018). History and definition of hazing. In S. Knight & M. L. Boettcher (Eds.), *Critical perspectives on hazing in colleges and universities* (pp. 23–33). Oxfordshire, UK: Routledge.

Sasso, P. A., & DeVitis, J. L. (2015). Fraternities and sororities: Developing a compelling case for relevance in higher education. In *Today's college students: A reader* (pp. 241–255). Bern, Switzerland: Peter Lang.

Seabrook, R. C., Ward, L. M., & Giaccardi, S. (2018). Why is fraternity membership associated with sexual assault? Exploring the roles of conformity to masculine norms, pressure to uphold masculinity, and objectification of women. *Psychology of Men Masculinity, 19*(1), 3–13.

Shea, C. (1994, June 22). Wall of silence. *The Chronicle of Higher Education*. https://www.chronicle.com/article/Wall-of-Silence/90513

Sims, S., Luebsen, W., & Guggiari-Peel, C. (2017). Exploring the role of co-curricular student engagement in relation to student retention, attainment and improving inclusivity. *Journal of Educational Innovation, Partnership and Change, 3*(1), 93–109.

Snell, M. (2017, November 27). Hazed and abused—my Sigma Lambda Gamma experience. *Nonsense & Shenanigans Blog.* https://nonsenseandshenanigansblog.wordpress.com/2017/11/27/ hazed-and-abused-my-sigma-lambda-gamma-experience/

Social Sciences Feminist Network Research Interest Group. (2017). The burden of invisible work in academia: Social inequalities and time use in five university departments. *Humboldt Journal of Social Relations, 39*(1), 228–245.

Strayhorn, T. L. (2015). *Student development theory in higher education: A social psychological approach.* Oxfordshire, UK: Routledge.

Strayhorn, T. (2019). *College students' sense of belonging* (2nd ed.). Oxfordshire, UK: Routledge.

Syrett, N. L. (2009). *The company he keeps: A history of White college fraternities.* Chapel Hill, NC: The University of North Carolina Press.

Texas State University. (2020, August 17). *Hazing memorandum.* https://fsl.dos.txstate.edu/Hazing.html

Tingley, K., Crumb, L., Hoover-Plonk, S., Hill, W., & Chambers, C. R. (2018). Sorority and fraternity attitudes towards initiation and hazing. *Oracle: The Research Journal of the Association of Fraternity/Sorority Advisors, 13*(2), 46–60.

Turner, J. C. and Oakes, P. J. (1986), The significance of the social identity concept for social psychology with reference to individualism, interactionism and social influence. *British Journal of Social Psychology, 25*(3), 237–252.

Yeung, K. (2009). Challenging the heterosexual model of brotherhood: The gay fraternity's dilemma. In C. L. Torbenson & G. Parks (Eds.), *Brothers and sisters: Diversity in college fraternities and sororities* (pp. 184–209). Plainsboro, NJ: Associated University Presses.

CHAPTER ELEVEN

Bridging the Gap between Culturally-Based Sororities and Fraternities within Larger SFL Communities

TRACE CAMACHO

Sorority and fraternity life (SFL) share similar challenges to the campuses on which they reside with regard to diversity and inclusion. Like many institutions of higher education, SFL communities and their governing organizations were not constructed or intended for more diverse, contemporary student populations, and have long struggled to support students from historically marginalized backgrounds (Gillon, Beatty, & Salinas, 2019; Hughy, 2010; Jayakumar & Museus, 2012).

It cannot be overlooked that many sororities and fraternities have historically and intentionally excluded individuals from marginalized backgrounds (Gillon et al., 2019; Syrett, 2009). In response to these exclusionary practices, several SFL organizations were founded. These SFL organizations include Jewish individuals, People of Color, and those who identify as queer and transgender (Kimbrough, 2003; Ray & Rosow, 2013). As new organizations cropped up, existing sororities and fraternities resisted the integration of their chapters by explicitly denying membership to individuals from historically marginalized groups through codified exclusionary clauses or unwritten recruitment practices, including white-only clauses in governing documents (Joyce, 2018). Until recently there were still schools where culturally-based sororities and fraternities were not advised by the SFL office. Culturally-based sororities and fraternities were instead advised by offices of multicultural student affairs. Being advised by two separate offices created both a physical and metaphorical separation between culturally-based and historically white sororities and fraternities.

Historically white sororities and fraternities have had a major influence in the growth and development of SFL offices, as well as SFL communities on college campuses. Early administration of historically white sororities and fraternities was the responsibility of either the Dean of Men or Women on each campus (Anson & Marchesani, 1991). These historically white chapters were primarily affiliated with the North American Interfraternity Conference (NIC) and National Panhellenic Conference (NPC). Over time, sorority and fraternity advising became a functional area within student affairs and grew to include staff positions whose sole responsibility was to advise sororities and fraternities (Camacho, 2020).

SFL offices have traditionally centered around advising historically white NPC sororities and NIC fraternities. As such, many programs such as recruitment, awards and community events including Greek Weeks, and physical office space in SFL offices have been structured to serve and promote historically white sororities and fraternities. This chapter will explore ways that SFL offices and communities can examine their practices, policies, and programs to bridge the gap between culturally-based sororities and fraternities and historically white sororities and fraternities.

As a scholar-practitioner it is important to identity my positionality as it relates to SFL. I am a cisgender gay Latino man who is a member of a Latinx/o-based fraternity. Professionally I have served as an advisor to culturally-based and historically white sororities and fraternities for over 13 years, primarily at large public institutions. In this chapter, I first provide an overview of SFL recruitment, the use of physical space on campus, and programs. I also offer suggestions for creating more collaborative and equitable SFL communities. I conclude with reflective questions for SFL practitioners to explore the ways they can bridge gaps within their respective communities and organizations.

Recruitment

Panhellenic sorority recruitment and IFC fraternity recruitment is often unaffiliated students' first exposure to a campus's sorority and fraternity community (Camacho, 2020; Salinas, Gillon, & Camacho, 2019). Prospective members are given a small glimpse into SFL on their campus through multi-day or multi-week recruitment processes connecting chapters and their new prospective members usually near the beginning of the fall semester. From my personal experience, recruitment processes can influence a prospective member's perspectives on individual organizations and subsequent decisions on which, if any, to join. These recruitment processes may also unintentionally or intentionally perpetuate or mitigate inequalities and differences between culturally-based sororities and fraternities and traditionally white sorority and fraternity chapters.

Recruitment may begin before a student even touches foot on the college campus through virtual or print marketing. For most campuses, this is usually done through a prospective member section on their SFL website, a brochure, or direct mailing that introduces new students to the campus sorority and fraternity community. In these marketing pieces, campuses can work to promote equity and inclusion by highlighting the rich experiences culturally-based organizations offer and providing a general overview of SFL alongside profiles of traditionally white sororities and fraternities. The ordering of the organizations in the marketing pieces can be interpreted as a reflection of organizational prestige or importance. If culturally-based chapters are placed near the back of marketing pieces rather than throughout, it could convey that these organizations are an afterthought. In addition, if it is left up to individual chapters to supply content and photos, those chapters who have the money to have professional photo shoots will have more polished content.

Further using language in marketing and publications that does not omit culturally-based chapters is important to inform current and prospective members that cultural chapters are part of, rather than separate from, the campus sorority and fraternity community. The terms sorority and fraternity are often associated with historically white sororities and fraternities. A good practice is using the terms "Panhellenic Sorority Recruitment" and "Interfraternity Council Recruitment" rather than sorority recruitment and fraternity recruitment. Labeling general sorority recruitment "Panhellenic recruitment" implies the recruitment process is for anyone interested in joining a Panhellenic-affiliated sorority and that not all sororities will be participating. A nonspecific label implicitly and explicitly can signal to students and campus that if an organization does not participate in the sorority recruitment process, it is not a real sorority.

For current members of culturally-based sororities and fraternities, not being seen as part of the broader fraternity and sorority community places them at a deficit in the recruitment of new members if there is a perception that the experience they offer is not seen as equal to that of historically white sororities and fraternities. In addition, since Panhellenic and Interfraternity Council recruitment often happen early in the semester, if not before the beginning of the semester, culturally-based organizations could be denied the opportunity to expose prospective members to their organizations. A prospective member going through the Panhellenic and Interfraternity council recruitment processes may feel that the experience a culturally-based organization offers may be more in line with what they seek from an SFL experience. Students sometimes realize later in their college career that a culturally-based sorority or fraternity offers an experience more closely aligned with what they were looking for rather than a historically white chapter experience; however, because they join a historically white organization, they often are not able to join another sorority or fraternity. Even if a prospective member does not want to join a culturally-based sorority or fraternity, early exposure through marketing and Panhellenic and IFC recruitment processes (specifically by making clear that sorority and fraternity recruitment is not limited solely to NPC and IFC chapters) is one way to show that culturally-based organizations are an integral part of a campus sorority and fraternity community.

Campuses can also work to create more inclusive recruitment practices by focusing on marketing the whole sorority and fraternity community, rather than leaving it to individual councils to fund and produce their own marketing material. Given the size of some governing councils, the practice of relegating the weight to individual councils creates a monetary inequity due to chapter size and resources. More financially resourced councils can produce well-intentioned marketing pieces such as brochures and flyers that can often leave out information on other councils and fail to provide a full scope of the sorority and fraternity experience on campus. For campuses with limited recruitment oversight, this may cause problems.

SFL offices and staff delegate much of the planning and execution of recruitment and other major events to the individual SFL governing councils. Because each council has very different expectations from their affiliated national umbrella groups with regards to recruitment practices, minimally supervised recruitment processes can lead to myopic planning and the creation of barriers to bridging the gap between culturally-based sororities and fraternities and historically white sororities and fraternities. SFL councils and offices can work together in planning recruitment to ensure prospective members are being exposed to all councils without infringing on their preferred method of recruitment. In a formal recruitment process that involves a structured open house round in which chapters and prospective members narrow down their selections, campuses can intentionally include culturally-based chapters as part of that round. An example of this is having open houses in classes, rooms, or other campus space that allows all organizations equitable access to space. In addition, SFL offices and councils can make sure that in any pre-recruit communications and in-person orientations, they include information on culturally-based chapters in order to increase their exposure to prospective members.

Though campuses must work to ensure that they promote equity in recruitment processes and in marketing information, culturally-based organizations must also be willing to share information in order to help students make educated choices on which organization may be the best fit for them. This is not to mean it is beholden to culturally-based organizations to remind campus SFL communities and offices of their existence when it comes to marketing and recruitment processes, but is instead a call for SFL offices and administrators to work collaboratively with culturally-based organizations on their promotion and recruitment. Culturally-based organizations thus must be willing to provide accurate and transparent information regarding membership requirements, financial expectations, and new members processes. Not doing so does not give prospective members an accurate representation of the rich experience culturally-based chapters can offer and places more of the burden on the prospective member to seek out and initiate the recruitment process.

SFL recruitment processes provide many opportunities to bridge the gap between culturally-based chapters and historically white SFL chapters. The experience in a historically white chapter and a culturally-based chapter are different but both valid and meaningful to their members. It is important during the recruitment process to show that both types of membership opportunities will provide a rich and fulfilling experience to prospective members. SFL offices and communities can do this in an intentional way in bridging the gap through inclusive marketing and examining and updating their recruitment practices to make sure prospective members are exposed to information on all councils and chapters.

Physical Space

When SFL members think of physical space in relation to the SFL experience, many might quickly point to sorority and fraternity houses on largely residential campuses. Sorority and fraternity houses can be the center of social and chapter life for many members and are often seen as a key part of the sorority and fraternity experience. Culturally-based chapters, however, rarely have chapter houses, and as such do not have the symbolic physical presence a chapter house provides (Harris, Barone, & Finch, 2019). Strange and Banning (2001) discussed how the physical environment is a representation of campus values and priorities; sorority and fraternity houses are one manifestation of this. This telegraphing of campus and community values includes both the size and physical location of buildings such as academic colleges or cultural centers, as well the upkeep and renewal of buildings. A new building close to the center of campus is symbolic of that department, program, or college's prestige or value to the university. Student and community members can easily see the difference between brand new athletic facilities close to campus when compared to an academic college or department being housed in an older, run-down building near the edge of campus.

For SFL communities, this physical display of values and priorities is evident through both sorority and fraternity chapter's houses and physical space within SFL offices. When driving into a college campus, one may see a street or streets lined with sorority and fraternity houses serving as a gateway to campus. These houses may even be located physically on campus, showing how SFL is ingrained and entwined in the campus experience. These sorority and fraternity houses most often belong to chapters affiliated with historically white sororities and fraternities. These massive structures are physical symbols of power and prestige, particularly on campuses where housing proximal to the campus can be incredibly costly and inaccessible to average students. Though not every historically white sorority and fraternity community or chapter in the country has a chapter house, houses are often symbolic and physical representation of the SFL experience.

As chapter houses are physically representative of the SFL experience on campus, culturally-based SFL chapters are often left out in terms of visible representation and valuation (Harris et al., 2019). This invisibility leads to common questions during recruitment and even between current SFL members like "where is your chapter house" and is often followed by "why don't you have a chapter house?" In reality, the reason culturally-based chapters regularly do not have a chapter house is largely a monetary one. In addition, there have been culturally-based chapters who have existed on campuses for many years but were not permitted to purchase homes due to discriminatory housing practices (Torbenson & Parks, 2009). Although there is the sheer cost of building and maintaining a chapter house, which usually requires chapters to recruit and maintain a minimum number of dues-paying members, the primary monetary factor driving chapter housing inequality is insurance. Insuring sororities and fraternities is expensive due to their high-risk nature, particularly due to hazing. In addition, the cost of insuring a fraternal organization greatly increases if that organization has physical property, including a house. The high cost of insurance is not just because the physical structure of the chapter house must be insured but an organization must also secure insurance to cover the liability of members and non-members injuring themselves on chapter property.

In addition to the symbolic nature of an SFL chapter house, houses also serve functional purposes such as a physical place for chapter members to gather, study, meet, and hold programs. Culturally-based chapters in contrast must reserve meeting rooms and event space through a campus events office. Sometimes this space comes at a cost to the culturally-based chapter who, due to membership size, often have a smaller budget than historically white chapters. In addition to cost, culturally-based chapters must also deal with the availability or rather lack of availability of campus space. Besides formal meetings and events, culturally-based chapters must find informal gathering spaces, like student unions or space in the library, to socialize.

In order to bridge the gap in the disparity in physical space resources, many campuses have invested in general-use space and storage for their culturally-based SFL chapters. Arizona State University (Arizona State University, n.d.) built a sorority and fraternity village that contains both chapter houses and a multi-use facility with event and meeting space for chapters. The University of North Texas has an SFL center that contains offices for SFL staff and meeting and event space for chapters (University of North Texas, n.d.). These types of spaces provide culturally-based chapters physical space with which to conduct business, hold events, and signal their participation in their campus community. In addition to meeting space, campuses have built physical monuments to showcase and highlight the culturally-based chapters on their campus. Northwestern University created banners that hang throughout campus that show all of the culturally-based organizations on campus. Texas Christian University constructed pillars in a common area on campus dedicated to historically African American chapters. The University of Arizona Greek Heritage Park is another example of campus physical space dedicated solely to the SFL community (Smith, 2016). The Greek Heritage Park is located in close proximity to chapter houses and is an event space that culturally-based chapters can use for step and stroll competitions as well as new member presentations. Having an event space near to or integrated with SFL chapter houses can provide symbolic representation that culturally-based chapters are part of, rather than separate from, the broader SFL community.

The other physical space which can be utilized to bridge the gap between culturally-based SFL chapters is a campus SFL office or office space. SFL offices may have space allocated for council and student leader use. Often, this space is used for meetings and for council officers and other SFL leaders to work on projects related to their duties as officers. Though the SFL office may allocate the space and computers, other supplies in the space are purchased by the governing councils through their own budgets creating a sense of ownership over the space. Culturally-based governing councils may not be able to provide funds to purchase computers for council officer use as well as other supplies. In addition, SFL students who frequently use the space for programming and meetings may give off a perceived sense of ownership over the space, limiting its use for other chapters.

SFL offices can work to bridge the gap in their physical space by ensuring equitable access to meeting space in the office, particularly for culturally-based chapters that may have no other office or meeting spaces.

In addition to providing meeting spaces, if possible, SFL offices can assist culturally-based chapters by helping provide storage space for important supplies and materials. This change would allow a central university space for cultural chapters to store materials related to chapter operations such as important documents, ritual equipment, and marketing and recruitment materials. Culturally-based chapters often must find alternative methods for storing chapter-related materials as they do not have a chapter house. These options can be renting a storage unit or passing the materials between different chapter member's residences. These alternatives can lead to the loss of important chapter-related documents and materials. By providing storage space for culturally-based chapters, SFL offices can ensure that materials and artifacts are preserved. Similarly, having storage space might also incentivize culturally-based chapters to frequent SFL offices, further integrating them into the campus community through interactions with SFL staff and other chapter leadership.

Space is a resource and SFL communities must realize that in order to bridge the gap between culturally-based SFL chapters and historically white chapters, they will need to be creative in providing equitable access to space, particularly as culturally-based chapters regularly do not have the same access to space as their historically white counterparts. Given the financial cost of creating new space, SFL communities should look to the spaces they currently have to envision ways culturally-based chapters may be able to utilize them. Further, if the opportunity arises to create or renovate existing SFL community space, care should be taken to make sure the space needs of culturally-based chapters are examined through dialogue with these chapters.

Programs and Services

SFL is based around four core principles: friendship, leadership, service, and scholarship (Camacho, 2020). Friendship is the sisterhood, brotherhood, or siblinghood that creates deep and close interpersonal bonds amongst members. Sororities and fraternities seek to develop leaders through formal and informal opportunities for their members, such as serving as a chapter, regional or national officer, or taking part in a leadership development program. Service is evidenced through the giving of time or money to local or national causes. Many sororities and fraternities have a national service project such as Habitat for Humanity or a philanthropic partner such as St. Jude's Children's Research Hospital. SFL chapters promote the final principle of scholarship by providing scholarships and academic skills to their members to promote scholastic achievement.

SFL leadership programs are sponsored by both individual chapters and campus SFL offices. These programs provide multiple opportunities to bridge the gap between culturally-based SFL chapters and the broader SFL community on campus. Philanthropy and service is a central piece of all SFL chapters by providing an opportunity for chapters to come together to raise money and provide service. Many chapters put on events to raise money for their respective national charities but often the advertising and promotion of such events does not go beyond the SFL community or their respective councils. It is not uncommon for Panhellenic sororities to invite only other Panhellenic chapters and IFC chapters to come to their philanthropy events. These philanthropy events are an opportunity to not simply raise money but also for chapter members to interact. Historically white sororities and fraternities can be more intentional about inviting culturally-based chapters. Extending the invitation for participation or collaboration is an opportunity for culturally-based chapters to enter into and engage social space that allow both connection and integration. However, this opportunity often goes overlooked (Beatty, McElderry, Bottoms, & Gray, 2019). Several chapters in both types and councils have the same or very similar national philanthropies. For example, St. Jude Children's Research Hospital is affiliated with both historically white and culturally-based organizations. This overlap provides an opportunity for chapters to come together and collaborate to host events to raise money for the hospital rather than holding individual events. Collaborating around shared philanthropic causes provides opportunities for members from different chapters to work together towards common pursuits and provides more opportunities for members of culturally-based and historically white chapters to interact. Research on students in higher education shows that greater cross-racial and intergroup interaction has been shown to lead to increased feelings of belonging and the development of cross-racial friendships (Chang, Astin, & Kim, 2004). Interactions between historically white and culturally-based chapters are a great place to start. These interactions can be facilitated by SFL offices through programming around the shared principles of SFL chapters.

Similar to philanthropy programming, SFL communities can bridge the gap between culturally-based chapters and historically white chapters by partnering for hands-on service projects. These service projects can be sponsored by the governing councils or the SFL office and provide an opportunity to bring students together for service-learning experiences. Examples of this include an

SFL community-based service project such as participating in a campus wide day of service or volunteering for a large event or relief effort in their local community.

Scholarship in addition to service is also an important component to SFL organizations (Camacho, 2020). In order to promote scholarship, many SFL chapters encourage study hours, tutoring, and connect members with on campus academic resources. These approaches to scholarship are universal across both culturally-based and historically white chapters. Academics provides an opportunity for SFL councils and offices to encourage cooperative scholarship programming by bringing students together and network across academic similarities. This collaboration could be done by connecting students in similar majors or courses. In addition, SFL offices, in conjunction with chapters, can sponsor programming on topics such as applying to graduate or professional school. Scholarship programming is a low to no cost way to engage members from all councils across the one thing they all have in common: that they are all college students.

Bridging the gap between culturally-based and historically white sororities and fraternities will only happen through inclusive and strong leadership from both SFL members and SFL offices (Beatty et al., 2019). Inclusive leadership can be cultivated by utilizing the many leadership programs that exist at the chapter, communal, and community level to educate members on inclusive leadership. Creating an inclusive SFL community that bridges the gap between culturally-based and historically white SFL chapters' needs should include education on diversity and inclusion; this should start during a SFL chapter's new member process.

Historically white sororities and fraternities have varying levels of requirements for their new member processes. If an organization truly wants to create inclusive global leaders, a new member process needs to include some type of training on diversity and inclusion (Beatty et al., 2019). Doing this shows new members that diversity and inclusion are important values of an SFL organization. In addition, including diversity and inclusion in new member education provides a baseline understanding of difference. Understanding difference can help members confront possible racist, homophobic, sexist practices that may exist in their respective organizations. If members confront and work to eliminate these practices, this may help to create an environment where culturally-based organizations are more likely to interact and program with historically white organizations. Not confronting these racist, homophobic practices creates an unwelcome environment for members and chapters that come from historically marginalized backgrounds and reiterates the historic need for culturally-based chapters.

Creating inclusive SFL communities through programming and education is difficult because members must confront organizational history that is built on exclusion and chapter behavior that promotes and enables racist and homophobic attitudes (Beatty et al., 2019; Beatty & Boettcher, 2019). For example, there is a longstanding practice of excluding membership in historically white sororities and fraternities from People of Color and Jewish people (Syrett, 2009). Organizations have specifically written exclusionary clauses into their charters and governing documents throughout history to this effect (Syrett, 2009). If an organization historically would not accept a member from a marginalized group, reflecting on how they currently maintain that exclusion may be difficult.

Historically white SFL chapters not only have to look to their past for barriers to bridging the gap between culturally-based SFL chapters and historically white ones. In recent academic years, there have been several high-profile incidents of chapters promoting or allowing racist behavior to occur. The Oklahoma chapter of Sigma Alpha Epsilon sang a song with racist lyrics on their way to a chapter formal (New, 2015). Chapters have held social events demeaning Black and Latinx/a/o people (e.g., MLK Cookouts with blackface, Cholo and Chola parties), and chapters have even been exposed for still practicing racial exclusion in their recruitment practices.

Campuses can help to curb these exclusionary and harmful practices by holding chapters accountable for not adhering to campus and SFL community values. Additionally, SFL communities and councils can speak out against racist and homophobic incidents that happen with in their community. Bringing light to these incidents can show culturally-based organizations that SFL communities are willing to work towards creating a more inclusive environment.

Leadership Programs

In addition to using new member education and accountability measures, SFL organizations can bridge the gap between historically white chapters and culturally-based chapters by embedding diversity and inclusion training in leadership programs. Many SFL national organizations host yearly leadership programs that bring together chapter leaders from across the country in order to learn to be better leaders on their respective campuses (Camacho, 2020). These leadership programs should include modules on inclusive leadership that focus on examining participants' privilege and how their actions and the actions of their chapters can promote racism, sexism, homophobia and other forms of oppression. These leadership programs should be offered to both historically white and culturally-based chapters. Once members are able to recognize different forms of oppression, the leadership program should provide them resources for working to eradicate these different forms of oppression within their organization. These programs could teach members about how to collaborate with historically marginalized communities along shared interests (like their philanthropies).

SFL offices can also utilize leadership programs they host to educate members of historically white sororities and fraternities on working to eliminate various forms of oppression that may exist in their communities. Many campus SFL offices host leadership training for new council officers and chapter presidents. During these leadership programs, council and chapter leaders can work to develop action planning on making their SFL communities more welcoming to students from historically marginalized backgrounds and building stronger relationships between culturally-based and historically white chapters. This can be achieved by having councils and chapters explore ways to eliminate barriers to collaboration amongst different chapters and remove exclusionary practices from their own chapters. During these leadership programs, students can develop short- and long-term plans to increase equity in their respective chapters and councils.

Conclusion

Bridging the gap between historically white chapters and culturally-based chapters will only happen if historically white chapters and SFL offices take the responsibility to build stronger relationships with students and chapters from historically marginalized backgrounds. Historically white chapters must acknowledge the historical barriers their organizations have created both intentionally and unintentionally that prevent collaboration with culturally-based organizations. SFL offices must create opportunities to bring together chapters from different councils to collaborate around shared interests and educational programming. In addition, SFL offices and councils must examine ways they are creating inequities through recruitment and marketing between culturally-based and historically white SFL chapters.

Questions for Reflection

- What policies, practices, and programs exist within your SFL office or community that create or sustain inequality between culturally-based and historically white chapters?
- How does systemic oppression exist in SFL communities? How does that affect the experience of culturally-based chapters and their members?

- What role can student affairs professionals play in identifying and interrupting practices that further marginalize culturally-based organizations.
- What role can students play in bridging the gap between culturally-based and historically white chapters through programming, relationship building, and activism?

References

Anson, J. L., & Marchesani, R. F., Jr. (Eds.). (1991). *Baird's manual of American college fraternities* (20th ed.). Indianapolis, IN: Baird's Manual Foundation.

Arizona State University. (n.d.). *Greek housing courtyard*. https://greekvillage.asu.edu/

Beatty, C. C., & Boettcher, M. L. (2019). My culture is not a costume: Institutional practices and racism. In K. E. Gillon, C. C. Beatty, & C. Salinas Jr. (Ed.), *Critical considerations of race, ethnicity, and culture in fraternity & sorority life* (New Directions for Student Services, no. 165, pp. 39–49). Hoboken, NJ: Jossey-Bass.

Beatty, C. C., McElderry, J. A., Bottoms, M., & Gray, K. (2019). Resisting and responding to racism through fraternity and sorority involvement. In K. E. Gillon, C. C. Beatty, & C. Salinas Jr. (Ed.), *Critical considerations of race, ethnicity, and culture in fraternity & sorority life* (New Directions for Student Services, no. 165, pp. 99–108). Hoboken, NJ: Jossey-Bass.

Camacho, T. (2020). Fraternity and sorority life. In M. David & M. Amey (Eds.), *The Sage encyclopedia of higher education* (Vol. 1, pp. 569–571). Thousand Oaks, CA: Sage.

Chang, M. J., Astin, A. W., & Kim, D. (2004). Cross-racial interaction among undergraduates: Some consequences, causes, and patterns. *Research in Higher Education*, 45(5), 529–553.

Gillon, K. E., Beatty, C. C., & Salinas, C., Jr. (2019). Race and racism in fraternity and sorority life: A historical overview. In K. E. Gillon, C. C. Beatty, & C. Salinas Jr. (Ed.), *Critical considerations of race, ethnicity, and culture in fraternity & sorority life* (New Directions for Student Services, no. 165, pp. 9–16). Hoboken, NJ: Jossey-Bass.

Harris, J. C., Barone, R. P., & Finch, H. (2019). The property functions of whiteness within fraternity and sorority culture and its impact on campus. In K. E. Gillon, C. C. Beatty, & C. Salinas Jr. (Ed.), *Critical considerations of race, ethnicity, and culture in fraternity & sorority life* (New Directions for Student Services, no. 165, pp. 17–27). Hoboken, NJ: Jossey-Bass.

Hughey, M. W. (2010). A paradox of participation: Nonwhites in White sororities and fraternities. *Social Problems*, 57(4), p. 652–679.

Jayakumar, U. M., & Museus, S. D. (2012). Mapping the intersection of campus cultures and equitable outcomes among racially diverse student population. In S. D. Museus & U. M. Jayakumar (Eds.), *Creating campus cultures: Fostering success among racially diverse student population* (pp. 1–29). Boca Raton, FL: Taylor & Francis.

Joyce, S. B. (2018). Perceptions of race and fit in the recruitment process of predominantly white fraternities. *Oracle: The Research Journal of the Association of Fraternity/Sorority Advisors, 13*(2), 29–45.

Kimbrough, W. M. (2003). *Black Greek 101: The culture, customs, and challenges of Black fraternities and sororities.* Vancouver, British Columbia, Canada: Fairleigh Dickinson University Press.

New, J. (2015, March 9). Fraternity caught on video singing racist song. *Inside Higher Ed.* https://www.insidehighered.com/quicktakes/2015/03/09/fraternity-caught-video-singing-racist-song

Ray, R., & Rosow, J. A. (2012). The two different worlds of Black and White fraternity men: Visibility and accountability as mechanisms of privilege. *Journal of Contemporary Ethnography, 41*(1), 66–94.

Salinas, C., Jr., Gillon, K. E., & Camacho, T. (2019). Reproduction of oppression through fraternity and sorority recruitment and socialization. In K. E. Gillon, C. C. Beatty, & C. Salinas Jr. (Ed.), *Critical considerations of race, ethnicity, and culture in fraternity & sorority life* (New Directions for Student Services, no. 165, pp. 29–38). Hoboken, NJ: Jossey-Bass.

Smith, K. (2016, September 28). *Celebrating the history and future of UA Greek Life.* https://arizonaalumni.com/article/celebrating-history-and-future-ua-greek-life

Strange, C. C., & Banning, J. H. (2001). *Educating by design: Creating campus learning environments that work.* Hoboken, NJ: Jossey-Bass.

Syrett, N. L. (2009). *The company he keeps: A history of white college fraternities.* Chapel Hill, NC: University of North Carolina Press.

Torbenson, C. L., & Parks, G. (Eds.). (2009). *Brothers and sisters: Diversity in college fraternities and sororities.* Plainsboro, NJ: Associated University Presses.

University of North Texas. (n.d.). *Home.* https://studentaffairs.unt.edu/cfsl

CHAPTER TWELVE

Interweaving Culturally-Based Sororities and Fraternities into the Campus Imagination

CRYSTAL E. GARCIA AND ANTONIO DURAN

As we consider the topic of interweaving culturally-based sororities and fraternities into the campus imagination, we believe it is of utmost importance to first begin by recognizing the contexts that sorority and fraternity life (SFL) communities are situated in today. At the time of writing this chapter, we are in the midst of a global pandemic as COVID-19 continues to affect the health and lives of people around the world, disproportionately so for Black, Indigenous, and People of Color within the U.S. Furthermore, the murders of Tony McDade, Breonna Taylor, Ahmaud Arbery, George Floyd and countless other Black lives have called attention to acts of racial terror and police brutality stemming from anti-Blackness, inciting demands for racial justice.

Campus communities and more specifically, SFL, have always been connected to these oppressive dynamics. The call for racial justice has also come to light through SFL in what has been called the "Abolish Greek Life" movement. Within this movement, members of SFL organizations across the nation have asked to end historically white sororities and fraternities arguing that they serve to perpetuate systems of privilege and oppression. Increasingly, sorority and fraternity (inter)national leadership across organization types have stepped forward to offer statements in response to the state of the world and racial justice in particular. Although we cannot know how the Abolish Greek Life movement will affect SFL in the future, it is apparent that SFL has found itself at a crossroads.

Will historically white SFL organizations choose to ignore the issues that have been presented to them or will they decide to address them head on?

Despite its challenges, we do not propose to abandon SFL. Rather, given the power that rests within SFL communities, we wonder what it would mean to holistically transform SFL to leverage this power to cultivate a more equitable world; we envision that culturally-based sororities and fraternities can be leaders in this endeavor. To be clear, we do not view the equity work that is needed in SFL solely as a historically white or culturally-based sorority and fraternity issue. Rather, we argue that each organization has particular work to do to examine structures, behaviors, and perceptions that cause harm to Black, Indigenous, People of Color as well as other minoritized identities such as ability, gender, nationality, religion, sexuality, and socioeconomic status among others.

We want to take the opportunity that has been afforded us through this text to share some of our thoughts on how SFL organizations can transform their communities and center culturally-based sororities and fraternities (CBSFs) in these efforts. Writing can be liberatory and can provide a way to allow our imaginations to construct other possibilities. Through this chapter we center the concept of critical hope (Freire, 1970), a term that Bozalek, Leibowitz, Carolissen, and Boler (2014) described "as a unitary and unified concept which cannot be disaggregated into either hopefulness or criticality" (p. 1). Adopting a frame of critical hope will provide us the opportunity to consider possibilities and hope for the future while still recognizing ways power, privilege, and oppression play a role in this endeavor.

In writing this chapter, we recognize that CBSFs are already cultivating change within their spheres of influence. However we also argue that all too often their capacity to do so at a chapter level, particularly within historically white institutions, can be stifled by a lack of recognition and resources from the campus community broadly. Therefore, we first discuss the need for campus and local communities to recognize the strength of CBSFs. We then unpack ways CBSFs can (and often do) serve as leaders for SFL communities in centering humanizing practice among members and as leaders for social change and justice.

Recognizing the Strengths of CBSFs

Noted above, CBSFs are frequently overlooked within the broader SFL landscape. Thus, we begin this chapter by arguing that campus communities need to acknowledge the strengths that CBSFs possess.

Examining Histories of Oppression

In order for campus communities to develop a complex understanding of CBSFs, they must first recognize histories of oppression and privilege that have shaped the foundational purposes of these organizations as well as the experiences of minoritized students within their institution. It is important to note that these discussions may reveal unpleasant and uncomfortable dynamics; it is for this precise reason that it is important to address them directly. This learning should focus on organizational histories by exploring why and how the organizations formed and what their legacies of inclusion and exclusion has looked like in the time since their founding. Discussions of historical legacies of oppression and privilege should also include an exploration of the institutional SFL history. For instance, when did CBSFs begin at the institution? What challenges did they face as they were established on campus? Depending on when chapters were established, it is also imperative to examine how policies and laws at the time affected how they operated. For instance, were CBSFs permitted to purchase land or houses for their members? Finally, histories are not only relevant as they apply directly to organizations and institutions. Colleges and universities are also situated within local communities and these communities have an important role in students' off-campus experiences. Therefore, understanding how the community has engaged with minoritized communities including People of Color is crucial to understanding contemporary community contexts.

Increasing Awareness of CBSFs

In addition to recognizing the histories tied to privilege and oppression, it is vital to bring in educational pieces to inform the campus community about the work CBSFs are doing. In Chapter Eleven, Trace Camacho shared thoughtful considerations in this vein regarding organizational recruitment. SFL offices and student affairs divisions should additionally do their part to educate the campus community about CBSFs. This work can begin with questioning ways the institution at a broad level recognizes the work done by student organizations then more specifically interrogate the extent that CBSFs are part of these conversations. Furthermore, university administrators should engage in efforts to show students that they are seen by individuals at high levels within the institution. Vice presidents of student affairs divisions are in a particularly useful position to do so by coordinating lunches and informal meetings with leaders of CBSFs to ask them what initiatives they are working on, how they are doing in their roles as students and student leaders, and if they feel supported in this work. Other spaces such as faculty senate should also offer opportunities for student groups to inform the institutional faculty about their organizations and the work they do. If indeed the intent of the university community is to support students in and out of class, faculty are incumbent to recognize out of class experiences that are meaningful to students.

Additional considerations in increasing awareness of CBSFs is thinking critically about where information is made available about the organizations and how that information is framed. One primary place this education occurs is within online spaces such as websites and social media. Crystal conducted a study alongside William Walker, Samantha Jenkins, and Kathleen Smith focused on exploring SFL websites at 18 public predominantly white research universities in the Southeastern U.S. (Garcia, Walker, Jenkins, & Smith, in press). They found that institutions frequently did not represent historically white and culturally-based SFL councils equitably. Often, information for Multicultural Greek Councils and National Pan-Hellenic Councils was incomplete, missing active links, and had fewer active social media accounts when compared to Panhellenic Council (PC) and Interfraternity Councils (IFC). Furthermore, when councils created their own websites separate from the university's, these sites were inequitably structured as historically white councils more often had professionally constructed sites while NPHC and MGC groups did not. These findings underscore the need for SFL and student affairs offices to take an equity centered approach by providing additional resources to ensure CBSFs are made visible as PC and IFC groups are through online spaces.

This section focused on increasing awareness of CBSFs, but ultimately students, faculty, and staff can be aware of CBSFs without actually supporting them; unfortunately this is all too often the case. Often, CBSFs host workshops, panels, and featured speakers to raise cultural awareness and to address difficult topics like matters of race/ethnicity, gender, and sexuality. Research has shown that members of CBSFs expressed that it is uncommon for individuals outside of their councils to attend their events, which means they rarely see white students, faculty, and professional staff support their initiatives (see Garcia 2019a, 2019b). Campus community members must recognize the labor these students expend in planning and overseeing these events for the benefit of others. We encourage campus communities including students, staff, and faculty to make a concerted effort to attend these events and engage in learning about these important topics.

Racial Change in HWSFs and Campus Community

Our final recommendation for campus communities to recognize the strength of CBSFs falls to historically white sororities and fraternities. These organizations must do the work to critically examine ways their racialized histories have and continue to cause harm to Students of Color broadly, and CBSFs more specifically. HWSFs must reckon with ways these organizations have perpetuated violence against minoritized communities by ignoring the existence of CBSFs (Garcia, 2019b) and should work towards changing this culture. As noted in Chapter Eleven, one way HWSFs can increase awareness of CBSFs is including education on culturally-based SFL during their education processes. They should also pursue opportunities to develop meaningful relationships and collaborations with culturally-based SFL organizations, not simply to tokenize these groups.

Culturally-Based Sororities and Fraternities as Leaders in Humanizing Practice

Mentioned time and again throughout this text, CBSFs were founded with the aims to serve minoritized communities. Even though many of these organizations were focused on singular issues of race/ethnicity or sexuality in relation to their roles as gendered organizations, there is ample opportunity for these groups to serve as leaders in humanizing practice more broadly for campus communities by adopting these practices within their membership. When we use the term humanizing practice we refer to behaviors, policies, and perspectives that recognize individual as holistic beings and honor those unique identities. Much of these considerations were unpacked in Chapter Nine; however we offer some additional thoughts here for organizations to center in their equity work.

Reflecting on Organizational Values

Before discussing these suggestions, we want to share an important item of reflection. In a study we recently conducted exploring the experiences of Queer Women of Color in culturally-based sororities (Duran & Garcia, 2021; Garcia & Duran, 2021), one of our participants, Cecelia who is a member of a Historically Native American Sorority, described her organization's aversion to directly address the topic of transgender membership. This led her to assert that the sorority was intended to serve, "women, but it's only, I guess, the Native women. The standard Native woman. A straight Native woman." We share Cecelia's sentiments because they point to an imperative question for CBSFs to reckon with. Who is your organization intended to serve? Asking these questions directly will help CBSFs center their values and purposes and guide their engagement in humanizing practice.

Culturally-based sororities and fraternities should not consider themselves incapable of perpetuating harm to other minoritized populations, and instead should openly critique themselves and question ways their organizational culture has reinforced systems of oppression and what it would mean to transform these cultures into more equitable spaces for all members. We assert that culturally-based organizations have the opportunity to be at the forefront of such practices on their campuses. In doing this work, we challenge CBSF members to dig deeply and consider perhaps a nuanced version of the vision their founders had for their organizations to serve this purpose. We note this may be a nuanced version because although it is important to consider foundational values, it is also imperative to question the context during which organizations were founded and how that may have dictated other forms of exclusion that society promoted at the time. In other words, if organizations were founded in times when overt hostilities toward queer and transgender people were prevalent, that does not mean that organizations must continue those legacies.

Gender and Sexuality Considerations

Gender and sexuality refer to distinct aspects of one's identities, yet these terms are often conflated and used as an indicator for one another, even within CBSFs (Duran & Garcia, 2021; Garcia & Duran, 2020). It is necessary that culturally-based SFL organizations critically examine ways they interact with gender and sexuality. For instance in terms of sexuality, in our research exploring the experiences of Queer People of Color in CBSFs, participants have shared stories of chapters planning date parties pairing men and women together or implementing process regulations such as "no dating boys" for sorority members. Patterns of heteronormativity can also be perpetuated within conversations that embed assumptions about members' sexuality and minimize those that are not straight. Members must question, for instance, whether when asking new members about romantic interests if they ask questions or phrase statements that assume their partner is the opposite sex. Additionally, members can interrogate whether they show the same level of interest in queer members' relationships that they do with heterosexual siblings.

We also encourage CBSF membership to question what it would mean for culturally-based SFL organizations to deeply consider the gendered norms they perpetuate at the (inter)national organization level as well as within chapters. We recommend that organizational leadership guide chapters to review the images the (inter)national organization and chapters portray in official organizational materials as well as on social media. Are there ways these send explicit or implicit messages about who can be a member of the organization? For instance, are all members portrayed as embodying the "ideal" feminine image? Additionally, conversations regarding gender would not be complete without directly addressing the organization's stance on membership for transgender individuals. Prior to making these decisions, we urge (inter)national organizations and chapters to educate themselves and their membership about what it means to be a transgender person to dispel myths and perpetuate harmful ideologies that serve to other transgender individuals. SFL offices and student affairs divisions can further support students as they engage in work unpacking dynamics around gender and sexuality in relation to their organizations by providing educational sessions, referring students to resources, and celebrating the work CBSFs do.

Ability Considerations

In addition to issues of gender and sexuality, CBSFs must critically examine their accessibility to people with disabilities. For instance, are the locations used for chapter or new member education meetings accessible to individuals with physical disabilities? As CBSFs plan events, such as yard shows or new member showcases, do members consider how to ensure these spaces are accessible? Exploring these considerations is important for current members as well as for individuals that may want to attend these events. SFL offices and student affairs divisions must provide resources that assist students in thinking through accessibility logistics. This could take the form of accessibility consideration guides alongside professional development opportunities. However, workshops should not only engage students in thinking about formalized events, but also in how accessibility comes into play in their everyday organizational culture.

In addition to considerations regarding individuals with physical disabilities, CBSFs should also address ways they serve students with mental disabilities. For instance, do organizational practices and policies cause harm to students with learning disabilities by overprogramming and detracting from the additional study time some individuals may need? Furthermore, have organizational leaders and members intentionally engaged in conversations about mental health? As discussed by Douglas N. Case in Chapter Six, LGBTQ individuals often face mental health challenges as a result of hostilities they face from others in response to their gender performance and sexuality. Similarly, racially/ethnically minoritized individuals may also experience forms of violence based on their race/ethnicity. These hostilities can take the form of microaggressions or overt acts of discrimination and can be accumulating and wearing on the mental health of Students of Color (Lewis, Mendenhall, Harwood, & Browne Huntt, 2013; Pérez

Huber & Cueva, 2012). Given our current societal climate, this is a particularly important consideration for Black students as tensions around the Black Lives Matter movement intensify.

Ultimately, institutional leadership is responsible for addressing dynamics of racism, sexism, and trans oppression among others on campus. They can begin this work by naming forms of systemic oppression and equipping students with language to make sense of these dynamics. These educational moments must be frequent; it is absurd, for example, to expect organizational change as a result of offering one diversity workshop to students each year. Until institutions take charge of shifting racial climates, Black, Indigenous, and Students of Color are left to grapple with the ramifications of a hostile climate. CBSFs can center humanizing practice by destigmatizing mental health issues within their organizations. To do so, membership must first recognize and discuss these realities and the effects they have on members. Furthermore, organizational leaders and members can normalize help-seeking and encourage members to use campus counseling and other services to support students as they navigate the consequences of systemic oppression.

Race/Ethnicity and Religion Considerations

Although CBSFs have a well-documented history of lifting up racial/ethnically minoritized communities, that does not mean they are incapable of reproducing harm towards Black, Indigenous, and People of Color. Referring back to previous discussions raised by Keith Garcia in Chapter Nine, membership must consider questions like, are there ways our organization centers monolithic views of particular racial or ethnic experiences? For instance, within the scope of Asian American sororities and fraternities, how often do conversations disrupt monolithic assumptions about a Pan Asian identity? Furthermore, are there ways our blanket assumptions about individuals' experiences ignore members that identify with nationalities outside of the U.S.? For example, a Latinx/o-based fraternity may promote their members to commit to vote in an upcoming election without considering whether all members actually have the ability to vote. In addition to navigating considerations of legality, nationality affects individuals' experiences within our society in unique ways. Members and organizations broadly must recognize and address differences, for example, in the ways Black students may understand their positionality and navigate U.S. society distinctly from African international students. Within these discussions, members should recognize that individuals for whom English is not their first language may speak with a discernible accent, which may open them to particular forms of discrimination based on their identities as People of Color, nationality, and language.

Perhaps as an extension of nationality and culture, organizations should also be intentional in recognizing non-dominant religious and cultural holidays. Some ways these dynamics manifest is through organization parties, posts, and recognized holidays (for attendance and scheduling purposes as mentioned in Chapter Eight). As previously discussed, members of CBSFs must revisit their organizational purposes and values. If the purpose of the organization is not to promote Christianity, membership should examine organizational practices, policies, and culture to determine if there are ways they prioritize Christianity and marginalize members that identify with religions outside of Christianity.

Culturally-Based Sororities and Fraternities as Leaders for Social Change and Justice

Culturally-based sororities and fraternities have expansive networks that stretch around the globe. NPHC sororities and fraternities alone comprise an estimated 1.5 million graduate and undergraduate members (TAMUC, 2020). Other younger umbrella associations are smaller in size but still possess strong member bases. NALFO for instance reports current undergraduate membership of over 5,500 and more than 30,000 alumni (NALFO, 2019–2020). We share these numbers to recognize the work these groups have done to build their organizational networks over the years, however we also recognize that strength is not drawn from numbers alone. Strength is also derived from a shared commitment to values, movements, and communities. It is crucial to recognize the power CBSFs possess and how this power has already been yielded to contribute to social change and justice in significant ways including through developing members' critical consciousness, engaging in equity centered philanthropic efforts, and committing to social justice causes.

Developing Critically Conscious Members

As described in the introduction of this text, CBSFs have positively contributed to student experiences in significant ways. Considering findings that underscore the connection between membership in these organizations and outcomes associated with leadership and racial/ethnic identity development (Atkinson, Dean, & Espino 2010; Guardia & Evans, 2008), CBSFs are in a unique position to contribute to students' development as critically conscious leaders. Freire (1970) described critical consciousness or conscientização as "learning to perceive social, political, and economic contradictions, and to take action against the oppressive elements of reality" (p. 35). Because CBSFs were created in response to systems of oppression, their organizational fabric likely already attends to dynamics that are directly connected to the identities associated with the founding of the organization. However, as noted previously in the discussion of humanizing practices, there are additional ways CBSFs can engage in work uncovering societal oppression. Historically white sororities and fraternities, as well as other student-based organizations, should look to CBSFs as they lead the way in cultivating critical consciousness within their membership.

As reflected in Freire's (1970) definition of critical consciousness, it is important to recognize that this concept involves more than just raising awareness, but also involves compelling individuals to action to address societal inequities. Engagement in activism is one way individuals may respond; in fact, students with minoritized identities, and those within CBSFs in particular, have a long history of engaging in activism in response to social inequities (Garcia, Walker, Dorsey, Werninck, & Johns, in press; Jones & Reddick, 2017; Linder & Rodriguez, 2012; Logan, Lightfoot, & Contreras, 2017; Parks & Hughey, 2020). (Inter)national organizational leadership must recognize the costs students risk to engage in activism and recognize that these decisions are not made lightly nor do they have light ramifications for the individual (Linder, 2019). Increasingly, more organizations are allowing members to wear their letters as they engage in forms of activism, though these decisions have been controversial (Grigsby Bates, 2014). It is important that (inter)national organizations, colleges, and universities not only allow their members to engage in forms of activism in promotion of social justice, but also make intentional efforts to support these members (see Linder, 2019).

Engaging in Equity Centered Philanthropy

Campus communities have much to learn from CBSFs in terms of their leadership in contributing to philanthropy that is tied to addressing inequities in our society. Although we cannot possibly identify all the ways organizations have done so within the scope of this chapter, we want to take a moment to highlight a few examples. Sigma Gamma Rho Sorority Inc., an NPHC organization, shared their commitment to multiple philanthropic initiatives including a focus on breast cancer awareness due to their recognition that "African Americans bear a disproportionate burden of cancer—the highest mortality rate of any ethnic group" (Sigma Gamma Rho Sorority, Inc., n.d., p. 2). Alpha Pi Omega Sorority

Inc., a historically Native American organization, selected the National Indian Education Association as its philanthropy, an organization that "strives to keep Indian Country moving toward educational equity" (Alpha Pi Omega Sorority, Inc., 2016, Our Philanthropy section). Beta Chi Theta Fraternity, Inc., a NAPA organization, began a commitment to "Beating Heart Disease," a health issue the fraternity is committed to because of its disproportionate effects on the South Asian community (Beta Chi Theta Fraternity, Inc., n.d.). Many CBSFs already make significant contributions to philanthropic endeavors that address systemic inequities and they continue to have the opportunity to lead campus communities in doing the same.

Commitment to Social Justice Causes

Currently, Crystal and Dr. Michael Goodman are working on a critical discourse analysis of sorority and fraternity (inter)national organization social media messaging on topics of social justice. They selected 37 SFL organizations from each broader organizational type—Native American, NALFO, NAPA, NMGC, NPHC, NPC, and NIC—and identified the organization's most followed social media platform collecting every post made to the account over the span of 4 years. Perhaps unsurprisingly, preliminary results show that CBSFs more often and more explicitly addressed and advocated for social justice issues. CBSFs have the opportunity to continue to lead campus communities in their commitments to social justice causes.

As mentioned previously, CBSFs often engage in initiatives to advocate for social justice and to educate campus communities about social justice related issues. For instance, many CBSFs have demonstrated their commitments to the queer and transgender community by participating in and showing their support of members that participated in Pride marches and events. Organizations have also hosted or co-hosted panels and workshops to examine the experiences of queer and transgender people in an effort to address heteronormative expectations and practices that serve to reinforce the gender binary. In our research exploring the experiences of Queer People of Color within CBSFs, participants expressed that it was not only individually affirming when their organizations engaged in such practices, but it was also an indicator to them that their organization's values aligned with their own (Duran & Garcia, 2021; Garcia & Duran, 2020). Organizations can similarly show their support of other social justice causes such as the Black Lives Matter movement, efforts to increase accessibility, women's marches, rallies in support of DACA and protections for undocumented people. As noted before, committing to these efforts contributes to the action piece of critical consciousness. Furthermore, these efforts are important in working toward a more equitable society and can also affirm current and future members' identities.

Conclusion

Our intent in writing this chapter was to highlight ways that culturally-based SFL organizations should be recognized and how they can, and do, serve as leaders within SFL communities and society as a whole. This chapter called attention to ways these organizations are doing so by cultivating critically conscious leaders, engaging in equity based philanthropy, and committing to social justice causes. However, in order for campus communities to learn from the work CBSFs are engaging in and to show they truly value this labor, they must first ensure the campus community educates itself on the histories and contributions of CBSFs. Therefore, we want to end this chapter by revisiting the concept of critical hope. In our minds, we envision a campus where prior to the start of the semester, all students receive information about CBSFs on campus through multiple and accessible modes. The information explains the history of sororities and fraternities broadly, drawing attention to how historical and contemporary legacies of sexism, racism, homophobia, transphobia, and the centralization of Christianity have shaped the organizations that exist on campus today. The materials further explain why multiple councils exist, the purpose they serve, and the multitude of ways the councils collaborate with one another to make the campus community a more equitable place. Culturally-based sorority and fraternity members are leaders on campus in providing a place for students to connect in siblinghood with one another and to engage in humanizing practice. We realize that to achieve this future, campus communities, SFL offices, (inter)national organizations and umbrella associations all have work to do to contribute to these aims.

Questions for Reflection

- How can you use the concept of critical hope to shape the future of culturally-based sororities and fraternities?
- In what ways can campus communities support efforts to highlight the contributions of culturally-based sororities and fraternities?
- What initiatives can culturally-based sororities and fraternities engage in to serve as leaders in their commitments to social justice and equity centered philanthropy?

References

Alpha Pi Omega Sorority, Inc.. (2016). *About us.* http://www.alphapiomega.org/About.html#Philanthropy

Atkinson, E., Dean, L. A., & Espino, M. M. (2010). Leadership outcomes based on membership in multicultural Greek council (MGC) organizations. *Oracle: The Research Journal of the Association of Fraternity/Sorority Advisors, 5*(2), 34–48.

Beta Chi Theta Fraternity, Inc. (n.d.). *Beating heart disease.* https://betachitheta.com/beatingheartdisease

Bozalek, V., Leibowitz, B., Carolissen, R., & Boler, M. (Eds.). (2014). *Discerning critical hope in educational practices.* Oxfordshire, UK: Routledge.

Duran, A., & Garcia, C. E. (2021). Quaring sorority life: Identity negotiation of Queer Women of Color in culturally-based sororities. *Journal of College Student Development, 62*(2), 186-202.

Freire, P. (1970). *Pedagogy of the oppressed.* New York City, NY: The Continuum International Publishing Group Inc.

Garcia, C. E. (2019a). Climates for ethnic and racial diversity: Latina/o sorority and fraternity member perspectives. *Journal of Student Affairs Research and Practice.* Advance online publication. https://doi.org/10.1080/19496591.2019.1631836

Garcia, C. E. (2019b). "They don't even know that we exist": Exploring sense of belonging within sorority and fraternity communities for Latina/o members. *Journal of College Student Development, 60*(3), 319–336. https://doi.org/10.1353/csd.2019.0029

Garcia, C. E., & Duran, A. (2021). Regulating sexuality through gender-based rhetoric: The experiences of Queer Women of Color in culturally-based sororities. *Journal of Diversity in Higher Education. Advance online publication.* doi: 10.1037/dhe0000312

Garcia, C. E., & Duran, A. (2020). "In my letters, but I was still by myself": Highlighting the experiences of Queer Men of Color in culturally based fraternities. *Journal of Diversity in Higher Education.* Advance online publication. https://doi.org/10.1037/dhe0000167

Garcia, C. E., Walker, W., Dorsey, C., Werninck, Z., & Johns, J. (in press). Culturally based sororities and fraternities as spaces of activism within predominantly white institutions. *Oracle: The Research Journal of the Association of Fraternity/Sorority Advisors.*

Garcia, C. E., Walker, W., Jenkins, S., & Smith, K. (in press). Culturally-based fraternities and sororities: Representation via institutional websites. *Journal of College Student Development.*

Grigsby Bates, K. (2014, December 13). Black fraternities and sororities split on protest policy. *NPR.* https://www.npr.org/sections/codeswitch/2014/12/13/370427539/black-fraternities-and-sororities-split-on-protest-policy

Guardia, J. R., & Evans, N. J. (2008). Factors influencing the ethnic identity development of Latino fraternity members at a Hispanic serving institution. *Journal of College Student Development, 49*(3), 163–181.

Jones, V. A., & Reddick, R. J. (2017). The heterogeneity of resistance: How Black students utilize engagement and activism to challenge PWI inequalities. *The Journal of Negro Education*, *86*(3), 204–219.

Lewis, J. A., Mendenhall, R., Harwood, S. A., Browne Huntt, M. (2012). Coping with gendered racial microaggressions among Black women college students. *Journal of African American Studies*, *17*, 51–73.

Linder, C. (2019). Power-conscious and intersectional approaches to supporting student activists: Considerations for learning and development. *Journal of Diversity in Higher Education*, *12*(1), 17–26. http://doi.org/10.1037/dhe0000082

Linder, C., & Rodriguez, K. L., (2012). Learning from the experiences of self-identified Women of Color activists. *Journal of College Student Development*, *53*(3), 383–398.

Logan, G., Lightfoot, B. A., & Contreras, A. (2017). Black and Brown millennial activism on a PWI campus in the era of Trump. *The Journal of Negro Education*, *86*(3), 252–268.

NALFO. (2019–2020). *Member organizations*. https://nalfo.org/member-organizations/

Parks, G. S., & Hughey, M. W. (2020). *A pledge with a purpose: Black sororities and fraternities and the fight for equality*. New York, NY: NYU Press.

Pérez Huber, L., & Cueva, B. M. (2012). Chicana/Latina testimonios on effects and responses to microaggressions. *Equity & Excellence in Education*, *45*(3), 392–410.

Sigma Gamma Rho Sorority, Inc.. (n.d.). *Project reassurance*. https://celectcdn.s3.amazonaws.com/files/0037/0882/ProgramUpdate_12.23.14.pdf

TAMUC NPHC. (2020). *Council history*. https://nphc.tamu.edu/council-history/

CHAPTER THIRTEEN

Moving Forward: Concluding Thoughts on the Future of Culturally-Based Sororities and Fraternities

ANTONIO DURAN AND CRYSTAL E. GARCIA

Since their founding, culturally-based sororities and fraternities have uplifted and centered minoritized communities who experienced exclusion in sorority and fraternity life (SFL) communities, college campuses, as well as in society broadly (Torbenson & Parks, 2009). As noted throughout this text, the histories of these organizations have been documented in scholarly works (e.g., Brown, Parks, & Phillips, 2012; Dosono, Badruddin, & Lam, 2020; Miranda, Garcia, & Guardia, 2020; Oxendine, Oxendine, & Minthorn, 2013; Parks & Hughey, 2020). And yet, understanding these legacies only provides individuals part of the story of how these culturally-based sororities and fraternities play a major role in helping individuals thrive on and beyond college campuses. Recognizing this point, this text represented our attempt to center the voices of practitioners who have long been helping to move these organizations forward, especially in contemporary times where racism and other forms of oppression are still rampant in and outside of higher education settings (Gillon et al., 2019). Whether it was focusing on specific types of organizations or addressing issues that span the landscape of culturally-based SFL communities, the collective guidance offered by authors in this book offer needed perspective for those looking to work alongside these groups in modern times.

In this chapter, we offer some ruminations on the text as a whole, providing a broader perspective on how we hope this book intervenes into the SFL literature.

To start, we offer a brief overview of the themes we saw emerge across chapters that warrant the attention of readers. Following this analysis, we then make the case for increased attention to culturally-based sororities and fraternities in research. Namely, it is our belief that additional scholarship on these organizations will only better inform practice in the future. Finally, we conclude with our personal reflections on the standing relevance of culturally-based sororities and fraternities in these times, making the case that these organizations are still as necessary as they were when they were founded.

Themes Present across the Chapters

The beauty of this text stemmed from the wide array of points-of-view offered by the chapter authors, those who have dedicated their careers to ensuring the success and thriving of members in culturally-based sororities and fraternities. Throughout their chapters, these individuals detailed the challenges that they see organizations facing, especially within larger SFL communities. And still, authors made it a point to provide the continued possibilities that culturally-based sororities and fraternities hold for transforming the lives of individuals and campus communities at large. Thus, in the following sections, we highlight some of the most notable arguments that were present across the various chapters of this book such that readers are able to easily identify what it takes to continue to move culturally-based sororities and fraternities forward.

Challenges Facing Culturally-Based Sororities and Fraternities

Though culturally-based sororities and fraternities are significant organizations for minoritized students on college campuses, these groups face numerous obstacles as they attempt to actualize their values and goals. In the chapters penned by the authors of this text, several key challenges emerge as being particularly important to address moving forward. These include: having incongruent policies established in SFL offices, lacking financial resources, and requiring education for advisors of these groups.

Incongruent Policies Established in SFL Offices

Although they possess some similarities to historically white SFL organizations, culturally-based sororities and fraternities are also different in ways that warrant further attention by SFL offices. Highlighted in several chapters, culturally-based sororities and fraternities are frequently held to the same standards established for historically white SFL organizations despite their important differences. For example, in Chapter Eight, Symphony and Derek Oxendine detailed how institutional policies on expansion, chapter sizes, or grade point average (GPA) requirements inherently disprivilege Native American Fraternities and Sororities. And the reality is that this disenfranchisement of culturally-based sororities and fraternities exists across the various organizational types. What is concerning about this pattern is that culturally-based sororities and fraternities are required to meet requirements that are created by organizations that intrinsically have more privilege and capital, especially at historically white institutions. As a direct result, culturally-based sororities and fraternities are once again marginalized in the broader SFL community. To advocate for culturally-based SFL organizations means to reckon not only with their historical legacies of exclusion but to also understand how these groups continue to be marginalized on and beyond college campuses.

Lack of Financial Resources

As communicated in Chapter Eleven, many culturally-based SFL organizations do not have access to the appropriate resources that would allow them to thrive. Whether it is the need for physical space or financial assistance, culturally-based sororities and fraternities often do not possess the capital afforded to historically white sororities and fraternities. Though the circumstances under which these organizations function are different, especially as it relates to membership dues, culturally-based sororities and fraternities deserve to receive assistance from SFL offices to support their initiatives. Fostering a sense of belonging for individuals requires people believing that they matter to a larger group (Strayhorn, 2019) and one way to accomplish this goal is by financially supporting their labor. Articulated by Trace Camacho in Chapter Eleven, providing culturally-based sororities and fraternities with appropriate resources may take the form of creating collaborations across councils that may have already have more capital.

Need for Advisor Education

Though not as explicitly stated as the challenges above, underlining most of the chapters was the reality that advisors working with culturally-based sororities and fraternities may not have the education necessary to adequately support these organizations. As highlighted in the previous subsections, when advisors are not prepped to know the ways that culturally-based sororities and fraternities function, they are less likely to challenge and perhaps more likely to produce policies that push these organizations to the margins within the SFL landscape and that lead to their extinction on college campuses. Consequently, one major challenge that exists and that requires addressing is the availability of educational opportunities on how to properly advise and support culturally-based sororities may be lacking. As a result, professional associations dedicated to SFL professionals should take heed of the recommendations provided throughout this text in order to offer professional development that is more tailored toward the contemporary needs of culturally-based sororities and fraternities.

Future Possibilities for Culturally-Based Sororities and Fraternities

Important to acknowledge is that the perspectives provided by this book's chapter authors signal not only the places where culturally-based sororities and fraternities encounter barriers, but also to imagine new ways of moving these organizations into the future. It is in these possibilities that we see a tremendous amount of promise, recommendations that professionals can use to inform their practice. In the following sections, we highlight three key possibilities: revisiting policies and integrating organizations in larger SFL communities, taking steps toward challenging the gender binary, as well as working with students and organizations to better these sororities and fraternities.

Revisiting Policies and Integrating Organizations in Larger SFL Communities

Highlighted above, one of the challenges that those working with culturally-based sororities and fraternities encounter is the fact that too many SFL offices function from a place of centering historically white organizations. Consequently, practices and policies are created without considering the unique ways that culturally-based SFL organizations function. Acknowledging this reality leads us to name our first future possibility. Rather than relegating culturally-based sororities and fraternities as afterthoughts in the day-to-day operations of SFL offices, practitioners must start from a place of attending to their needs. Trace Camacho's chapter mentioned above provides a useful starting point for professionals interested in doing this work and who seek to bridge the gap between culturally-based and historically white SFL organizations. Related to this point, we highly encourage SFL practitioners to conduct audits on their practices and policies in an attempt to locate those that inherently disprivilege culturally-based sororities and fraternities. Expanded on more below, this work should be done in concert with the students and perhaps other members of the organizations in order to ensure that their voices are heard.

Part of this aim also involves making more intentional efforts to shine a light on culturally-based sororities and fraternities in broader SFL spaces. Drawing on our personal experiences, research, and the lessons provided by the practitioners in this text, too often, members of historically white sororities and fraternities do not know that culturally-based SFL organizations exist. In this lies a great inequality. While members of culturally-based sororities and fraternities are expected to know about historically white SFL groups, the reverse is not the same. Hence, SFL professionals must incentivize members of historically white sororities and fraternities to learn about and/or collaborate with culturally-based SFL organizations. Importantly, this kind of encouragement must be paired with providing individuals affiliated with historically white sororities and fraternities with the proper cultural competency needed to work across councils. Although these initiatives are not necessarily easy, they are crucial to centering culturally-based sororities and fraternities.

Challenging the Gender Binary

Finally, we find it important to acknowledge the continued ways that culturally-based sororities and fraternities wrestle with their intention to support members in accordance with their gendered realities while at the same time, embracing more gender-expansive ways of thinking. In Chapter Six, Douglas N. Case introduced this very dilemma that has been progressively taken up by organizations in recent years. Specifically, with the exception of a few co-educational fraternities, SFL organizations are inherently gendered organizations. However, as noted in Chapter Six, this has oftentimes rendered transgender and non-binary individuals invisible when they make considerations about member recruitment on the basis of sex assigned at birth. Thus, a positive advancement has been groups that have expanded their constitutions to allow for individuals who were not assigned a particular sex at birth to join their organizations, a reality communicated in Chapter Five written by Juan Guardia.

Therefore, we are hopeful that additional organizations will allow for transgender and non-binary individuals to join and still, we would be remiss not to state that these types of changes are insufficient if the culture of these groups do not also operate in gender-expansive manners. What we mean by this point is that it is not enough to simply allow transgender and non-binary people to join culturally-based sororities and fraternities. To further create inclusive and equitable environments, leaders of culturally-based SFL organizations must ensure that the gender binary is not reinforced in the practices, rituals, and traditions of these groups in manners that are oppressive. Consequently, we believe that a future possibility for culturally-based sororities and fraternities involves taking a critical look at who is eligible for membership based on gender, in addition to conducting intentional audits on how they support individuals of diverse gender identities and expressions.

Working with Students and National Organizations to Better Experiences

Implicit in all of the chapters in this book is the recommendation to listen to those affiliated with culturally-based sororities and fraternities in order to better serve these communities. Perhaps this is an overly simplistic future possibility, but as evidenced by the arguments made throughout this text, it is an implication that must be more seriously taken up by SFL professionals. Practitioners should make it a point to engage in critical reflection about their own areas of bias and places where they may lack the understanding to adequately advocate for culturally-based sororities and fraternities. Related to this point, practitioners should take the initiative to not only position the burden of education on members themselves but to also reference the growing body of research on culturally-based SFL organizations in order to engage this learning process. For instance, individuals can reference the scholarship cited in Chapter Two. Moreover, practitioners could also connect with the volunteers and staff of national organizations when applicable. Relationship building with both students, as well as the national organizations, is a vital step in effectively attending to the needs of culturally-based sororities and fraternities.

Need for Further Research

Reflecting on the recommendations provided by chapter authors throughout this text, we as authors were reminded that culturally-based sororities and fraternities are ever-evolving and require professionals to be response to these changing realities. As such, we also assert that scholars interested in SFL contexts must similarly attend to culturally-based organizations by conducting up-to-date research on these groups. Informed by the extant literature covered in Chapter Two of this text, as well as by the chapters that followed, we identified a few areas of research that may be of particular importance for practitioners moving forward.

Other Culturally-Based Sororities and Fraternities and Different Institutional Types

In curating this book, we made an intentional decision to highlight organizations that seek to uplift Communities of Color, as well as Lesbian, Gay, Bisexual, Transgender, and Queer (LGBTQ) individuals. This scope resembles others' conceptualizations of culturally-based sororities and fraternities. However, we would be remiss not to acknowledge the other types of SFL organizations that exist whose mission are to advocate for other minoritized groups. Though regrettably not as common as the groups highlighted in this text, these sororities and fraternities require the attention of practitioners and scholars alike. For instance, Stapleton and Nicolazzo (2019) explored the experiences of those in a culturally Deaf sorority, attending to a group that is not oftentimes thought of within SFL communities. Additionally, given the long history of anti-Semitism in the United States, Jewish sororities and fraternities represent other organizations that have created space for marginalized individuals (Sanua, 2003). Similar to the groups attended to in this book, these organizations are still serving valuable functions on college campuses. And yet, empirical research on these sororities and fraternities is few and far between. The same pattern holds true for Black sororities and fraternities that are not a part of the NPHC as well as culturally-based sororities and fraternities that serve populations not included in larger umbrella associations and categorizations offered in this text such as those for Armenian, Muslim, Persian, and Italian Americans. Consequently, we argue that scholars should take further notice of these organizations in order to understand their continued influence on the lives of minoritized people and how these groups combat oppressive realities to this day.

Additionally, it is not our desire to suggest that culturally-based sororities and fraternities are only meaningful at institutions that are historically white. Such an argument would obscure the histories of organizations founded at Historically Black Colleges and Universities (HBCUs). With this in mind, another line of inquiry that scholars can engage in involves understanding how the influence of culturally-based sororities and fraternities differs depending on institutional type. For example, what does it mean to join a chapter of a Latinx/a/o-based organization at a Hispanic-Serving Institution versus a historically white college or university? Where are Multicultural Greek Organizations more concentrated and how does this affect the experiences that members have? These are simply but a couple of questions that researchers can pose in order to further add depth into the scholarly landscape on culturally-based sororities and fraternities.

Experiences of Members On- And Off-Campus

Underscored through the vignettes written by members of culturally-based sororities and fraternities in this text, these organizations represent lifelong bonds and forms of community for minoritized individuals. This hallmark differentiates these groups from other culturally-based organizations on college campuses (e.g., student clubs) as formal ties to these communities usually dissipate after an individual graduates. For those in culturally-based sororities and fraternities, however, lifelong membership adds tremendous value for many. Yet, a shortage of research exists on members' experiences of their culturally-based sororities and fraternities beyond the symbolic college gates. In other words, studies frequently explore campus-based perspectives of individuals, shining attention on their undergraduate and graduate years. What is concerning about this is that some members do not join as students and it also obscures the long-term benefits of these organizations.

Thus, researchers should continue to expand their investigations to comprehend how members of culturally-based sororities and fraternities report their engagement with organizations on a broader level. For instance, how connected are these individuals to their siblings across the country and what are the ways that organizations facilitate these relationships? How does knowledge of these bonds help improve how practitioners on campuses understand these organizations, their influence, and the lives of their students? Furthermore, this body of research would also benefit from more long-term studies that potentially employ a longitudinal design exploring life outcomes for members of culturally-based sororities and fraternities. Such knowledge could be helpful as members and campus-based professionals describe what is to be gained by affiliating with culturally-based sororities and fraternities.

Addressing Intersectional Forms of Oppression

Articulated in Chapter Nine authored by Keith Garcia, these organizations still have a way to go in order to adequately support those who identify with minoritized groups not explicitly centered in the group's mission. Guided by an attention to intersectional forms of oppression using the analytic coined by Crenshaw (1989, 1991), Keith Garcia argued that these organizations would better serve their members. Existing scholarship on culturally-based sororities and fraternities suggests a similar need, especially as it pertains to LGBTQ individuals within organizations established to uplift racially minoritized communities (DeSantis & Coleman, 2008; Duran & Garcia, 2020a, 2020b, 2021; Garcia & Duran, 2020; Jenkins, 2012; Literte & Hodge, 2012; Williams, 2017). Therefore, we contend that researchers should continue to examine how culturally-based sororities and fraternities address issues of heterosexism, in addition to attending to trans oppression—a topic not frequently explored (see Epps, 2020 for an exception). Moreover, few examples exist in the scholarly literature of how SFL communities address ableism in their environments. To address this omission, scholars could take the lead of perspectives shared by Stapleton and Nicolazzo (2019) who showcased how members of a Deaf sorority resisted ableism, and audism specifically, through their organization. Whether it is investigating ableism, trans oppression, heterosexism, classism, settler colonialism, or other forms of marginalization, researchers should strive to add nuance to the ways that power and oppression works within the context of culturally-based sororities and fraternities in order to address structural inequities.

Although we firmly believe that scholars should critically examine how culturally-based sororities and fraternities address intersecting forms of oppression, we also caution individuals doing this work from presenting these communities in a deficit light in which they are seen as more oppressive than their white counterparts. For instance, Mahoney (2019) argued that it is not that BGLOs are more inherently more homophobic than other groups, but rather that histories of anti-Blackness and a necessity to enact respectability politics has led to behaviors that deem queer people as deviant within these spaces. Similarly, scholars have warned against presenting BGLOs in ways that vilify blackness (e.g., Hughey, 2008; Hughey & Hernandez, 2013). Though these perspectives are specific to BGLOs, we argue that their implications should be applied to culturally-based sororities and fraternities broadly. We certainly encourage people to critically examine the ways that these organizations perpetuate marginalization themselves, but ask that people do so while keeping in mind the legacies of oppression that have shaped the behaviors and beliefs of minoritized communities.

Supporting Culturally-Based Sororities and Fraternities

Additionally, another area of research that requires further attention involves understanding how those advising culturally-based sororities and fraternities gain the skills, knowledges, and abilities necessary to do this work effectively. The very impetus for this text stemmed from a desire to provide professionals some tools to comprehend the needs of these often-overlooked SFL organizations, especially when they have little to no previous experience with these groups. And still, much more research is required in order to better assist practitioners who are in a position to advocate for these communities. What does exist in the scholarly literature largely focuses on Black Greek-Letter Organizations (BGLOs) (e.g., Parks & Spencer, 2013; Patton & Bonner, 2001; Strayhorn & McCall, 2012). Therefore, future researchers can take the cue from these pieces of literature to elaborate on this line of inquiry.

For instance, scholars can expand their scope in order to illustrate how SFL professionals on college campuses are prepared to advise different types of culturally-based sororities and fraternities including the organizations represented in this text. Such research could take a specific look at how individuals are on-boarded, how advisors turn to other practitioners for support, and what kinds of professional development opportunities are especially meaningful for these individuals. Moreover, using the work of Strayhorn and McCall (2012) as an example, researchers should ask critical questions about how individuals develop cultural competency necessary to assist these organizations. This scholarly inquiry should take a critical stance, examining how professionals' social identities and backgrounds influence their ability to effectively relate to students in these organizations. For example, how do white advisors avoid falling into the trope of the white savior when advising culturally-based sororities and fraternities whose aims include uplifting racially minoritized communities? How do non-Black People of Color consider their own roles in perpetuating anti-Blackness in advising organizations? These questions are important springboards for this area of research.

Furthermore, scholars could investigate how campus-based professionals collaborate and partner with individuals outside of higher education institutions when advising these organizations. Examples of this could include conducting studies to analyze how campus-based professionals work with sororities and fraternities' national organizations, especially as it relates to questions of how certain groups get established at postsecondary institutions. Researchers may pose inquiries such as: how do campus-based practitioners build effective partnerships with organizational leadership in order to ensure the success of culturally-based sororities and fraternities? Answers to this question and others would be valuable for professionals moving forward as they navigate working with different stakeholders in order to continue moving culturally-based sororities and fraternities.

The Relevance of Culturally-Based Sororities and Fraternities

Communicated in the preceding chapter, culturally-based sororities and fraternities continue to exist in a U.S. society that is deeply oppressive toward those who hold minoritized communities. Namely, the lives of racially minoritized individuals, as well as those in the LGBTQ community, are still threatened. Additionally, these communities still lack access to basic needs and face inequitable systems in work, housing, and education. In many ways, the realities that gave rise to culturally-based sororities and fraternities are present to this day.

Thus, when we reflect on recent "Abolish Greek Life" movements that argue that SFL communities are at their very root inequitable (Marcus, 2020), we both agree with the oppressive histories of SFL and at the same time, argue for the relevance of culturally-based sororities and fraternities. Both ideas are not mutually exclusive. In fact, as detailed in this text, culturally-based sororities and fraternities were started given the exclusive practices and clauses adopted by historically white organizations (Gillon, Beatty, & Salinas, 2020). Nevertheless, what emerged are sororities and fraternities that validate people's racial/ethnic identities (e.g., Delgado-Guerrero, Cherniack, & Gloria, 2014; Garcia, 2020a; Guardia & Evans, 2008; Orta et al., 2019) while also providing them with the skills and networks necessary to succeed in college (Delgado-Guerrero & Gloria, 2013; McClure, 2006; Moreno & Banuelos, 2013).

In times when these types of spaces are not always guaranteed for students with minoritized identities (Quaye, Harper, & Pendakur, 2020), the importance of these organizations cannot be understated. In addition, because these organizations provide lifelong relationships to individuals different from student clubs on campus (Hughey, 2007), they offer a unique experience for Students of Color, LGBTQ individuals, and many more. Consequently, culturally-based sororities and fraternities occupy a meaningful place in higher education settings and beyond. For this reason, practitioners must be more well-prepared to make sure that these organizations thrive and as Trace Camacho reminded us in Chapter Eleven that they are better integrated into the landscape of SFL communities. When professionals are able to provide these organizations with the adequate time, resources, and assistance, it is then that we will really see these organizations thrive.

Conclusion

The future of culturally-based sororities and fraternities is bright, as these organizations continue to provide those with minoritized identities the opportunity to make valuable connections with individuals who hold similar values (Delgado-Guerrero et al., 2014; Greyerbiehl & Mitchell, 2014) and to offer a place of refuge from the oppressive realities that exist on college campuses (e.g., Arellano, 2020; Tran & Chang, 2013). However, these organizations are also still erased and overlooked within higher education settings, a sentiment shared by members themselves (Garcia, 2020). This text hopes to function as an intervention into this pattern, encouraging professionals to take notice and adequately attend to culturally-based sororities and fraternities. It is not enough to rely on practices believed to be positive for any member of a SFL organization. Instead, practitioners must make a concerted effort to learn the needs of culturally-based sororities and fraternities specifically. By listening to the voices centered in this book, professionals may be better equipped to engage in this work. And still, learning from this text should be only one step in a long journey of educating oneself to be a proper advocate of culturally-based sororities and fraternities as they progressively move into their futures.

References

Arellano, L. (2020). Why Latin@s become Greek: Exploring why Latin@s join Latino Greek-letter organizations. *Journal of Hispanic Higher Education, 19*(3), 280–302.

Brown, T. L., Parks, G. S., & Phillips, C. M. (Eds.). (2012). *African American fraternities and sororities: The legacy and the vision* (2nd ed.). Lexington, KY: University Press of Kentucky.

Crenshaw, K. (1989). Demarginalizing the intersection of race and sex: A Black feminist critique of antidiscrimination doctrine, feminist theory, and antiracist politics. *University of Chicago Legal Forum, 140*, 139–167.

Crenshaw, K. (1991). Mapping the margins: Intersectionality, identity politics, and violence against Women of Color. *Stanford Law Review, 43*, 1241–1299.

Delgado-Guerrero, M., Cherniack, M. A., & Gloria, A. M. (2014). Family away from home: Factors influencing undergraduate Women of Color's decisions to join a cultural-specific sorority. *Journal of Diversity in Higher Education, 7*(1), 45–57.

Delgado-Guerrero, M., & Gloria, A. M. (2013). La importancia de la hermandad Latina: Examining the psychosociocultural influences of Latina-based sororities on academic persistence decisions. *Journal of College Student Development, 54*(4), 361–378.

DeSantis, A. D., & Coleman, M. (2008). Not on my line: Attitudes about homosexuality in Black fraternities. In G. Parks (Ed.), *Black Greek-letter organizations in the twenty-first century* (pp. 291–312). Lexington, KY: The University Press of Kentucky.

Dosono, B., Badruddin, B., & Lam, V. W. H. (2020). History of Asian American Greek-letter organizations. In P. A. Sasso, J. P. Biddix, & M. L. Miranda (Eds.), *Foundations, research, and assessment of fraternities and sororities: Retrospective and future considerations* (pp. 25–37). Gorham, ME: Myers Education Press.

Duran, A., & Garcia, C. E. (2020a). Narratives of Queer Men of Color in culturally-based fraternities making meaning of masculinities. *International Journal of Qualitative Studies in Education*. Advance online publication. doi: 10.1080/09518398.2020.1828652

Duran, A., & Garcia, C. E. (2020b). Post-undergraduate narratives of Queer Men of Color's resistance in culturally-based fraternities. *Journal of Student Affairs Research and Practice*. Advance online publication. doi: 10.1080/19496591.2020.1772083

Duran, A., & Garcia, C. E. (2021). Quaring sorority life: Identity negotiation of Queer Women of Color in culturally-based sororities. *Journal of College Student Development, 62*(2), 186–202.

Epps, S. A. Y. (2020). *Experiences of transgender men who joined National Pan-Hellenic sororities pre-transition* (Unpublished doctoral dissertation, Louisiana State University, Baton Rouge, LA).

Garcia, C. E. (2020). "They don't even know we exist": Exploring sense of belonging within sorority and fraternity communities for Latina/o members. *Journal of College Student Development, 60*(3), 319–336.

Garcia, C. E., & Duran, A. (2020). "In my letters, but I was still by myself": Highlighting the experiences of Queer Men of Color in culturally based fraternities. *Journal of Diversity in Higher Education*. Advance online publication. http://dx.doi.org/10.1037/dhe0000167

Gillon, K. E., Beatty, C. C., & Salinas, C., Jr. (2019). Race and racism in fraternity and sorority life: A historical overview. In K. E. Gillon, C. C. Beatty, & C. Salinas Jr. (Eds.), *Critical considerations of race, ethnicity, and culture in fraternity & sorority life* (New Directions for Student Services, no. 165, pp. 9–16). Hoboken, NJ: Wiley.

Greyerbiehl, L., & Mitchell Jr., D. (2014). An intersectional social capital analysis of the influence of historically Black sororities on African American women's college experiences at a predominantly white institution. *Journal of Diversity in Higher Education, 7*(4), 282–294.

Guardia, J. R., & Evans, N. J. (2008). Factors influencing the ethnic identity development of latino fraternity members at a Hispanic serving institution. *Journal of College Student Development, 49*(3), 163–181.

Hughey, M. W. (2007). Crossing the sands, crossing the color line: Non-Black members of Black Greek Letter Organizations. *Journal of African American Studies, 11*(1), 55–75.

Hughey, M. W. (2008). Brotherhood or brothers in the "hood"? Debunking the "educated gang" thesis as Black fraternity and sorority slander. *Race, Ethnicity & Education, 11*(4), 443–463.

Hughey, M., & Hernandez, M. (2013). Black, Greek, and read all over: Newspaper coverage of African-American fraternities and sororities, 1980–2009. *Ethnic & Racial Studies, 36*(2), 298–319.

Jenkins, R. D. (2012). Black fraternal organizations: Understanding the development of hegemonic masculinity and sexuality. *Journal of African American Studies, 16*(2), 226–235.

Literte, P. E., & Hodge, C. (2012). Sisterhood and sexuality: Attitudes about homosexuality among members of historically Black sororities. *Journal of African American Studies, 16*, 674–699.

Mahoney, A. D. (2019). *Queering Black Greek-lettered fraternities, masculinity and manhood: A Queer of Color critique of institutionality in higher education* (Paper 3286) (Doctoral dissertation University of Louisville, Louisville, KY). University of Louisville Electronic Theses and Dissertation.

Marcus, E. (2020, August 1). The war on frats. *The New York Times*. https://www.nytimes.com/2020/08/01/style/abolish-greek-life-college-frat-racism.html

McClure, S. M. (2006). Voluntary association membership: Black Greek men on a predominantly white campus. *Journal of Higher Education, 77*(6), 1036–1057.

Miranda, M. L., Garcia, K. D., & Guardia, J. D. (2020). NALFO: A retrospective y hacia adelante. In P. A. Sasso, J. P. Biddix, & M. L. Miranda (Eds.), *Foundations, research, and assessment of fraternities and sororities: Retrospective and future considerations* (pp. 39–46). Gorham, ME: Myers Education Press.

Moreno, D. R., & Banuelos, S. M. S. (2013). The influence of Latina/o Greek sorority and fraternity involvement on Latina/o college student transition and success. *Journal of Latino-Latin American Studies (JOLLAS), 5*(2), 113–125.

Orta, D., Murguia, E., & Cruz, C. (2019). From struggle to success via Latina sororities: Culture shock, marginalization, embracing ethnicity, and educational persistence through academic capital. *Journal of Hispanic Higher Education, 18*(1), 41–58.

Oxendine, D., Oxendine, S., & Minthorn, R. (2013). The historically Native American fraternity and sorority movement. In H. J. Shotton, S. C. Lowe, & S. J. Waterman (Eds.), *Beyond the asterisk: Understanding Native students in education* (pp. 67–80). Sterling, VA: Stylus.

Parks, G. S., & Hughey, M. W. (2020). *A pledge with purpose: Black sororities and fraternities and the fight for equality.* New York, NY: NYU Press.

Parks, G. S., & Spencer, D. (2013). Student affairs professionals, Black "Greek" hazing, and university civil liability. *College Student Affairs Journal, 31*(2), 125–138.

Patton, L. A., & Bonner, F. A., II. (2001). Advising the Historically Black Greek Letter Organization (HBGLO): A reason for angst or euphoria? *National Association of Student Affairs Professionals Journal, 4*(1), 17–30.

Quaye, S. J., Harper, S. R., & Pendakur, S. L. (Eds.). (2020). *Student engagement in higher education: Theoretical perspectives and practical approaches for diverse populations* (3rd ed.). Oxfordshire, UK: Routledge.

Sanua, M. R. (2003). *Going Greek: Jewish college fraternities in the United States, 1895–1945.* Wayne State University Press.

Stapleton, L. D., & Nicolazzo, Z. (2019). Sorority life reimagined: Deaf culture and mainstream sorority life. In K. E. Gillon, C. C. Beatty, & C. Salinas Jr. (Eds.), *Critical considerations of race, ethnicity, and culture in fraternity & sorority life* (New Directions for Student Services, no. 165, pp. 87–98). Hoboken, NJ: Wiley.

Strayhorn, T. L. (2019). *College students' sense of belonging: A key to educational success for all students* (2nd ed.). Oxfordshire, UK: Routledge.

Strayhorn, T. L., & McCall F. C. (2012). Cultural competency of Black Greek-Letter Organization advisors. *Journal of African American Studies, 16*(4), 700–715.

Torbenson, C. L. & Parks, G. S. (Eds.). (2009). *Brothers and sisters: Diversity in college fraternities and sororities.* Cranbury, NJ: Rosemont Publishing & Printing Corp.

Tran, M. C., & Chang, M. J. (2013). To be mice or men: Gender identity and the development of masculinity through participation in Asian American interest fraternities. In S. D. Museus, D. C. Maramba, & R. T. Teranishi (Eds.), *The misrepresented minority: New insights on Asian Americans and Pacific islanders, and the implications for higher education* (pp. 67–85). Sterling, VA: Stylus.

Williams, J. M. (2017). *Ostracized insiders: Exploring the experiences of Black gay men in historically Black Greek letter fraternities* (Doctoral dissertation, Texas A&M University, College Station, TX). Texas A&M University Libraries. https://oaktrust.library.tamu.edu/

About the Authors

Editors

Crystal E. Garcia, Ph.D., is an Assistant Professor in the Department of Educational Administration at the University of Nebraska-Lincoln. Her research critically examines the mechanisms by which racially minoritized college students experience campus environments, specifically focusing on campus climates and the role of student affairs in student experiences. Her sorority and fraternity life research projects have included a critical content analysis of institutional SFL websites, an examination of the experiences of Queer People of Color in culturally-based sororities and fraternities, and an exploration of the role of Latinx/a/o-based sororities and fraternities in students' sense of belonging among others.

Crystal is a Class of 2021–2023 ACPA Emerging Scholar-Designee and was awarded the 2020 NASPA Latinx/a/o Knowledge Community Outstanding Faculty Award, the 2018 AERA Hispanic Research Issues SIG Dissertation of the Year Award, and the 2018 ACPA Burns B. Crookston Doctoral Research Award. Her work has been published in journals including *The Journal of College Student Development*, *The Review of Higher Education*, *The Journal of Diversity in*

Higher Education, and *Oracle: The Research Journal of the Association of Fraternity/Sorority Advisors*. She currently serves as a member of the Editorial Boards for the *Journal of College Student Development*, the *Journal of Student Affairs Research and Practice*, and the *College Student Affairs Journal*. She earned her Ph.D. in Educational Studies specializing in Educational Leadership and Higher Education at the University of Nebraska-Lincoln. Originally from Texas, she obtained her B.S. and M.S. degrees from Texas A&M University-Commerce.

Antonio Duran, Ph.D., is an Assistant Professor of Administration of Higher Education at Auburn University. His research agenda examines two main areas: a) how historical and contemporary legacies of oppression influence college student development and experiences and b) how student affairs professionals use knowledge of these systems to influence their practice. Specific to sorority and fraternity life, he has collaborated with Dr. Garcia on research projects including a study looking at the experiences of Queer People of Color in culturally-based organizations, as well as a project examining the professional preparation of FSL professionals who advise culturally-based sororities and fraternities. He is also currently the advisor for the Auburn University colony of Omega Delta Phi.

Antonio has had his work published in journals such as the *Journal of College Student Development (JCSD)*, *Journal of Student Affairs Research and Practice (JSARP)*, *International Journal of Qualitative Studies in Education (QSE)*, and *Journal of Diversity in Higher Education (JDHE)*. Every year, he submits and presents findings from his studies at the annual meetings of the Association for the Study of Higher Education (ASHE), Student Affairs Professionals in Higher Education (NASPA), College Student Educators International (ACPA), and the National Conference on Race and Ethnicity in American Higher Education (NCORE). He received his B.A. in English and American Literature from New York University, his M.S. in Student Affairs in Higher Education from Miami University, and his Ph.D. in Higher Education and Student Affairs from The Ohio State University.

Contributors

Bilal Badruddin is a doctoral student in the Higher Education Leadership & Policy Studies Program at Howard University. Prior to pursuing his doctoral degree, Badruddin worked as a student affairs practitioner at Eastern Washington

University (2013–2015) and Colgate University (2015–2017). In addition to his work on college campuses, Badruddin serves as the national president and C.E.O. of Delta Epsilon Psi Fraternity, Inc., which is a South Asian interest fraternity, and has served on the NAPA Board. He earned a B.A. in Advertising Research from Temple University (2011) and an M.Ed. in Higher Education from Loyola University Chicago (2013).

Cameron C. Beatty, Ph.D. is an assistant professor in the Educational Leadership and Policy Studies Department at Florida State University. Dr. Beatty teaches courses in the undergraduate leadership studies certificate and higher education graduate program, as well as conducts research with the Leadership and Learning Research Center. Dr. Beatty's research foci includes exploring the intersections of gender and race in leadership education, leadership development of Students of Color on historically white campuses, and experiences racial battle fatigue for Black and Latinx students. His recent publications center on topics that include: race and racism in fraternity and sorority life, supporting undergraduate Black women through Sister Circles, gains in leadership capacity for high-achieving Black men leaders, and supporting undergraduate men in leadership education through liberatory pedagogy.

Trang Bui is pursuing her Master of Educational Psychology with an emphasis in Higher Education/Student Affairs at Wichita State University. Trang currently works in the Office of Student Success and the Office of Applied and Experiential Learning. She is a founding sister of Sigma Psi Zeta Sorority at Wichita State University, where she also completed her Bachelor of Arts in Education. Trang worked as an elementary classroom teacher in Wichita USD259 (2016–2019). She currently serves as Secretary of the NAPA Board.

Trace Camacho, Ph.D. is currently the Director of Student Life and Development at California State University, Long Beach overseeing a broad portfolio of student involvement areas. Dr. Camacho has over 12-year experience advising fraternities and sororities at various institutions including Michigan State University and the University of Arizona. Dr. Camacho is a member of Sigma Lambda Beta International Fraternity Inc.

Douglas N. Case is currently the coordinator for Campus Pride's Lambda 10 Project/Out & Greek Initiative which promotes visibility, inclusion and safety for LGBTQ students participating in sorority and fraternity life. He retired from San Diego State University where he worked in the Division of Student Affairs from 1979 - 2015, most of that time as Coordinator of Fraternity and Sorority Life. Doug was very active in the Association of Fraternity/Sorority Advisors, serving as President in 1991 and was the recipient of the association's prestigious Robert H. Shaffer Award given to a person working in higher education demonstrating a long-term commitment to fraternities and sororities. Doug served as the chapter advisor for the San Diego chapter of Delta Lambda Phi from its founding at SDSU in 1992 until 2020. He has also served on the international fraternity's volunteer staff as Risk Management Director and as Director of University Relations. Doug has co-authored two research projects on the experiences of LGBGTQ members in social sororities and fraternities and has been involved in the LGBTQ equality movement, twice serving as president of San Diego Democrats for Equality. He currently serves as Political Affairs Director for openly lesbian California State Senate President Toni Atkins.

Bryan Dosono, Ph.D. is the Director of Research and Development of the National APIDA Panhellenic Association and International President of Lambda Phi Epsilon International Fraternity, Inc. His dissertation research uncovered ways in which Asian Americans and Pacific Islanders negotiate collective action in the context of their online identity work. He earned his Bachelor of Science degree with honors in Informatics (Human-Computer Interaction) from the University of Washington and a Doctor of Philosophy in Information Science and Technology from Syracuse University.

Keith D. Garcia currently serves as an Assistant Director of Fraternity and Sorority Life at the Northwestern University in Evanston, IL. In his role he advises the Multicultural Greek Council as well as chapters across the Interfraternity Council, Multicultural Greek Council, National Pan-Hellenic Council, and Panhellenic Association. He is also responsible for harm reduction education across the fraternity and sorority community on campus. Beyond Northwestern University he is involved as a leadership educator and consultant. Keith teaches within the Leadership Minor at the University of Minnesota-Twin Cities and travels the country supporting campuses, fraternal organizations, and community groups in tackling issues related to leadership from a lens of justice and equity. His education includes a Bachelor of Business Administration from the City University of New York's Bernard M. Baruch College and a Master of Arts in Educational Administration-Student Affairs from the University of Nebraska–Lincoln. He is a member of La Unidad Latina, Lambda Upsilon Lambda Fraternity, Inc. and credits his membership as a catalyst for his journey into this work. He has served his fraternity in various capacities from the local to the national levels, most recently having served as a member of the Board of Directors.

Christopher C. Graham joined Alpha Phi Alpha while attending Winston-Salem State University. He earned his Master of Science in Counseling, with an emphasis on student development in higher education from the University of North Carolina at Greensboro and went on to work professionally within the fraternity and sorority advising profession. Chris has worked at Florida State University for the past eight years, the last five he has served as Director of Fraternity and Sorority Life. In his role, he has led one of the largest fraternal communities in the country. He also has extensive experience serving as a consultant and volunteer for several universities and fraternity and sorority headquarters in a variety of capacities, including educational programs, curriculum development, organizational structure, and more. He has served on the Board of Directors and is the current President for the Association of Fraternity and Sorority Advisors (AFA).

Juan R. Guardia, Ph.D. has been in the field of student affairs for over 20 years in various administrative roles. He is currently the Assistant Vice President for Student Affairs and Dean of Students at the University of Cincinnati where he oversees the African American Cultural & Resource Center, Bearcat Bands, Dean of Students Office, Ethnic Programs & Services, LGBTQ Center, Parent & Family Programs, Resident Education & Development, and Student Conduct & Community Standards. He has also worked at a variety of institutions, including Northeastern Illinois University, Florida State University, and George Mason University. Juan has also served as adjunct faculty in the higher education programs at Loyola University Chicago, Florida State University, and the University of Cincinnati. His research interests focuses on Latinx/a/o college students, college students racial and ethnic identity development, Hispanic-serving institutions, and Latinx/a/o fraternities and sororities. Juan is former chair of the National Association of Latino Fraternal Organizations and a proud, lifetime member of Phi Iota Alpha Fraternity, Inc.

Marcos Guzman has spent his student affairs professional career working with fraternity and sorority organizations and students. He received his M.Ed. in Student Affairs in Higher Education from Texas State University and a B.S from New Mexico State University. For the past 5 years, Marcos has worked at the University of Arizona where he currently serves as the Assistant Dean of Students and Director of Fraternity and Sorority Programs. He regularly serves as a volunteer with his own fraternity, the Sigma Chi International Fraternity, and with the Association of Fraternal Leadership and Values. He is active within the Tucson community where he serves on the Board of Directors for the southern Arizona non-profit Emerge! Center Against Domestic Abuse.

Vigor W. H. Lam currently works at City College of San Francisco as a consultant on the program and construction management team for Kitchell CEM to implement the facilities master plan for an $845M bond program. Prior to this role, he worked in various student affairs functional areas, including academic affairs, campus activities and life, multicultural affairs, and residential life. He has conducted prior research and examined the experiences of members in Asian American Greek-Letter Organizations (AAGLOs). He has held leadership positions and presented at ACPA, AFA, AFLV, NACA, and NASPA. He earned a M.Ed. in Postsecondary Administration and Student Affairs from University of Southern California (2015) and a B.S. in Landscape Architecture from The Ohio State University (2012). He is a member of Pi Delta Psi Fraternity, Inc. and has served on the NAPA Board and his national fraternity for several years.

Heather L. McMillan Nakai is an enrolled member of the Lumbee Tribe of North Carolina. Heather received her A.B. from Dartmouth College in History and Native American Studies and her J.D. from the University of California at Los Angeles with a concentration in Indian law and corporate law. Heather is licensed to practice law in North Carolina and practices federal Indian law full time. In her personal capacity, Heather is engaged in litigation against the United States seeking enforcement of individual Indian rights as her effort to correct unjust treatment of Lumbee people.

Javier Mena currently serves as the National Treasurer of the National Multicultural Greek Council and Psi Sigma Phi Multicultural Fraternity, Inc. Since joining in the Fall of 2011 he has done a lot of advocacy work, specifically in the immigrants' right movement. Over the years he has served on several roles within his chapter, the region, and the national level. Javier has helped rebrand the organization as part of the brand committee. He also led as the National Expansion Director and expanded the organization to schools across NJ & in Virginia. Currently, he works in higher education at a New Jersey university. He joined higher education to be a part of the solution in creating a more equitable system. Javier enjoys working with students & helping them navigate college.

Jenny Nirh, Ph.D. works with communication and outreach efforts focused on undergraduate student success and retention at the University of Arizona. Previously, she worked in fraternity and sorority life for many years also at the University of Arizona. She has conducted research focused on hazing within student organizations and her current work has a focus on cultivating belonging. She has been an active volunteer with Alpha Chi Omega. Jenny has a PhD and MA in Higher Education from the University of Arizona, and a BA in Political Science from the University of New Mexico.

Nadrea Njoku, Ph.D. works as Senior Research Associate for the Frederick D. Patterson Research Institute. Her research foci include student success and career pathways at Historically Black Colleges and Universities, with a specific focus on the influence of campus environments and student development theory. She positions this work in a critical race and feminist framework that is devoted to disrupting issues of race and gender within the postsecondary education context. She's a proud graduate of Xavier University of Louisiana and Indiana University.

Derek Oxendine, Ph.D., Lumbee, is the Director of the Bachelor of Interdisciplinary Studies (BIS) program at the University of North Carolina at Pembroke and he has spent his entire professional career working in student affairs and student success units. He received his Ph.D. in Educational Studies with a concentration in Higher Education and a doctoral minor in Educational Research Methodology from the University of North Carolina at Greensboro, where he also received his M.Ed. in Student Personnel Administration in Higher Education. He received his B.A. in Psychology from the University of North Carolina at Chapel Hill. His research and scholarship areas include student success, experiences of first-year college students, the impact of college on ethnic identity development, experiences of American Indian students and staff in higher education, Historically Native American Fraternities and Sororities, structural equation modeling, and Indigenous research methods. He is a member of Phi Sigma Nu Fraternity, Inc. and served for 15 years in the roles of Chief Dean of Ma'enos and Chief President on the fraternity's Chief Council.

Symphony Oxendine, Ph.D. is Cherokee/Choctaw from Tulsa, Oklahoma. Dr. Oxendine is an Assistant Professor in Higher Education at the University of North Carolina Wilmington and also the coordinator for the Ed.D. in Educational Leadership specialization in Higher Education. She spent 6 years as a student affairs practitioner before pursuing her doctorate and becoming faculty in a student affairs/higher education graduate preparation program. She received her Ph.D. in Educational Studies with a concentration in Higher Education and her M.Ed. in Higher Education Administration at the University of North Carolina at Greensboro where she also received. She received her B.A. from Oklahoma State University in Applied Sociology. As an Indigenous quantitative scholar, Dr. Oxendine's research is centered on the social and institutional issues that affect the educational performance and institutional support of Indigenous peoples and other underrepresented groups within postsecondary education institutions, graduate preparation programs, Historically Native American Fraternities and Sororities, student involvement and its impact on retention, leadership development, and appreciative inquiry. She is a member of Alpha Pi Omega Sorority, Inc. and has served for 15 years as a Grand Keeper of the Circle in various roles including Grand President and is currently the Grand Treasurer.

Jessica Peñaranda has served as the National President of the National Multicultural Greek Council since 2018. She is a member of Theta Nu Xi Multicultural Sorority, Inc. since the Fall of 2005. She is one of seven founders of her home chapter—the Alpha Gamma chapter at The College of New Jersey—and has served the national organization as former Regional Director for the Northeast region, held multiple Graduate/Alumnae/Professional chapter positions, and is the first co-chair of the organization's Gender Justice Working Group, leading national efforts on gender inclusion. Since becoming a member, Jessica continues to nuance and push the boundaries of how we understand, define, and practice multiculturalism within her national organization, the NMGC, and in our communities. She is a longtime social justice activist, social service provider, and strategist who values creativity and innovation to inspire social change. Jessica is passionate about collective leadership and creating communities of care through healing justice centered through an intersectional, anti-oppressive framework with an emphasis on building relationships, cultural humility, mutual community aid, and transformative justice practices that are informed by her lived experiences as a Queer (Im)migrant Woman of Color.

Janel Ramos is a recent graduate of the University of South Florida. She is a proud sister of Omega Phi Beta Sorority, Inc. where she became the first Founder-Daughter legacy in the organization. In her first year as a member, Janel received the "Pillar of the Community: Leadership" award from the Office of Fraternity/Sorority Life. She went on to become the president of the Beta Eta Chapter and the president of the Multicultural Greek Council where she oversaw 15 organizations. As a senior Janel received "NALFO's Undergraduate Excellence Award" and "NALFO's Campus Leadership Excellence Award" for her work in Fraternity/Sorority Life.

Hannah L. Reyes is a master's student in the Administration of Higher Education Program at Auburn University. Prior to pursuing her master's degree, Hannah worked as a student affairs practitioner at Mississippi State University. Her department, as well as the organizations she advised, worked closely with the Office of Sorority and Fraternity Life for programming and involvement efforts. She has also been involved in numerous research projects and conference presentations centering the experiences of students and practitioners involved with culturally-based sororities and fraternities.

Cristobal Salinas Jr., Ph.D. is an assistant professor in the Educational Leadership and Research Methodology Department at Florida Atlantic University. His research promotes access and equality in higher education and explores the social and political context of education opportunities for historically marginalized communities. Dr. Salinas is the Founder and Editor for the *Journal Committed to Social Change on Race and Ethnicity*, and Social Media Editor for the *Community College Journal of Research and Practice*. In his 5 years as professor, he has published 21 peer-review articles, 5 books, over 25 book chapters, among other creative scholarship. Dr. Salinas has received over 25 international and national awards for his commitment to social justice, diversity, equity, and inclusion. His research has been featured in CNN, CNN *Español*, NPR, and Good Morning America.

Jessica Snell has served as the University Liaison for the National Multicultural Greek Council since 2019. She became a member of Lambda Tau Omega Sorority, Inc. in Fall 2012 at William Paterson University – Geminate Beta chapter. Upon graduation, Jessica has served in various capacities as an alumnae for her organization such as Alumnae Advisor for various chapters and Academic Affairs Director for her National Governing Board. In her current position as a campus-based professional at a university in New Jersey, she continues to advocate and support the fraternal world each and every day. Her experiences and knowledge help fuel her line of work as she hosts workshops and training for other professionals in the fraternal community. Using her platform within higher education and her volunteer roles, she aims to continue amplifying the voices of the marginalized.

Avery Willis (they/he) is a Trans Chicanx student and organizer. They received their Bachelor of Social Work from Georgia State University in May of 2020 and are currently enrolled in the University of Southern California Master of Social Work program. Avery has been involved in activism communities since high school, with notable experience through the Transgender Law Center and national GSA Network. Avery served two terms as the Active-at-Large on the Board of Directors for Delta Lambda Phi Fraternity and currently serves as one of the Alumni-at-Large Directors.

Ebony Wofford is a Coordinator in the Department of Fraternity and Sorority Life at Florida State University where she is responsible for advising and supporting the National Pan-Hellenic Council. She received her B.A. in Political Science from North Carolina A&T State University and a M.Ed. in Higher Education from the University of North Carolina Wilmington. Throughout her time in FSL, Ebony has been an active volunteer with the Association of Fraternity/Sorority Advisors, Association of Fraternal Leadership and Values, and as a member of Zeta Phi Beta Sorority, Incorporated.

Index

A

Abolish Greek Life movement 207, 230
academic xvi, 170, 186, 197–198, 201–205
 excellence 99, 124
 experience 170
 performance & persistence 3, 28
 support & mentorship 63, 95–96, 136
acceptance 111, 119
 of Black Greek-Letter Organizations 24
 of queer individuals 31, 110–114, 117, 119
accountability 131–132, 185, 203
achievement 42, 84, 149, 152, 201
ACPA (American College Personnel Association), 149, 164, 171, 235–236, 240
activism 62
activities
 campus 4, 46, 88, 94, 97, 104, 240
 expansion 68, 96, 97–98, 115, 118, 137, 145–147, 223

Greek life, (see: hazing)
Greek Week 117–118
 plan prevention 182, 185–187
 tailgating 104
 toxic 183
advancement 70, 225
African-American, (see: Black)
alcohol consumption, (see: hazing)
ancestors 75, 144
anti-Black, (see: discrimination)
Asian-American Greek Letter Organizations (AAGLOs), 65
 Chinese 6, 65–66, 75
 criteria 70
 dismantling stereotypes 76–78
 modern day 68
 timeline 65–68
 values 71–75
Asian Pacific Islander Desi Americans (APIDAs), 70, 75–77, 129
 National APIDA Panhellenic Association 9, 65, 67

awareness
  anti-bullying 117
  cultural 75, 77, 125
  Latinx/a/o, cultural 92
  Native American, cultural 136
  raising 73, 209–211, 216
  self- 62

B

backgrounds
  cultural 23
  influence of 230
  marginalized 193, 202, 204
  similar 24, 51
  socioeconomic 76, 184
behaviors
  anti-Blackness 188, 229
  anti-Queer 7–8, 229
  harmful to BIPOC 208
  hazing, *(see: hazing)*
  hegemonic masculine, *(see: masculinity)*
  hypersexual 25
  inclusivity 7, 107, 149, 150, 164, 165–170, 195, 202, 203
  oppressive, *(see: oppression)*
  problematic 3, 23
  root cause 58, 180
  straight-acting 110
beliefs 6, 25, 30–31, 61, 139–141, 143, 161, 229
  hegemonic masculinities 25
  homophobia, *(see: discrimination)*
  Native American, cultural 143
  oppressive, *(see: oppression)*
biases, *(see: discrimination)*
Black Greek Letter Organizations (BGLOs)
  acceptance of 24
  experiences 47, 51
  institutional dynamics 52–53
  nature of 32, 46, 59
  recruitment 56
  timeline 46
Black, Indigenous, and People of Color (BIPOC) 124, 130, 207–208, 214
Black
  community members 159–163, 165
  feminist 42, 161
  Greek Letter Organizations, *(see: Black Greek-Letter Organizations)*
  men 237
  students 179, 237
  women 165, 171–172, 237
Black Lives Matter 159, 217
bonds,
  Indigenous 144
  Latinx/a/o 94, 97
  LGBTQ 111, 115
  siblinghood 12, 16–17, 19, 21, 24–25, 50, 83, 118, 166, 168, 179, 212, 218, 228
boundaries 135, 137, 242
burden 151, 169, 197, 216, 226

C

camaraderie 103, 111
caucasian, *(see: white)*
causes, philanthropic & social justice 68, 200–201, 215, 217–218
Culturally Based Sororities & Fraternities (CBSFS) 4–6, 8–9, 12–14, 208–218
ceremonies 74, 143–144
cisgender 31, 91, 108, 113–114, 160, 162, 166, 168, 194
  cishet *(cisgender, heterosexual)* 166
colonization 30, 137, 140, 150–151, 229
Communities of Color 9, 12, 14–15, 23–24, 66, 68, 97, 127, 211, 214–215, 226, 230, 242–243
competition 98, 115, 117, 147
confronting injustice 139, 151, 167, 202

D

Deferred Action for Childhood Arrivals (DACA) 217
dangers, *(see: hazing)*
deaf communities 76, 169, 227, 229
death 68, 113, 177–178, 190
decolonization 139, 142, 145, 151
delegitimization 130, 146
disabilities 160, 169, 213
discrimination 4, 6–7, 25, 68, 71, 76–77, 80, 115, 119, 133, 146–147, 179–180, 213, 215, 229
    ableism 30, 228–229
    elitism 4, 24, 48
    exclusion 4–6, 8, 45–46, 76, 95, 162, 167, 180, 193, 203–204, 209, 212, 221, 223
    homophobia 31, 76, 163, 203, 218
    racism 13, 30, 43, 45, 50, 55, 68, 75, 124, 150, 162–163, 179–181, 185, 188, 202–203, 206, 214, 218, 221, 237
    segregation 45–46, 71
    sexism 46, 181, 202–203, 214, 218
    stereotypes 63, 76
    supremacy 30–31, 46, 130, 139, 159
    transphobia 117, 218
disenfranchisement 179, 223
diversity 21, 62, 100, 179

E

economics 6, 139, 142, 216
elitism, *(see: discrimination)*
empowerment 88, 92–93, 123, 175, 184–185
engagement (student, leadership) 12, 27–28, 51, 53, 55, 91, 96, 113, 144, 147, 169–170, 172, 184, 211, 216, 228, 234
environments
    affirming 26, 59, 119, 167, 180, 225
    equitable 225, 228
    oppressive 16, 21, 35, 162–163, 180
ethnicity 214
excellence 68, 84, 124
exclusion, *(see: discrimination)*
expectations
    financial 197
    gender expression, *(see: gender)*
    hegemonic 8, 25, 183
    heteronormative, *(see: gender)*
    Latinidad 165
    Native American 135
    organizational 54, 135, 148, 165–166, 169, 183–184, 196–197, 217

F

femininity 26, 77, 109–110, 166, 183, 213
    flamboyant 109
feminism 42, 184
feminist 42, 161, 171, 241
fraternities, *(see: Sorority & Fraternity Life communities)*
friendship 23, 66, 111, 179, 200–201

G

gaps (limitations) 22, 33, 57, 149, 160, 171, 194
gatekeeping 4
gender
    -affirming 12, 26, 94, 115, 217
    binary 25, 45, 106–107, 217, 224–225
    cisgender, *(see: cisgender)*
    exclusion 5, 7
    identity 24
    inclusion 107–108, 115
    neutral 106, 118
    non-binary, *(see: transgender)* 104, 108, 110, 115, 168
    non-conforming, *(see: transgender)*

stereotypes 25
variant 106
trans-, *(see:* transgender)
generational differences 111–113
Greek-letter 15, 29, 33–35, 45–46, 77, 179

H

habits 178
hazing 7, 13–14, 22, 29–30, 32, 36, 41–42, 56, 109, 175–191, 198, 234, 241
   anti-hazing 9, 115, 119, 182, 186–187, 189
   "fagging" 176
Historically Black Colleges & Universities (HBCUs) 5, 41–42, 45–46, 48, 52, 227
heteronormativity 117, 165–166, 212, 217
heterosexism 7, 16, 26, 30, 109, 113, 181, 229
heterosexual 31, 111–113, 166, 191, 212
Hispanic 14–16, 18, 33, 35–36, 87, 90–91, 94, 163, 183, 227, 239
   History 88–89
   Latinidad 162, 164–165, 171
   Latino Greek-Letter Organizations (LGLOs) 23, 74–75, 89
   Latinx 83, 87–88, 90, 92, 99, 101
   sorority & fraternity timeline 88–89
   perspective 91–98
historicizing 3
holistic 48, 63, 96, 98, 183, 211
homeless 46, 117
homophobia, *(see: discrimination)*
homosexuality, *(see: queer)*
humanizing 208, 211, 214, 216, 218

I

ideologies 76, 213
incentivizing 57, 164, 167, 169, 172, 225, 200

inclusivity, *(see: behaviors)*
Indigenous 130, 139–140, 142–144, 150–153, 155, 183, 207–208, 214, 241–242
   Cherokee 241
   Choctaw 241
inequalities 149, 184, 191, 195, 204, 210, 216–217, 220, 229–230
influences 28, 37, 75, 101, 162
interactions 24, 42, 58, 110, 136, 149, 161, 201

L

labels 12
LGBTQIA, *(see: Queer)*
   LGBTQIA-interest, *(see: Queer-interest)*

M

manhood, *(see: masculinity)*
marginalization 30–31, 159, 161–164, 167, 171–172, 229
masculinity 13, 15, 17, 25, 34–35, 36, 183–184, 232–233
media 4, 13, 68, 113, 176, 210, 212, 217, 243
mental health 51, 114, 119, 175
   destigmatization 214
microaggressions 50, 213

N

National Pan-Hellenic Council (NPHC) 4, 6, 10–11, 17, 42, 46–57, 59, 71, 105, 165, 179–180, 210, 215–217, 227
norms
   campus 42
   change 167
   gendered 25, 108, 161–162, 183, 212

societal 161–162, 171
White cultural 144

O

operations 49, 52, 66, 68, 172, 200, 224
opportunities
   alleged ensured equality 46
   expansion 68
   for LGBTQ interests, *(see: Queer)*
   involvement 90–92
   lack thereof 45
   leadership 62, 93, 98
   to network 95
oppression 7–8, 21, 24–25, 28–31, 127, 130, 132, 145, 147, 149–150, 159, 162, 164–165, 167–168, 181–182, 185, 188, 203–205, 207–209, 212, 214, 216, 221, 225, 227–231, 236
outreach 96, 116, 187

P

parents 119, 160, 169–170, 187, 239
passions 47, 85, 123–124
pathways 14, 47, 62, 68, 71, 94, 115, 164, 241
patriarchy 43, 162
patterns 8, 25, 74, 143, 212
perceptions 32, 43, 109, 113, 208
performance 3, 74–75, 166, 213, 242
philosophies 93, 143
pledge, *(see: recruits)*
police 55, 129, 131, 207
politics 6, 31, 42, 52, 67, 76, 131, 216, 229, 243
   Black feminist, *(see: feminism)*
   respectability 31, 229
populations 4–6, 12–13, 31, 115, 144, 147, 154, 180, 193, 212, 227
preferences 16, 24, 104, 117, 196

prejudice, *(see: discrimination)*
problematic behaviors, *(see: behaviors)*

Q

Queer (LGBTQIA)
   bisexual 4, 26, 94, 105–106, 110–111, 115, 126, 180, 226
   campus climate 112–114
   counseling 119
   fraternity 109–110
   gay 4, 26, 94, 109, 112–115, 179–180, 194, 226
   history 105–106
   lesbian 4, 15, 19, 26, 94, 105–106, 110, 115, 180, 226, 238
   LGBTQIA-interest 105–109, 112, 114–119
   sorority & fraternity interest 110–112
   transgender 4, 7, 19, 26, 94–95, 105–106, 108, 110, 112, 115, 119, 121, 126, 166, 180, 193, 211–213, 217, 225–226, 232, 244
   pre-transition 23
   transitioning 23, 123
   trans-inclusive 94, 100, 166
   transphobia, *(see: discrimination)*
   treatment of 12, 173, 240
queerness 31
queer-spectrum 113, 120

R

racist, *(see: discrimination)*
recruits 36, 41, 52, 72, 119, 220, 234
relationships 3, 22–23, 48, 50, 54, 56, 72, 77, 83, 117–118, 127–128, 131–132, 142–145, 151, 179, 181, 183, 188, 204, 211–212, 228, 231, 242
religion 5, 109, 160, 162, 164, 208, 214
representation 62, 197–199, 219

reproduction 37, 121, 179, 185, 206, 214
resistance 6, 8, 33–34, 72, 75, 117, 132, 140, 163, 173, 220
respect 65, 93, 126, 135, 142–143, 148, 153, 161, 169, 178, 181

S

scholars 12, 21–22, 24–30, 32, 142, 145, 166, 226–230
scholarship 7, 12–13, 21–22, 25–27, 32–33, 66, 141–142, 148, 150, 169, 190, 200–202, 222, 226, 228, 241, 243
sensitivity 94, 117, 118
service 63, 84, 124, 200
sexual 26, 94, 124
sexuality 13, 26, 103, 212
straight, *(see: heterosexual)*
siblinghood, *(see: bonds, cultural)*
slander 233
societal 108, 112–113, 162, 166, 180, 214, 216
socioeconomic 76, 88, 160, 162, 168, 208
Sorority & Fraternity Life (SFL) communities
    historically white fraternities 8, 10, 198
    historically white sororities 8, 195, 198
Spanish 87, 93, 165
spirituality 91, 144, 153
stances 7, 127, 213, 230
standards 23, 25, 68, 76, 129, 143, 145, 147–149, 222, 239
stigmatizations 110, 128
Stonewall 113
struggles 18, 36, 52, 128, 132, 140, 164, 234
supremacy, *(see: discrimination)*
sustainability 129, 185, 187

T

teacher 62, 237
themes 22, 42, 46, 72, 185, 222
theories 62, 74, 101, 151, 173
tradition 42, 52, 56, 72–74, 178
trans, *(see: Queer)*

U

underclassmen 175, 178
undergarments 184
underrepresented 115, 242
upperclassmen 175, 178

V

values 61, 65, 71, 84, 211
violence 35, 173, 177, 179–180, 183, 211, 213, 232
volunteers 47–48, 77, 142, 163, 171, 226

W

white
    -adjacent 75
    non-white 130–131, 163
    privilege, white 185, 203, 209
    whiteness xvi, 31, 161, 163

www.ingramcontent.com/pod-product-compliance
Ingram Content Group UK Ltd.
Pitfield, Milton Keynes, MK11 3LW, UK
UKHW021850210426
5322IPUK00022B/573